Lead←Grow→Shape:
A Prescription for Life-Long Leader Development
Workbook *2017*

« STUDENT EDITION »

A workbook for emerging pharmacy leaders…

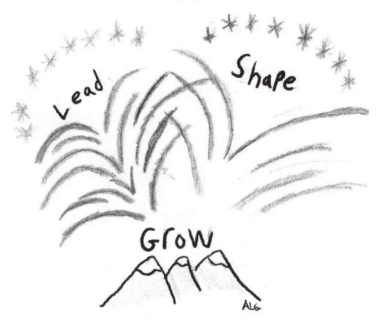

Editorial Board:

Nancy A. Alvarez, PharmD

Gary J. Keil, II, PhD

Michael J. Negrete, PharmD

John D. Grabenstein, PhD (Colonel, Retired, U.S. Army)

Illustrations by A. L. Grabenstein

Pharmacy Leadership & Education Institute, Inc.

Pharmacy
Leadership &
Education
Institute

Version 2017-S-2.00   1 January 2017

ORDER INFORMATION

For print copies, go to http://plei.org/lead-grow-shape/, order from the CreateSpace options, and select preferred shipping speed.

For Kindle® editions, go to smile.amazon.com/Kindle, search for **Lead-Grow-Shape** by Alvarez *et al.*, select *Student Edition*, and order. Immediate access, no delay.

▸

Studying with a Kindle® or Kindle® App

Many readers will purchase this book as an e-book (electronic book) for projection using a Kindle® or Kindle® app. If you do not already have the latest version of the Kindle® app on your laptop (version 1.17.1 or higher), you can download it **for free** at https://www.amazon.com/kindleapps.

Follow the instructions for your combination of (a) the Kindle® app version you use and (b) your computing device. The guidelines below should help you use a Kindle® e-book in a classroom setting.

<u>**Viewing Basics**</u>. We typically recommend <u>landscape</u> orientation, single column. Choose font size, words per line, brightness, margins, and color mode as you prefer. Smaller font size allows more words per line (helpful to view tables). Use the toolbar to widen the viewable content (stretch margins outward), thus minimizing empty space at the left and right sides of viewable pages. Test these options now.

<u>**Location**</u>. Kindle books **do not have page numbers**. This is beyond our power to change. Instead, you will find location numbers (a numerator and a denominator) at the bottom of the reading screen. Learn to recognize and recall the location of any given text segment. Practice these functions now.

Appendices 1 and 2 for details, including how the Modules of this Workbook map to the relevant standards and competencies).

Self-awareness – Examine and reflect on personal knowledge, skills, abilities, beliefs, biases, motivation, and emotions that could enhance or limit personal and professional gro[ ]

Leadership – Demonstrate responsibi[ ]ieving shared goals, regardless of position.

Innovation & entrepreneurship – En[ ]ties by using creative thinking to envision[ ]ishing professional goals.

Professionalism – Exhibit behaviors and values that are consistent with the trust given to the profession by patients, other healthcare

<u>**Movement**</u>. Use the Table of Contents button [marked with "1" in next graphic] to reveal the Workbook's major sections. Tap the icon again to make the list disappear. Tap the entries ["3"] to move quickly to the selected point. Use the "Go To" function ["2"] to move to specific segments specified in the Table of Contents (i.e., Modules and major parts) to move around the Workbook. You can use the Search function to seek specific words. Hotlinks with the Table of Contents portion of the reading frame ["4"] may also be useful to help you move. Test these functions now.

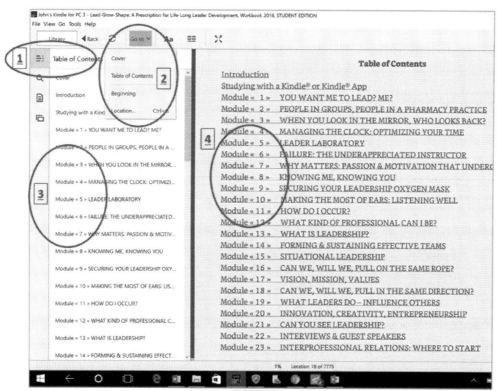

How to highlight within a Kindle® app. To highlight a passage of several words, long-press the desired text with two fingers, then spread the highlight with another finger. Or, using one finger, long-press (or double click) a word to select it, then use the drag-handles to expand the selection. If you are using a mouse, left click and drag the cursor in the usual way, to highlight the desired passage. These actions also trigger a pop-up box allowing choices to make a note, create a highlight, or share a passage. Practice highlighting text on your personal device now.

> | Highlight | Note |
>
> And don't forget — this is a process! Publish
> Kindle is easy and takes only 5 minutes of y(
> — but correctly preparing your book for suc(
> Kindle takes time and effort. Don't worry; if
> follow the steps we outline here, you should
> confident you'll end up with a successfully d
> and formatted book and one you will be pro
> see for sale on Amazon. You will even be abl
> verify this with our Previewer!
>
> Let's get started!

How to take notes within a Kindle® app. Tap and hold your finger down on text where you want to make a note. If you are using a mouse, double click a word and drag the cursor, as desired. Type your note in the window—it can hold more text than what appears at any one time. On the Kindle® device, you should select "Create Note" before you start. On other devices, the option may say "Add Note" or simply "Note." Use the laptop or on-screen keyboard to enter your note. On the Kindle® Keyboard, you can just begin typing to enter your note. Save your note. View all the notes you have taken for a book by opening the Kindle® menu and selecting the appropriate icon. The Kindle® Fire will show your notes directly in the menu, but with other models you need to select the option "View Notes and Marks," "Notes/Marks" or "Go To | Notes."

Practice entering a note on your personal device now. If all else fails (but it shouldn't), keep your notes progressively in a word-processing document, noting the Module, Annex, or section numbers as you go.

Retrieving notes (annotations). Annotations are saved both on your device and your Amazon account, so all highlights and notes from all your e-books can be viewed in one spot and saved elsewhere. The support URL for this function is: https://kindle.amazon.com/your_highlights. If you are using a Kindle® device, you can create a "My Clippings" TXT file.

How to print annexes. Follow instructions on your device on how to print selected sections of this book. For annexes where facilitators may want to distribute copies within a classroom, annex documents are available to facilitators upon request (LeadGrowShape@plei.org).

Functions. After you master the basics, be sure you test all the Kindle® function buttons, to make sure you aren't overlooking something. File | View | Go | Tools | Help.

- ▸ Table of Contents: You might want to show it or hide it.
- ▸ Bookmarks: Learn how to use them.
- ▸ Options: Check out auto-updating, auto-backup of annotations and other features
- ▸ Popular Highlights: You can toggle on or off the option to display passages that are frequently highlighted by other Kindle® users. This might help you, or might be distracting.
- ▸ Dictionary: You can enable a dictionary function that is activated by long-pressing a word.
- ▸ Flashcards: You can make your own flashcards to help yourself learn vocabulary.

Structure of each Module. Here is your guide to the **structure of each Module**:

- ▸ ☞ Learning Objectives
- ▸ #.1. Readings or activities <u>before class</u>
- ▸ #.2. Resources needed
- ▸ #.3. In-class activities
- ▸ #.4. Discussion questions
- ▸ #.5. After-class assignments
- ▸ #.6. Bibliography, references, & resources

Table of Contents

Notes on Revised Editions. This revision of *Lead←Grow→Shape* keeps the same basic structure, while refining and adding text. So, the Module numbers are unchanged, but the page numbers in the print editions will differ between earlier editions and this one.

Flashcards for *Lead←Grow→Shape,* via Quizlet.com

Flashcards make useful study aids for vocabulary and concepts. Never forget that the exercises in *Lead←Grow→Shape* emphasize self-reflection and group experiences, far more than mere vocabulary. Still, these flashcard games can make learning and differentiating basic concepts fun. Or you could use the flashcards to refresh your memory after class. The mobile apps described below could be useful to you, especially while traveling.

To jumpstart your leadership learning, we have prewritten flashcards for 40 categories from 31 of our Modules and Annexes. All in all, you have access to 318 term-and-definition pairs. All this is available to you **free**, without charge, at a website called Quizlet.com, regardless of whether you use our print or Kindle® versions. You will see advertisements (which underwrite the 'free' service). As you view the ads, consider the communication principles depicted in them (not least: how to convey a key message at a glance).

One cool thing about electronic flashcards is the variety of learning games you can play via Quizlet. Learners can use what works best for them and go at their own pace. You can choose from:

▸ Flashcards: Press the Options button; 'Start with definition' will usually be the preferred choice. At the beginning, you might want to select the 'Both Sides' option. Shuffle mixes up the order of terms. Play cycles through flashcards automatically. Use Audio functions to hear the text read out loud.

▸ Learn Mode: Tests your knowledge of a subject after you have studied it a few times, involving Correct and Incorrect buckets. Options: 'prompt with definition' will usually be the preferred choice.

▸ Test Mode: Provides practice tests; we suggest the matching, multiple-choice, and true/false formats. Options: 'start with definition' will usually be the preferred choice.

▸ Playing Match, also called Scatter or Make Everything Disappear: Match terms to their definitions, with accompanying timer.

▸ Playing Gravity: Type the term as the definition falls down the screen. Options: 'Start with definition' will usually be the preferred choice.

1. To access the Quizlet flashcard function, follow these steps:
   a. Go to Quizlet.com and select **Sign up**. Or go to https://quizlet.com/join/ZZdUj2K9t.
   b. Choose either the **Sign up with email** option, or use a Google or Facebook account.
   c. Follow these steps to quickly create an account:
      1. Enter your birthday. This is needed to comply with the Children's Online Privacy Protection Act.
      2. Pick a unique username.
      3. Enter your e-mail address.
      4. Pick a secure password.
      5. Read (and agree to) the Quizlet Terms of Service.
      6. If asked, indicate whether you are a student or a teacher.
      7. Select **Sign Up.**
   d. After the signup process, Quizlet sends a confirmation email. Select **Confirm your email** to confirm the account. You may begin using Quizlet.
   e. Mobile App: consider downloading the Quizlet mobile application from the Apple Store or Google Play. These apps can help you study the content off line, which can be useful when traveling.

2. After setting up your Quizlet account, you will want to search for our "class" and its "sets" of flashcards. Simply tap the magnifying glass icon and type "Lead-Grow-Shape class" into the text box at the top of the screen. Be sure to specify "class" in your search, to avoid a long list of hits. Then tap the magnifying glass icon and your results will appear below. Select PLEI's *Lead←Grow→Shape* entry.

Or try going to https://quizlet.com/class/3716098/

3. Once you are inside the *Lead←Grow→Shape* class, we suggest sorting the sets alphabetically. Tap on a set title and select a mode (e.g., Flashcards, Learn, Test, Match, Gravity). See above for tips for each mode.

4. Explore all the function buttons, including Print.

5. Take advantage of the Help Center, which explains the many features of Quizlet.

6. Have fun and happy learning!

Here is a list of Quizlet sets for various portions of the *Lead←Grow→Shape* workbook.

Module « 1 » Aspects of Each Pharmacist » 5 terms
Module « 3 » Values-Interests-Strengths-Needs (VISN) » 4 terms
Module « 5 » Leadership Styles » 14 terms
Module « 6 » Reasons Why People Fail (Maxwell) » 10 terms
Module « 7 » Emotional Intelligence (Goleman, etc) » 7 terms
Module « 9 » Crucial Conversations (Patterson) » 6 terms
Module « 10 » Listening Principles & Tools » 16 terms
Module « 10 » Annex 10-1. Listening-Skills Lexicon » 9 terms
Module « 11 » Annex 11-1. Johari Window » 4 terms
Module « 12 » Professionalism » 11 terms
Module « 14 » Challenge-Skill-Task Wheel (Flow Pie, Csíkszentmihályi) » 8 terms
Module « 14 » Annex 14-3. Group-Development Lexicon » 9 terms
Module « 15 » Situational-Leadership Model (Hersey & Blanchard) » 8 terms
Module « 16 » Fords' Four Conversations » 4 terms
Module « 16 » Four Conversation Styles: What to Cover » 8 terms
Module « 16 » Four Conversation Styles: When To Use Which » 7 terms
Module « 17 » Mission, Values, Vision » 8 terms
Module « 18 » Fords' Four Conversations » 4 terms
Module « 18 » Four Conversation Styles: What to Cover » 8 terms
Module « 18 » Four Conversation Styles: When To Use Which » 7 terms
Module « 20 » Innovation, Creativity, Entrepreneurship » 17 terms
Module « 23 » Interprofessional: I Pass the Baton (TeamSTEPPS) » 10 terms
Module « 23 » Interprofessional: Key Principles » 5 terms
Module « 23 » Interprofessional: Mutual Support » 5 terms
Module « 23 » Interprofessional: SBAR » 4 terms
Module « 23 » Interprofessional: Team Events » 3 terms
Module « 23 » Interprofessional: Team Roles » 15 terms
Module « 24 » Followership-Delegation Lexicon » 10 terms
Module « 25 » Pharmacy Associations, Canada » 7 terms
Module « 25 » Pharmacy Associations, USA » 8 terms
Module « 26 » Communication-Skills Lexicon » 8 terms
Module « 27 » Communication Depth (Powell) » 5 terms
Module « 29 » Goal Alignment » 4 terms
Module « 30 » Group Dynamics » 8 terms
Module « 30 » Parliamentary Procedure, Robert's Rules of Order » 17 terms
Module « 31 » Problem-Solving Process » 8 terms
Module « 32 » Disciplined Decision-Making » 10 terms
Module « 33 » Conflict Types & Action Steps » 8 terms
Module « 33 » Annex 33-1. Conflict Resolution » 5 terms
Module « 35 » L-I-M-S » 4 terms

Introduction

The profession of pharmacy needs leaders now, more than ever. This is the considered opinion of multiple pharmacy membership societies, the American Association of Colleges of Pharmacy (AACP) and now the Accreditation Council for Pharmacy Education (ACPE). This Workbook is designed to help expand the leader skills of each student pharmacist.

Did we say all student pharmacists? Meaning each student pharmacist? Yes! Leaders are trained, not born. Each student pharmacist will be called on to deliver excellent care, improve their practice site, advance the profession as a whole, and mature in their personal lives. This Workbook is designed to help each and every student pharmacist grow from their current level of competency to the next level. And pharmacists with stronger skills at leading, growing, molding, and shaping their environment will be happier and more fulfilled.

In April 2016, new ACPE standards went into effect for America's pharmacy schools. Standard 4 (see Appendix 1) states that pharmacy curricula will impart "to the graduate the knowledge, skills, abilities, behaviors, and attitudes necessary to demonstrate *self–awareness, leadership, innovation and entrepreneurship, and professionalism*" (emphasis added). Further, the 2016 ACPE standards require graduates to exert influence as they collaborate with other healthcare professionals to deliver patient-centered care.

The 2016 ACPE Standards arise, in part, from earlier work by AACP and its Center for the Advancement of Pharmacy Education (CAPE). In 2013, CAPE revised the list of Educational Outcomes it offers as the target for evolving pharmacy curricula on each pharmacy campus. In the 2013 CAPE Outcomes, Domain 4 describes Personal & Professional Development, which describe in detail the learning objectives associated with *self-awareness, leadership, innovation and entrepreneurship, and professionalism* (see Appendix 2).

What are these four elements expected by AACP and ACPE of each graduating pharmacist?

Self-awareness – The graduate is able to examine and reflect on personal knowledge, skills, abilities, beliefs, biases, motivation, and emotions that could enhance or limit personal and professional growth.

Leadership – The graduate is able to demonstrate responsibility for creating and achieving shared goals, regardless of position.

Innovation and Entrepreneurship – The graduate is able to engage in innovative activities by using creative thinking to envision better ways of accomplishing professional goals.

Professionalism – The graduate is able to exhibit behaviors and values that are consistent with the trust given to the profession by patients, other healthcare providers, and society.

▸

To meet these standards and needs, we have adapted dozens of respected leadership principles for application in the pharmacy environment. We expect this Workbook will empower the on-campus facilitator (i.e., instructor, professor, volunteer experiential educator) in active learning activities (teaching, discussions, role-playing) occurring in classrooms, augmented with on-campus or in-community activities. We suggest various assignments, in the form of readings or instruments to complete, as well as an option for journal entries, to help the participant reflect and document their evolving understanding of themselves and of others.

Here is your guide to the structure of each Module:

▷ ☞ Learning Objectives
▷ #.1. Readings or activities <u>before class</u>
▷ #.2. Resources needed
▷ #.3. In-class activities
▷ #.4. Discussion questions
▷ #.5. After-class assignments
▷ #.6. Bibliography, references, & resources

▸

The AACP and ACPE priority for self-awareness matches our own view that the «Leader Within» must be well understood.

This Workbook equips the on-campus facilitator with enough Modules to support a 1- or 2-credit course (or major segments of a larger course). These Modules will be suitable for a full cohort of first-professional-year (P1) students. Based on what experiences students on any given campus have, various Modules will be suitable for students in each of the professional years, meeting the call for longitudinal engagement of participants throughout the pharmacy curriculum. Alternately, Modules can be selected for a capstone course for P4 students or an elective course elsewhere in a pharmacy curriculum. Likewise, they should help pharmacy residents and other inquisitive people.

▸

Hey, you're probably a Millennial. You don't have to read the Modules in order. Hop around. You can gain from a Module even if your esteemed facilitator doesn't lead you through it.

▸

Now, a request for the obsessive-compulsives among our readers (you know who you are). If you would like to keep a running list of the typos and misspellings and oddities you find as you use this Workbook, we would be delighted to give it to the obsessive-compulsives on our editorial team (they know who they are) so we can upgrade the next iteration of the Workbook. We will figure out some virtual way of saying thank you! See Appendix 8 for the feedback form for mere mortals. Use the contact info there to send us your list of fixes needed. Excelsior!

Module « 1 »   YOU WANT ME TO LEAD? ME?

☞ Learning Objectives:

Objective 1. To describe the relevance of self-awareness to personal development and actuation.
Objective 2. To describe the relevance of leadership to personal fulfillment and professional activity.
Objective 3. To describe how innovation and entrepreneurship can advance a pharmacist's goals.
Objective 4. To describe how individual pharmacists act within a professional covenant.

1.1. Readings or activities before class:

First class of semester – not applicable.

1.2. Resources needed:

A. Course syllabus (from facilitator)
B. Workbook Module 1.
C. Article: Posner BZ. From inside out: Beyond teaching about leadership. *J Lead Educ.* 2009;8(1):1-10.
   www.journalofleadershiped.org/attachments/article/208/JOLE_8_1_Posner.pdf

1.3. In-class activities:

Step 1. Facilitator describes course purpose and syllabus, sets expectations and timelines for the semester.
Step 2. Facilitator reviews text content of Module 1.
   a. Review AACP and ACPE applications of self-awareness, leadership, innovation, entrepreneurship, and
      professionalism.
   b. Discuss competencies within leadership development (Table 1-A).
   c. Discuss guiding principles for leadership development (Table 1-B).
   d. Discuss connections between CAPE Educational Outcomes and pharmacy leadership (Table 1-C).
Step 3.
   a. Read text below.
   b. Assignment(s) for next class.

By continually enhancing your knowledge of yourself, you will be happier, increasingly effective, and more influential. At its foundation, leadership = influence. We cannot promise you greater wealth, but we are reasonably confident you will become more satisfied and more fulfilled.

This is a Workbook about developing leadership and other personal skills. Yes, leadership is a skill. Everyone can take their current level of leadership skill and increase it. No matter what you think, no matter how shy or introverted you claim to be, you already have some leadership skill that can be enhanced. Everyone leads in some capacity, whether you realize it or not. There are the obvious leaders who lead externally at their workplace, within professional and community groups, at home, and within families. Let's call them leaders-with-gavels or leaders-at-podiums. And then there are the millions of ways informal leadership is expressed.

Look at the table of contents and you will see various topics highly relevant to the workplace. But we will not start with work-related topics.

Instead, we must start internally, with the leader that exists within each of us, the selves that lead our lives and exert influence over what we think, how we feel, how we react, what we do, and why we do. While you may not be able to fully control or influence your environment, you surely can control and influence your role in your surroundings.

That is where we will start. We will begin «Within». That is the purpose of this Workbook, to help you look inside and grow, and then shape the world around you.

With this in mind, the early Modules contain various exercises to help you better understand yourself. One of the sayings of Siddhãrtha Gautama (known as the Buddha) is relevant here:

> "First, one would get oneself established in what is proper;
> Then one would advise another. [Thus] the wise one would not suffer."
> The Dhammapada—The Sayings of the Buddha
> Chapter XII, The Self, Verse 158

Regardless of your religious preference, this reflection calls us to attend to the «Leader Within» before endeavoring to direct or instruct others. Another way to think about this is akin to preparing for takeoff inside a commercial airplane. Flight attendants advise us that if there is a change in cabin pressure and oxygen masks fall from their storage compartments, passengers should first secure their own mask, before helping those around them. Similarly, we contend that the foundation of leader development rests upon our ability to attend to our personal leadership oxygen supply first.

The leadership and other skills addressed in this Workbook deal with various roles you will take on in your professional life and your personal life: Self, Learner, Manager, Facilitator, Advocator, Collaborator, Communicator, Professional, Spouse, Parent. The readings and exercises will help focus on four aspects recognized by pharmacy's academic leaders as essential to your preparation to become a pharmacist: *self-awareness, leadership, innovation and entrepreneurship, and professionalism* (see Appendices 1 and 2 for details, including how the Modules of this Workbook map to the relevant standards and competencies).

Self-awareness – Examine and reflect on personal knowledge, skills, abilities, beliefs, biases, motivation, and emotions that could enhance or limit personal and professional growth.

Leadership – Demonstrate responsibility for creating and achieving shared goals, regardless of position.

Innovation & entrepreneurship – Engage in innovative activities by using creative thinking to envision better ways of accomplishing professional goals.

Professionalism – Exhibit behaviors and values that are consistent with the trust given to the profession by patients, other healthcare providers, and society.

It is no accident that the description of leadership above includes the phrase "regardless of position." The ability to lead can enhance each of the aforementioned roles, even if you believe that the role "Leader" does not fit your persona. Influence is exerted in myriad ways that are unrelated to job title or elected position. Thus, lower-case "leader" fits everyone. Be attentive and we will show you a few dozen of the myriad ways.

We will help you assess your own baseline of knowledge and understanding, and then help you measure your progress in knowledge, skills, abilities, behaviors, and attitudes. Our mutual goal is to help you apply self-awareness, leadership, innovation & entrepreneurship, and professionalism within a healthcare practice and in a personal life.

Many of pharmacy's recent academic leaders blazed a trail in 2013-2016 for us to follow in this inquiry into leadership and professionalism. Table 1-A shows a list of competencies that your college expects you and your peers to master. Fear not, each of them is within your grasp.

TABLE 1-A. 2013 DELPHI-DERIVED COMPETENCIES FOR PHARMACY STUDENT LEADERSHIP DEVELOPMENT

Leadership Knowledge

    Competency 1: Explain the importance of leadership in pharmacy.

    Competency 2: Recognize that leadership comes from those with and without titles.

    Competency 3: Distinguish between leadership and management.

    Competency 4: Describe the characteristics, behaviors and practices of effective leaders.

Personal Leadership Commitment

    Competency 5: Demonstrate self-awareness in leadership.

    Competency 6: Engage in personal leadership development.

Leadership Skill Development

    Competency 7: Develop a shared vision for an initiative or project.

    Competency 8: Collaborate with others.

    Competency 9: Lead members of a team.

    Competency 10: Develop knowledge of organizational culture.

    Competency 11: Outline change processes.

Source: Janke KK, Traynor AP, Boyle CJ. Competencies for student leadership development in doctor of pharmacy curricula to assist curriculum committees and leadership instructors. *Am J Pharm Educ.* 2013 Dec 16;77(10):222. www.ncbi.nlm.nih.gov/pmc/articles/PMC3872941/pdf/ajpe7710222.pdf

As you study leadership and enhance the lower-case leader within you, you will learn the many ways leadership is exhibited in a pharmacy practice. Leaders do not need a title to lead (to influence). You will learn how a Venn diagram of leadership and management would be drawn. From your own observations, you will describe how effective (and ineffective) leaders act.

As you dive into these learnings, you will come to realize what strengths of leadership you have now, and how you can reinforce or enhance other aspects. Dozens of leadership inventories are available and you will try out a few for yourself. Even when you have little enthusiasm to go boldly, you will be sufficiently skilled to recognize these traits in others or at least help them appreciate their strengths.

From your baseline, you will start experimenting in the real world with strengthening your leadership neurons and muscles and vocabulary. You will inspire others towards a common goal, lead small projects, learn about followership, learn about getting things done in complex organizations, learn how to get groups to agree on and implement change.

> *"...And any skill can be developed, strengthened and enhanced given the motivation and desire along with practice and feedback, role models, and coaching...." Posner BZ. J Lead Educ. 2009;8(1):1-10.*

We're talking about human nature here, so let's discuss fear. Which do you fear more: the mathematical skills needed for pharmacokinetic calculations or the social elements of working with others towards a common goal? We will leave pharmacokinetics to other experts and give you tips about human nature that will help you succeed. Fear not.

How should we approach programs to develop leaders among student pharmacists? Table 1-B offers a framework of guiding principles. To start, why bother? In fact, all student pharmacists need these skills, so that they may engage in patient-centered care or care for populations of people, no matter which practice setting they ultimately choose.

Next, what must we attend to when investing in leader development? First, we start with the self. We must consider in-classroom, on-campus, and in-community elements (the exercises in this Workbook will address each of these), from now until graduation (and beyond).

And what elements are essential? Experts agree that position is irrelevant, that each person can lead and must choose whether to lead, that we should aim for improvement of the common good, that none of us is an island, that there are many paths to the destination, and that leading is one of multiple roles we will play in our profession and in our lives.

Indeed, various leadership styles have been described, including authoritarian, democratic, laissez-faire, participative, paternalistic, servant, situational, transactional, transformational, and others. We will explore these, comparing and contrasting.

TABLE 1-B. GUIDING PRINCIPLES FOR PHARMACY STUDENT LEADERSHIP DEVELOPMENT

Motivation for Teaching & Learning

   Guiding Principle 1: Leadership is important for all student pharmacists to develop.

   Guiding Principle 2: Leadership can be learned.

Fundamental Precepts

   Guiding Principle 3: Student leadership development must focus on student self-development.

   Guiding Principle 4: Leadership development should take place in a wide variety of settings including didactic curriculum, experiential curriculum, and extra-curricular involvement.

   Guiding Principle 5: Leadership development requires many "teachers" from whom students can learn.

   Guiding Principle 6: A person's leadership development is continuous.

Core Tenets

   Guiding Principle 7: Anyone has the potential to lead regardless of background, position or title.

   Guiding Principle 8: Leadership is a choice.

   Guiding Principle 9: Leadership is principle-based and rooted in the common good.

   Guiding Principle 10: Leadership involves relationships with people.

   Guiding Principle 11: There is no single right way to lead.

   Guiding Principle 12: Leadership and management are distinct activities.

Source: Traynor AP, Boyle CJ, Janke KK. Guiding principles for student leadership development in the doctor of pharmacy program to assist administrators and faculty members in implementing or refining curricula. *Am J Pharm Educ.* 2013 Dec 16;77(10):221. www.ncbi.nlm.nih.gov/pmc/articles/PMC3872940/pdf/ajpe7710221.pdf

So, why teach leadership stuff to every member of a pharmacy class? Only one of us will be "class president..."

Because everyone can lead. And each of us will be called to lead in some way at some point in time. Because pharmacy would be a better place if more people led more often.

Because community, inpatient, long-term care, administrative, and other pharmacy-practice settings need more people who can organize teams to effect change and achieve shared goals, pharmacy managers must be able to organize teams toward pharmacy work goals.

Because patients need enhanced care from a collection of well-educated, highly skilled, compassionate and empathetic, interprofessional teams, pharmacists need to secure their proper place on the team to enhance the performance of the team.

Pharmacists need to engage in activities that actually deliver their potential value, increase access to and quality of care, and decrease costs as they ensure optimal medication use. That is our part – responsibility and accountability for medication optimization – and it enhances the role of others on the healthcare team.

Interprofessional teams of physicians, nurses, pharmacists, and others must build trust, contribute efficiently and effectively, and deliberate consciously. Researchers must choose between options, organize teams, and overcome obstacles. Academics must navigate organizational processes.

▶

How are we doing so far – to convince you that leadership can be learned and that there are leadership roles for everyone? Are we helping you see the utility and necessity of spending time developing your leadership neurons and muscles and vocabulary?

See Table 1-C for a deliberate list of examples of how leadership skills apply to the work of a pharmacy. Note that the learnings and the skills overlap.

TABLE 1-C. CONNECTIONS BETWEEN CAPE EDUCATIONAL OUTCOMES & PHARMACY LEADERSHIP

Foundational Knowledge (Learner 1.1): PharmD graduates should be able to explain the importance of leadership in pharmacy; recognize that leadership comes from those with and without titles; describe the characteristics, behaviors, and practices of effective leaders; distinguish between leadership and management; and be familiar with the leadership model/framework used by the school.

Medication Use Systems Management (Manager 2.2): To optimally evolve and manage medication use systems, PharmD graduates should be able to develop knowledge of an organizational culture; develop a shared vision for an initiative or project; and outline change processes.

Patient Advocacy (Advocate 3.3): PharmD graduates should be able to empower patients to take responsibility for their overall health outcomes; advocate for a health system that represents patient interests; and shift the paradigm of health delivery to a patient-centered, team-based approach.

Interprofessional Collaboration (Collaborator 3.4): PharmD graduates should be able to lead members of a team; apply leadership practices that support collaborative practice and team effectiveness; and collaborate with others.

Communication (Communicator 3.6): PharmD graduates should be able to develop skills of persuasion and influence; communicate a shared vision; and communicate clearly and concisely.

Self-awareness (Self-Aware 4.1): PharmD graduates should be able to demonstrate self-awareness in leadership.

Innovation and Entrepreneurship (Innovator 4.3): PharmD graduates should be able to embrace and advocate changes that improve patient care; develop new and innovative services and/or practices; and identify a customized training path if a predetermined one does not exist for a specific specialty or practice area.

Professionalism (Professional 4.4): PharmD graduates should be able to engage in ongoing personal leadership development and find opportunities for professional engagement through active membership and positional/nonpositional leadership roles.

Source: Janke KK, Nelson MH, Bzowyckyj AS, Fuentes DG, Rosenberg E, DiCenzo R. Deliberate integration of student leadership development in doctor of pharmacy programs. *Am J Pharm Educ*. 2016 Feb 25;80(1):2. www.ncbi.nlm.nih.gov/pmc/articles/PMC4776295/pdf/ajpe8012.pdf

Schools of pharmacy are in the pharmacist-development business. One might argue that leadership is inherent in the education of a pharmacist. We contend that, if that were the case, there would not be a deliberate need to focus upon leader development by the academic pharmacy community through standards and policy papers describing educational outcomes.

Leader development must be intentional and it starts with a focus on promoting the individual excellence of each student pharmacist. These Modules offer a series of primers on self-awareness, leadership, innovation, professionalism, management, communication, and other fundamental components for mastering pharmacy practice, in all its varied forms. We will just be scratching the surface, of course. Courses like this could run full-time for years.

First, be confident. Have faith in yourself. The trick lies in learning how to harness the skills already inside you and making them even better than they are right now. Student pharmacists are just a few steps away from that "magic moment" (i.e., licensure) when they will be pharmacy problem-solvers and decision-makers themselves. Developing skills beyond what we first understand is what will differentiate us from those with the same initial ability but who do nothing with it!

Realize that not all skills may have immediate utility or that a skill used today could apply tomorrow in a totally different situation. Tomorrow, you will be different too – older and wiser with greater curiosity and ultimately vision that helps to illuminate your blind spots and enables you to act to shape direction.

▸

Seen any good pharmacists lately? A good pharmacist is easy to recognize: a good patient-counselor and advocate, a reasoning problem-solver, a good decision-maker, a creative planner, a good manager of people, resources, and time. Anyone can be a better pharmacist than he or she is today. You can be even more of a leader in pharmacy than you are today.

Education, growth, and development are continual processes. We do not stop learning new facts about drugs the day we graduate. Life-long learning is essential for pharmacists, so that we remain competent to deliver direct or indirect patient-centered care; this is required of us until we live no more. Neither do we ever stop learning about people. And that is what leadership and management and communication are all about: people.

> *"Teaching about leadership is necessary to enable others to lead effectively,*
> *but it is not sufficient. Not sufficient in the sense that leadership requires **doing***
> *and leadership development therefore requires action-learning (or learning on the job)*
> *to find one's voice, develop, and hone one's skills."*
> Posner BZ. J Lead Educ. 2009;8(1):1-10.

We believe it, so multiple exercises in this Workbook will get you up out of your seats and send you into exercises and into communities to do the things of leadership. At the same time, you will be focused on being a leader, accepting where you are today while you are on your way to tomorrow.

1.4. Discussion questions:

Per facilitator

1.5. After-class assignments:

A. Review syllabus and enter key assignment dates into your calendar.
B. Read all portions of text above not discussed in depth during class.
C. Practice highlighting text and adding notes via the Kindle app functions specific to your personal device (see "Studying with a Kindle® or Kindle® App").
D. Read and be ready to discuss: Posner BZ. From inside out: Beyond teaching about leadership. *J Lead Educ.* 2009;8(1):1-10. www.journalofleadershiped.org/attachments/article/208/JOLE_8_1_Posner.pdf
E. [*Optional*] Read blogpost: Sze D. Maslow: The 12 Characteristics of a Self-Actualized Person, 21 Jul 2015. www.huffingtonpost.com/david-sze/maslow-the-12-characteris_b_7836836.html
F. Fulfill the before-class activities for the next Module assigned by your facilitator.

1.6. Bibliography, references, & resources:

Carter JR, Palihawadana M, eds. *The Dhammapada: The Sayings of the Buddha.* New York: Oxford University

Press, 2008.

Erhard W, Jensen MC, Granger KL. Creating Leaders: An Ontological/Phenomenological Model. In: Snook S, Nohria N, Khurana R, eds. *The Handbook for Teaching Leadership*. New York: Sage Publications, 2012. Harvard Business School NOM Unit Working Paper 11-037; Barbados Group Working Paper No. 10-10; Simon School Working Paper Series No. FR 10-30, http://ssrn.com/abstract=1681682.

Flashcards via Quizlet, https://quizlet.com/class/3716098/, Aspects of Each Pharmacist » 5 terms

Janke KK, Nelson MH, Bzowyckyj AS, Fuentes DG, Rosenberg E, DiCenzo R. Deliberate integration of student leadership development in doctor of pharmacy programs. *Am J Pharm Educ*. 2016 Feb 25;80(1):2. www.ncbi.nlm.nih.gov/pmc/articles/PMC4776295/pdf/ajpe8012.pdf

Janke KK, Traynor AP, Boyle CJ. Competencies for student leadership development in doctor of pharmacy curricula to assist curriculum committees and leadership instructors. *Am J Pharm Educ*. 2013 Dec 16;77(10):222. www.ncbi.nlm.nih.gov/pmc/articles/PMC3872941/pdf/ajpe7710222.pdf

Posner BZ. From inside out: Beyond teaching about leadership. *J Lead Educ.* 2009;8(1):1-10. www.journalofleadershiped.org/attachments/article/208/JOLE_8_1_Posner.pdf

Traynor AP, Boyle CJ, Janke KK. Guiding principles for student leadership development in the doctor of pharmacy program to assist administrators and faculty members in implementing or refining curricula. *Am J Pharm Educ*. 2013 Dec 16;77(10):221. www.ncbi.nlm.nih.gov/pmc/articles/PMC3872940/pdf/ajpe7710221.pdf

Module « 2 » PEOPLE IN GROUPS, PEOPLE IN A PHARMACY PRACTICE

☞ Learning Objectives:

Objective 1. To describe how people act alone or when they come together in groups.
Objective 2. To describe goals and communication methods within various groups.
Objective 3. To describe how individuals influence group efforts to achieve common goals.
Objective 4. To evaluate an individual pharmacy leader in an historic context and reflect on how that experience applies in contemporary settings.

Before we get too far into the essence of who you are and how you lead, we need to consider how individuals interact in teams, including pharmacy teams. After all, Stephen Covey encourages us to "begin with the end in mind." Thus, this Module helps you take inventory of people and how they interact with each other in colleges, in social settings, in a pharmacy practice, within a broader healthcare network, within the surrounding community, within the profession of pharmacy, within families.

Pharmacists are called on to exhibit leadership in a wide variety of patient-care settings. Regardless of their job title or position within an organization, pharmacists can set agendas, influence progress, enable change, and achieve goals.

2.1. Readings or activities before class:

Read and be prepared to discuss: Posner BZ. From inside out: Beyond teaching about leadership. *J Lead Educ.* 2009;8(1):1-10. www.journalofleadershiped.org/attachments/article/208/JOLE_8_1_Posner.pdf

2.2. Resources needed:

A. Posner BZ. From inside out: Beyond teaching about leadership. *J Lead Educ.* 2009;8(1):1-10. www.journalofleadershiped.org/attachments/article/208/JOLE_8_1_Posner.pdf
B. Annex 2-1. Leadership Roles in Various Settings
C. Annex 2-2. Brief Report on a Leading Figure in Pharmacy History

2.3. In-class activities:

Step 1. Questions?
Step 2. Stage-Setting.

2.4. Discussion questions:

Per facilitator

2.5. After-class assignments:

A. *Facilitator discretion*: Using Annex 2-2, read a succinct biography of a pharmacy leader or other medical leader and write a _-page report about that person and lessons to be gleaned for their personal life and professional life.
B. Fulfill the before-class activities for the next Module assigned by your facilitator.

2.6. Bibliography, references, & resources:

Covey SR. *The 7 Habits of Highly Effective People*. New York: Simon Schuster, 1989.

Posner BZ. From inside out: Beyond teaching about leadership. *J Lead Educ.* 2009;8(1):1-10.
www.journalofleadershiped.org/attachments/article/208/JOLE_8_1_Posner.pdf

Rickert DR, Smith RE, Worthen DB. The 'seven habits': Building pharmacist leaders. *Am Pharm.* 1992 Aug;32(8):48-52.

Annex 2-1. Leadership Roles in Various Settings

Separate annex documents available to facilitators upon request (LeadGrowShape@plei.org).

Discuss sections A and B of this Annex. Fill in blanks in section C and those other sections directed by your facilitator. For section D and section E, choose one or more groups you belong to. Sections F, G, H, and I offer opportunities to evaluate various pharmacy practice settings.

A. Group: Bee hive

Group goals:	Survival, propagation
Positional leader(s):	Queen bee
Informal leader(s):	---
Subteams of group:	Drones, workers, queens
Activities:	Pollen collection, honey production, egg management
Communication	
formal:	Antennae, dance, chemicals and odors
informal:	---

B. Group: Basketball teams (women's or men's)

Group goals:	Win game, win league championship
Personal goals:	Starting position, scoring record
Positional leader(s):	Captain, coach, general manager
Informal leader(s):	Point guard, more-experienced member, other ___
Subteams of group:	Offense, defense
Activities:	Inbounding, driving, defense, scoring, foul shots, *et cetera*
Communication	
formal:	Huddles, practices
informal:	Play calls

C. Group: School of Pharmacy

Group goals:	▶
Personal goals:	▶
Positional leader(s):	Dean of pharmacy
Informal leader(s):	▶
Subteams of group:	▶
Activities:	▶
Communication	

formal:	▸
informal:	▸

D. Group: Social group 1 ✍ _____ ⌨

(your choice: APhA-ASP chapter, Canadian Association of Pharmacy Students & Interns (CAPSI) chapter, sorority chapter, fraternity chapter, chess club, student government association, church choir, scout troop, ROTC battalion, newspaper, yearbook, sports team, Phi Lambda Sigma, Rho Chi, other)

Group goals:	▸
Personal goals:	▸
Positional leader(s):	▸
Informal leader(s):	▸
Subteams of group:	▸
Activities:	▸
Communication	
formal:	▸
informal:	▸

E. Group: Social group 2 ✍ _____ ⌨

(your choice: APhA-ASP chapter, CAPSI chapter, sorority chapter, fraternity chapter, chess club, student government association, church choir, scout troop, ROTC battalion, newspaper, yearbook, sports team, Phi Lambda Sigma, Rho Chi, other)

Group goals:	▸
Personal goals:	▸
Positional leader(s):	▸
Informal leader(s):	▸
Subteams of group:	▸
Activities:	▸
Communication	

formal:	▶
informal:	▶

F. Group: Community (ambulatory, outpatient) pharmacy

Group goals:	▶
Personal goals:	▶
Positional leader(s):	▶
Informal leader(s):	▶
Subteams of group:	▶
Activities:	▶
Communication	
formal:	▶
informal:	▶

G. Group: Inpatient pharmacy

Group goals:	▶
Personal goals:	▶
Positional leader(s):	▶
Informal leader(s):	▶
Subteams of group:	▶
Activities:	▶
Communication	
formal:	▶
informal:	▶

H. Group: Other pharmacy: ✍ _____

Group goals:	▸
Personal goals:	▸
Positional leader(s):	▸
Informal leader(s):	▸
Subteams of group:	▸
Activities:	▸
Communication	
formal:	▸
informal:	▸

I. Group: Healthcare institution ✎_____

Group goals:	▸
Personal goals:	▸
Positional leader(s):	▸
Informal leader(s):	▸
Subteams of group:	▸
Activities:	▸
Communication	
formal:	▸
informal:	▸

Annex 2-2. Report on a Leading Figure in Pharmacy History

Separate annex documents available to facilitators upon request (LeadGrowShape@plei.org).

Read a succinct biography of a pharmacy leader or other medical leader and write a short report about that person and lessons to be gleaned for your personal life and professional life.

The following list offers options for evaluating an historic leader in pharmacy. The list contains few historical figures who were women or members of ethnic minorities, largely because relatively few graduated from pharmacy programs until the second half of the 20th century. Certainly, many female leaders and leaders of color have made and are making their mark on pharmacy as a profession since then.

You may wish to select a figure based on contribution type (see themes below), historical era, or geographic or fraternal connection. Or you may want to select a figure relevant to your state, province, or school. If you would prefer to substitute a different historical figure for this exercise, please propose that leader to your facilitator. To suggest additional biographies to feature in this list in our next edition, email LeadGrowShape@plei.org.

Questions to address in your report:

- What were this person's leadership traits and behaviors?
- What catalysts (e.g., graduate degree, skills, talents, luck) for the perceived success can you identify?
- What lessons in innovation are offered by this individual?
- What lessons in professionalism are offered by this individual?
- What lessons did you take from this assignment related to your own self-awareness?
- No human is perfect. What negative traits or limitations are known about this person?
- If you had more time to investigate, what negative traits or limitations might you check for?

Themes:

Association Leadership: Andersen, Apple, Archambault, Chauncey Cooper, Dunning, Gloria Francke, Hynson, Kremers, Lascoff, Little, Newcomb, Parker, Parrish, Prescott, Procter, Runge, Schaefer, Smith, Swain, Tice, Whelpley, Whitney.

Community Practice: Beringer, Butler, Diehl, Dow, Dunning, Durham, Henry, Hynson, Lascoff, Proctor, Runge, Smith, Stewart, Swain.

Education: Beal, Coggeshall, Chauncey Cooper, Diehl, Ebert, Fischelis, Gibson, Kremers, Little, Lyman, Maisch, Newcomb, Parrish, Power, Prescott, Remington, Schaefer, Smith, Spease, Squibb, Tice, Weaver, Whelpley, Wulling.

Government: Andersen, Archambault, Craigie, Durham, Henry, Parrish.

Institutional Practice: Archambault, Don Francke, Gloria Francke, Latiolais, Parker, Rice, Spease, Stewart, Whitney, Wilbert.

Manufacturing: Craigie, Diehl, Dunning, Ebert, Hallberg, Lloyd, Maisch, Power, Powers, Remington, Squibb, Wellcome.

Military: Craigie, Kendig, Maisch, Squibb.

Publishing: Beringer, Diehl, Eberle, Fischelis, Don Francke, Lyman, Maisch, Newcomb, Procter, Remington, Rubin, Smith, Tice, Whelpley.

Standards, Ethics, Legislation: Archambault, Beal, Brodie, Christensen, Coggeshall, Zada Cooper, Costello,

Durham, Ebert, Gibson, Hallberg, Henry, Kebler, Kendig, Lascoff, Little, Lloyd, Maisch, Parrish, Prescott, Procter, Rice, Squibb, Stewart, Tice, Whelpley.

For pharmacy fraternity affiliations, see list below citations.

For Canadian pharmacists, see list further below.

American Women Pharmacists: Contributions to the Profession, 1st ed, Henderson ML. Binghampton, NY: Pharmaceutical Products Press (Haworth Press), 2002. See also: www.aphafoundation.org/sites/default/files/ckeditor/files/WIP%20mural%20descriptions.pdf

African-American Pharmacy Students: Bond G. Recovering and expanding Mozella Esther Lewis's pioneering history of African-American pharmacy students, 1870-1925 [including: History of the Negro in Pharmacy]. *Pharm Hist* 2016;58:3-35.

Andersen: Mary Louise Andersen. Between the 'No Longer' and the 'Not Yet': Leaders risking popularity safety gamble their lives to help create a better world. *JAPhA*. 2003;43(5):S6–S9. https://www.pharmacist.com/mary-louise-andersen-2003-remington-medalist-dies-85

Apple: William Shoulden Apple 1918-1983: Proponent of pharmacy's independence. Worthen DB. *JAPhA*. 2009 May-Jun;49(3):453-7.

Archambault: George Francis Archambault (1909-2001). Worthen DB. *JAPhA*. 2003 May-Jun;43(3):441-3.

Beal: James Hartley Beal (1861-1945): Educator-statesman. Worthen DB. *JAPhA*. 2005 Sep-Oct;45(5):629-32.

Beringer: George Mahlon Beringer, Sr. 1860-1928: Practical pharmacist. Worthen DB. *JAPhA*. 2008 May-Jun;48(3):417-20.

Black History Month: African-American Pharmacists. Worthen DB. *Pharmacy Practice News* 2007(Feb):28. See also: Culp RW. The genesis of black pharmacists in America to 1900. *Trans Stud Coll Physicians Phila*. 1975;42(Apr):401-11.

Black medical pioneers: African-American 'firsts' in academic and organized medicine. Part three. Epps CH Jr, Johnson DG, Vaughan AL. *J Natl Med Assoc*. 1993 October; 85(10): 777–796. PMCID: PMC2568213

Brodie: Donald Crum Brodie (1908-1994): Pharmacy theoretician. Worthen DB. *JAPhA*. 2004 May-Jun;44(3):403-6.

Butler: Henry Rutherford Butler (1862-1931), www.georgiaencyclopedia.org/articles/science-medicine/henry-rutherford-butler-1862-1931

Christensen: Henry C. Christensen (1865-1947): Advocate of reciprocal registration in pharmacy. Worthen DB. *JAPhA*. 2008 May-Jun;48(3):421-4.

Coggeshall: George Dilwin Coggeshall (1808-1891): First great American pharmacy school graduate. Worthen DB. *JAPhA*. 2010 Nov-Dec;50(6):766-9.

Cooper: Chauncey Ira Cooper (1906-1983): Champion of minority pharmacists. Worthen DB. *JAPhA*. 2006 Jan-Feb;46(1):100-3. See also Cooper CI. The Negro in Pharmacy. In: Elliott EC. *The General Report of the Pharmaceutical Survey, 1946-49*. Washington, DC: American Council on Education, 1950:181-7.

Cooper: Zada Mary Cooper (1875-1961). Worthen DB. *JAPhA*. 2003 Jan-Feb;43(1):124-6.

Costello: Patrick Henry Costello 1897-1971: Architect of reciprocal standards. Worthen DB. *JAPhA*. 2009 Sep-Oct;49(5):694-8.

Craigie: Andrew Craigie (1754-1819), America's first apothecary general. Worthen DB. *JAPhA*. 2002 Sep-Oct;42(5):811-3.

Diehl: Conrad Lewis Diehl (1840-1917): APhA's reporter on the progress of pharmacy. Worthen DB. *JAPhA*. 2004 Nov-Dec;44(6):721-4.

Dow: Cora Dow (1868-1915) – pharmacist, entrepreneur, philanthropist. Henderson ML, Worthen DB. *Pharm Hist*. 2004;46(3):91-105.

Dunning: Henry Armitt Brown Dunning (1877-1962): Pharmacy philanthropist and father of the APhA Foundation. Worthen DB. *JAPhA*. 2004 Sep-Oct;44(5):633-6.

Eberle: Eugene Gustave Eberle 1863-1942: Pharmacy's chronicler. Worthen DB. *JAPhA*. 2009 Jul-

Aug;49(4):560-4.

Ebert: Albert Ethelbert Ebert (1840-1906): Founder of American Pharmacy's oldest award. Worthen DB. *JAPhA*. 2005 Jan-Feb;45(1):103-6.

Fischelis: Robert Phillip Fischelis 1891-1981: Pharmacy activist. Worthen DB. *Pharm Hist*. 2006;48(4):155-60. See also Worthen DB. *JAPhA*. 2006 Mar-Apr;46(2):294-7.

Francke: Donald Eugene Francke (1910-1978): "Reformer by nature, doer by necessity." Worthen DB. *JAPhA*. 2003 Jul-Aug;43(4):538-40.

Francke: Gloria Niemeyer Francke (1922-2008): Pharmacy's first lady. Worthen DB. *JAPhA*. 2010 Jan-Feb;50(1):100-3. See also: *Am J Health-Syst Pharm*. 2009;66:258-78.

Gibson: Robert D. Gibson. 2006 Remington Lecture: the pursuit of dignity. *JAPhA*. 2006 Sep-Oct;46(5):550-4.

Hallberg: Carl Svanté Nicanor Hallberg (1856-1910): Pharmacy's rough diamond. Worthen DB. *JAPhA*. 2010 Mar-Apr 1;50(2):315-9.

Henry: Aaron Henry, http://mshistorynow.mdah.state.ms.us/articles/363/aaron-henry-a-civil-rights-leader-of-the-20th-century; www.nytimes.com/1997/05/21/us/aaron-henry-civil-rights-leader-dies-at-74.html; https://en.wikipedia.org/wiki/Aaron_Henry

Hynson: Henry Parr Hynson (1855-1921): Community pharmacist advocate. Worthen DB. *JAPhA*. 2007 Jan-Feb;47(1):100-3.

Kebler: Lyman Frederick Kebler (1863-1955): Foe to fakers. Worthen DB. *JAPhA*. 2010 May-Jun;50(3):429-32.

Kendig: Harvey Evert Kendig (1878-1950): Architect of the U.S. Army Pharmacy Corps. Worthen DB. *JAPhA*. 2009 Nov-Dec;49(6):821-4.

Kremers: Edward Kremers (1865-1941): Pharmaceutical education reformer. Worthen DB. *JAPhA*. 2005 Jul-Aug;45(4):517-20.

Lascoff: J. Leon Lascoff (1867-1943): Champion of professionalism. Worthen DB. *JAPhA*. 2005 May-Jun;45(3):404-7.

Latiolais: Clifton J. Latiolais, MSc, DSc, Profiles in Leadership. White S, Godwin HN, Weber RJ. *Hosp Pharm*. 2013 September; 48(8): 697–702. See also *JAPhA*. 2010 Sep-Oct;50(5):650-5.

Little: Ernest Little (1888-1973): Champion of the American Foundation for Pharmaceutical Education. Worthen DB. *JAPhA*. 2006 Sep-Oct;46(5):641-4.

Lloyd: John Uri Lloyd 1849-1936: Wizard of American plant pharmacy. Worthen DB. *JAPhA*. 2009 Mar-Apr;49(2):342-4, 346.

Lyman: Rufus A. Lyman: Pharmacy's lamplighter. Worthen DB. *Am J Pharm Educ*. 2009 Aug 28;73(5):84. See also: Rufus Ashley Lyman (1876-1957): A towering figure in the field of pharmaceutical education. Worthen DB. *JAPhA*. 2004 Jan-Feb;44(1):106-9.

Maisch: John Michael Maisch (1831-1893): Father of adequate pharmaceutical legislation. Worthen DB. *JAPhA*. 2003 Nov-Dec;43(6):732-5.

Newcomb: Edwin Leigh Newcomb 1882-1950: Pharmacy's many-sided man. Worthen DB. *JAPhA*. 2008 Sep-Oct;48(5):682-5.

Parker: Paul Frederick Parker 1919-1998: A visionary innovator. Worthen DB. *JAPhA*. 2009 Jan-Feb;49(1):117-21.

Parrish: Edward Parrish (1822-1872): Pioneer ethicist. Worthen DB. *JAPhA*. 2005 Nov-Dec;45(6):758-61.

Power: Frederick Belding Power 1853-1927: Pioneer pharmaceutical scientist. Worthen DB. *JAPhA*. 2008 Jul-Aug;48(4):550-3.

Powers: Justin Lawrence Powers (1895-1981): Champion of improved medication standards. Worthen DB. *JAPhA*. 2007 Mar-Apr;47(2):292-5.

Prescott: Albert Benjamin Prescott (1832-1905): Pharmacy education's revolutionary spark. Worthen DB. *JAPhA*. 2004 May-Jun;44(3):407-10.

Remington: Joseph Price Remington (1847-1918). Worthen DB. *JAPhA*. 2002 Jul-Aug;42(4):664-6.

Rubin: Irving Rubin (1916-1998): Tireless campaigner for pharmacy. Worthen DB. *JAPhA*. 2003 Sep-

Oct;43(5):653-5.

Runge: Mary Munson Runge, www.pharmacist.com/runge-devotes-storied-career-disenfranchised

Schaefer: Hugo Herman Schaefer (1891-1967): Pharmacy's volunteer. Worthen DB. *JAPhA*. 2007 May-Jun;47(3):416-9.

Smith: Daniel B. Smith 1792-1883: Patriarch of American pharmacy. Worthen DB. *JAPhA*. 2008 Nov-Dec;48(6):808-10, 812.

Smith: James McCune Smith (1813-1865), The education and medical practice of Dr., first black American to hold a medical degree. Morgan TM. *J Natl Med Assoc*. 2003 July; 95(7): 603–614. PMCID: PMC2594637

Spease: Edward G. Spease 1883-1957: Father of hospital pharmacy standards. Worthen DB. *JAPhA*. 2006 May-Jun;46(3):403-6.

Stewart: Ella Nora Phillips Stewart, https://en.wikipedia.org/wiki/Ella_P._Stewart

Swain: Robert Lee Swain (1887-1963): Pharmacy's elder statesman. Worthen DB. *JAPhA*. 2010 Jul-Aug;50(4):540-4.

Tice: Linwood Franklin Tice (1909-1996). Worthen DB. *JAPhA*. 2003 Mar-Apr;43(2):329-31.

Weaver: Lawrence Clayton Weaver 1924-2011: Shouldn't we try? Worthen DB. *JAPhA*. 2012 Sep-Oct;52(5):700-6.

Wellcome: Henry Wellcome's museum for the science of history. Skinner GM. *Med Hist*. 1986 October; 30(4): 383–418.

Whelpley: Henry Milton Whelpley (1861-1926): Association worker. Worthen DB. *JAPhA*. 2006 Jul-Aug;46(4):517-20.

Whitney: Harvey A. K. Whitney (1894-1957). Worthen DB. *JAPhA*. 2002 May-Jun;42(3):525-6.

Wilbert: Martin Inventius Wilbert 1865-1916: Bridge builder between pharmacy and medicine. Worthen DB. *JAPhA*. 2007 Nov-Dec;47(6):768-73.

Wulling: Frederick John Wulling 1866-1947: Fighter for increased professional educational standards. Worthen DB. *JAPhA*. 2007 Sep-Oct;47(5):656-8, 661.

Fraternity Affiliations:

AZΩ: [*awaiting reply from AZΩ national office*]

KE: Zada Cooper, Gloria Francke, Lyman, Runge. Need online biographies for Mary Lou Andersen, Gay Dodson, Joy Donelson, Metta Lou Henderson, Lucinda Maine, Evlyn Gray Scott, Marilyn Speedie, Evelyn Timmons

KΨ: Rubin, Schaefer, Tice

ΛKΣ: Need online biographies for Shirley P. McKee, Mary Jo Reilly, Sara White, Janet Engle, others

РПФ: Rubin. Need online biography for Phil Sacks

ΦΔX: Beal, Dunning, Don Francke, Kremers, Lyman, Newcomb, Parker, Powers, Prescott, Spease, Weaver, Whitney, Wulling

Canadian Pharmacist Biographies, via Dictionary of Canadian Biography, www.biographi.ca/en/

BAIRD, WILLIAM TEEL, pharmacist, office holder, militia officer, and author; b. c. 1819 in Fredericton

BOYD, JOHN, teacher, publisher, and pharmacist; b. 1823 at South River, Sydney County, N.S.

BRETT, ROBERT GEORGE, pharmacist, physician and surgeon, businessman, politician, and lieutenant governor; b. 16 Nov. 1851 near Strathroy, Upper Canada

BRUNET, WILFRID-ÉTIENNE (baptized Étienne-Wilfrid), pharmacist and politician; b. 21 Oct. 1832 at Quebec

DALTON, CHARLES, farmer, pharmacist, co-founder of the silver-fox industry in Prince Edward Island, politician, philanthropist, and office holder; b. 9 June 1850 in Tignish, P.E.I.

DEARIN, JOHN JOSEPH, pharmacist and politician; b. probably in 1818 at St John's, Nfld.

DÉNÉCHAUD, JACQUES, surgeon, apothecary, and landowner; b. 11 July 1728 in Saint-Savin, France

ELLIOT, ROBERT WATT, pharmacist and businessman; b. 26 July 1835 in Eramosa Township, Upper Canada

ELLIOT, WILLIAM, farmer, pharmacist and businessman; b. 22 Dec. 1812 in Hammersmith (London), England

FRASER, JAMES DANIEL BAIN, pharmacist, scientist, and entrepreneur; b. 11 Feb. 1807 in Pictou, N.S.

GRAY, HENRY ROBERT, pharmacist, politician, inventor, and businessman; b. 30 Dec. 1838 in Boston, England

HÉBERT, LOUIS, apothecary, first officer of justice in New France, first Canadian settler to support himself from the soil, b. Paris 1575?

KERRY, JOHN, pharmacist and wholesaler and manufacturer of pharmaceutical products; b. 1825 in London, England

LYMAN, BENJAMIN, pharmacist, chemist, drug wholesaler, and manufacturer; b. in Derby, Vermont, 11 June 1810

McLAUGHLIN, JOHN JAMES pharmacist and manufacturer; b. 2 March 1865 near Enniskillen, Durham County, Upper Canada

MILLER, HUGH, pharmacist, justice of the peace, and office holder; b. 2 June 1818 in Inverness, Scotland

SAUNDERS, WILLIAM, pharmacist, scientist, civil servant, and author; b. 16 June 1836 in Crediton, England

STEWART, GEORGE, editor, publisher, pharmacist, and author; b. 26 Nov. 1848 in New York City

TILLEY, Sir SAMUEL LEONARD, pharmacist, politician, and lieutenant governor; b. 8 May 1818 at Gagetown, N.B.

TOUPIN-FAFARD, MATHILDE (baptized Marie-Célina-Mathilde, and known also as Mathilda), teacher, Sister of Charity at the Hôpital Général of Montreal, nurse, and school administrator; b. 27 Dec. 1875 in Saint-Cuthbert, Que.

TRUDEAU, ROMUALD (he was baptized Denys-Romuald), pharmacist, merchant, author, and politician; b. 7 Feb. 1802 at Montreal, Lower Canada

VIGER, AMANDA, named Saint-Jean-de-Goto, Religious Hospitaller of St Joseph, pharmacist, and founder and director general of the Hôtel-Dieu of Tracadie, N.B.; b. 27 July 1845 in Boucherville, Lower Canada

WEINER, GERRY (1933-), Progressive Conservative Party of Canada MP and cabinet minister, president of Equality Party, mayor of Dollard-des-Ormeaux, Quebec, https://en.wikipedia.org/wiki/Gerry_Weiner

Please help us identify biographies of notable Canadian pharmacists by using the feedback form in Appendix 8.

Resources:

Worthen DB. *Heroes of Pharmacy: Professional Leadership in Times of Change, 2nd ed.* Washington, DC: American Pharmacists Association, 2012.

Worthen DB. Reflections: 2010 Kremers Award Lecture. *Pharm History* 2010;52:55-69.

Worthen DB. Pharmacy heroes—Pay it forward. *Pharmacy Student* 2004;1(Jul-Aug):24-26.

Dictionary of Canadian Biography [Dictionnaire biographique du Canada]; University of Toronto and Université Laval; www.biographi.ca/en/

Module « 3 »   WHEN YOU LOOK IN THE MIRROR, WHO LOOKS BACK?

☞ Learning Objectives:

Objective 1. To identify one's personal core values.
Objective 2. To describe the degree to which each of one's activities enable the expression of one's values.
Objective 3. To identify obstacles that prevent expression of core values.

This Module addresses how to understand one's self, before considering others. If you do not know about yourself, you cannot do much. You cannot do much for others nor with others!

This Module helps participants name and prioritize their personal core values. And participants explore how leadership is depicted in various social media.

3.1. Readings or activities before class:

A. Someone challenged novelist Ernest Hemingway to write a short story in only six words. Hemingway's six-word story read: "For sale: baby shoes, never worn." Poignant, to say the least.

Following in this tradition, you have two six-word writing tasks.

1. Write your six-word memoir (about your life up to this point).

2. Write your six-word résumé (where you want to go in life, or maybe your personal mission statement).

Exactly six words each. No more, and no less. You can make them humorous, tragic, obvious, or occult. But they must reflect you. You will be amazed at how people come to understand you better (and empathize with you) in such brief statements.

Some examples to get your juices flowing:

    a. To write. To serve. To protect.
    b. Bounded by images, titles and fears.
    c. With vaccines help people around globe
    d. Regret-Free Living! Aspirational... Challenging... Possible...
    e. Always forgive. Never forget. Question EVERYTHING!
    f. Living unapologetically, growing daily, surrendering everything
    g. My journey incomplete; clear road ahead
    h. Childhood not great. Wonderful life today.

Now, it is your turn:

B. **Your six-word memoir** (about your life up to this point).

✍ _____   ⌨

C. **Your six-word résumé** (where you want to go in life or your personal mission statement).

32

D. Read and be prepared to discuss this passage on "Big Rocks," adapted from: Covey SR. *First Things First*. New York: Free Press, 1996.

E. Review the Activity and Percentage table in the section marked "Where Does the Time Go?" and begin thinking about and jotting down your answers. You can refine these answers when you get to class.

THE BIG ROCKS OF LIFE

An instructor was talking with a group of students. She said, "Okay, time for a quiz."

The instructor pulled out a 1-gallon, wide-mouthed jar and set it on a table. Then she placed a dozen fist-sized rocks, one at a time, into the jar.

When the jar was filled to the top and no more rocks would fit inside, she asked, "Is this jar full?" Everyone in the class said, "Yes." Then she said, "Really?"

Next, she reached under the table and pulled out a bucket of gravel. She dumped some gravel in and shook the jar to work gravel pieces into the spaces between the big rocks.

She smiled and asked the group once more, "Is the jar full?" By this time the class was onto her. "Probably not," a man answered. "Good!" she replied.

So, she reached under the table and brought out a bucket of sand. She started dumping in the sand and shaking the jar, so the sand went into the spaces between rocks and gravel. Once more she asked the question, "Is this jar full?" "No!" the class shouted. She replied, "Good!"

Then she grabbed a pitcher of water and began to pour it in until the jar was filled to the brim. Then she looked up at the class and asked, "What is the lesson here?"

An eager student raised her hand and said, "No matter how full your schedule is, if you try really hard, you can always fit some more things into it!"

"No," the instructor replied, "The lesson is: If you do not put the big rocks in first, you'll never get them in at all."

What are the big rocks in your life? Remember to prioritize the Big Rocks first, or you'll never get to them at all.

3.2. Resources needed:

Annex 3-1. Living Your Core Values
Annex 3-2. Values-Interests-Strengths-Needs (VISN) Chart

3.3. In-class activities:

-"Ever more people today have the means to live, but no meaning to live for." *Viktor E. Frankl*

Step 1. Questions?
Step 2. Six words.
Step 3. Big Rocks.
Step 4. Quote.
Step 5. Exercise.

PERSONAL CORE VALUES

The goal of every human should be to live a life that is fulfilled. With ever increasing demands on our time, the real question we confront is not: "How full can I make my life?" Rather, it is: "What do I want my life to be filled with?"

a. PEAKS: Look back and identify one or more events you believe represent HIGH points in your life. These should be experiences, which upon reflection gave you some sense of significant meaning or purpose. In the space below, make a list of VALUES you believe were being expressed during those times.

✎ _____ ⌨

b. TROUGHS: Look back and identify one or more events you believe represent a LOW point in your life. These should be experiences, which upon reflection, left you feeling totally empty and hollow. In the space below, make a list of values you were not being allowed to express, or perhaps were even being violated.

✎ _____ ⌨

c. Circle or highlight EACH of the following terms that are important to you and add terms not already listed into the blank spaces.

Accountability	Elegance	Integrity	Risk-taking
Accuracy	Empowerment	Joy	Romance
Acknowledgment	Excellence	Justice	Self-expression
Action	Fame	Love	Service
Adventure	Focus	Loyalty	Spirituality
Aesthetics	Free spirit	Nurturing	Status
Authenticity	Free to choose	Orderliness	Success
Beauty	Growth	Participation	Tradition
Collaboration	Happiness	Partnership	Trust
Community	Harmony	Peace	Truth
Comradeship	Honesty	Performance	Vitality
Connectedness	Honor	Power	Wealth
Contribution	Humor	Productivity	Wisdom
Creativity	Independence	Recognition	Zest
▸	▸	▸	▸
▸	▸	▸	▸

d. Select your TOP EIGHT core values from above (including those you identified a few questions earlier) and write them below in PRIORITY order (#1 = top priority):

1. ✎ _____ ⌨

2. ✎ _____ ⌨

3. ✎ _____ ⌨

4. ✎ _____ ⌨

5. ✎ _____ ⌨

6. ✎ _____ ⌨

7. ✎ _____ ⌨

8. ✎ _____ ⌨

e. Transfer the top eight into Annex 3-1. Living Your Core Values, and complete the exercise there .

WHERE DOES THE TIME GO?

Step 6.

a. List the activities you perform in an average week. If you are tempted to say you study 80% of your waking life, subdivide that chunk of time by study methods or locations. Then approximate what percentage of your week each activity consumes.

Activity *	Percent
Sleep	33 %
Facebook, videogames tv	15 %
School	40 %
Studying	10 %
Eating/drinking	2 %
	%
	%
Miscellaneous	%
	TOTAL = 100%

* Activities may include: sleep, school, work, groups, family, friends, Facebook, video games, Netflix, exercise, eating/drinking, household activities, *et cetera*. If you sleep 8 hours per day, then 33% = sleep.

b. Now, use the circle below to sketch out a pie chart to reflect how you spend your time using the information from the table above. Note: Each slice in the figure below represents 5% of the total.

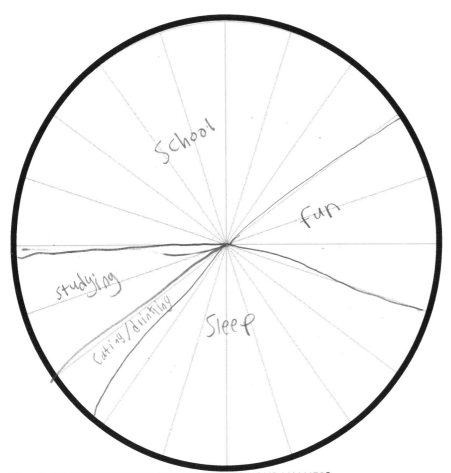

Step 7. TO WHAT DEGREE ARE YOU LIVING YOUR VALUES?

a. Refer to your pie chart. For each slice of your pie, list which value(s) you can express in the performance of that activity.

b. Find a partner near you, so you can pair-share your thoughts. Reflect on the following questions and pair-share your observations on each:

Pair-share 1:

    i. Do any of your core values repeatedly show up? Why could that be? Implications?

    ii. Which of your core values rarely show up, or do not show up at all? What might that say about those values or the activities you choose to perform?

    iii. Which slices of your pie have few or no core values attached? Why might you be spending time on those activities?

Notes: ___ 🖮

Pair-share 2:

    i. Are there certain slice(s) of your pie you would like to eliminate? If that is not possible, how might they be reduced? What is a first practical commitment you can make towards the reduction or elimination you seek?

    ii. Are there certain slices of your pie you would like to expand? How does that desire relate to your values? What is a practical first commitment you can make towards expansion of the slice (activity)?

    iii. After reflecting on your core values, what needs (and corresponding activities) are NOT currently present in your pie chart, if any? How could you make room for them in your pie? What is a practical first commitment you can make to accommodate needs missing from your pie chart that are tied to your core values?

Pair-share 3:

    i. Reflect on the various groups and organizations you belong to. Do any of those groups seem to struggle because of their inability to adequately express one of your core values? How might you assist them? What might the impact be for them and for you?

    ii. How will you deal with future opportunities and requests to take on new things that do not align with your core values?

c. List three commitments you will make to increase the amount of time spent on activities that solidly align with your values. Then share them with a partner:

By _____ (date) I commit to: ✍ _____ ▥

By _____ (date) I commit to: ✍ _____ ▥

By _____ (date) I commit to: ✍ _____ ▥

LEADER MINING ON THE WORLD-WIDE WEB

Step 8. Surf the web for "lead" or "leader" or "leading" or "leadership" for 5 minutes. Pay attention to how these terms are depicted.

Have one group explore Facebook, one group Instagram, one group Pinterest, one group LinkedIn, one group Twitter, one group Google, one group Snapchat, one group YouTube, *et cetera*, one group go rogue. Record what you see in the blanks below.

Most frequent: ✍ _____ ▥

Most curious: ✍ _____ ▥

Most useful: ✍ _____ ▥

What is similar, what is different across these media? ✍ _____ ▥

3.4. Discussion questions:

Per facilitator...
In what ways is it important for a pharmacist to understand personal core values?

3.5. After-class assignments:

A. Add a recurring entry to calendar to call your core values to your attention every morning at a time you select. Consider also adding a recurring entry for the end of the day, to spur you to reflect on how you spent your time.

B. Transfer your core values to the upper-left segment of the Values-Interests-Strengths-Needs (VISN) Chart in Annex 3-2. Transfer your priority activities to the upper-right segment.

C. Fulfill the commitments you made scheduling your priorities.

D. Fulfill the before-class activities for the next Module assigned by your facilitator.

3.6. Bibliography, references, & resources:

Center for Ethical Leadership, www.ethicalleadership.org

Co-Active Coaching Values Clarification Exercise, www.thecoaches.com

Covey SR. *First Things First*. New York: Free Press, 1996.

Fershleiser R, Smith L, eds. *Not Quite What I Was Planning: Six-Word Memoirs from Writers Famous & Obscure.* New York: Harper Perennial, 2008.

Flashcards via Quizlet, https://quizlet.com/class/3716098/, Values-Interests-Strengths-Needs (VISN) » 4 terms

Smith L, Fershleiser R, eds. *Six-Word Memoirs on Love and Heartbreak: by Writers Famous and Obscure.* New York: Harper Perennial, 2009.

Smith L, Fershleiser R, eds. *I Can't Keep My Own Secrets—Six-Word Memoirs by Teens Famous & Obscure.* New York: Harper Perennial, 2009.

Annex 3-1. Living Your Core Values

Separate annex documents available to facilitators upon request (LeadGrowShape@plei.org).

Name: ✍ _____ 🖮   Date: ✍ _____ 🖮

Let's evaluate how well you are living your core values – the attributes above that you identified as important and necessary for your life. Using the headers atop each column in Annex 3-1, evaluate each core value you listed.

a. Rate how well you express a value, using a scale of 1 to 10.

b. Provide example(s) of how this value shows up in your life. Describe what you do to express this value in your day-to-day living.

c. Identify any obstacles you face that prevent you from expressing your value to a greater extent.

d. What actions can you take to express your value more fully (i.e., to increase your score)?

Core Value	Score I express this value: 1-never to 10-always	Justification Describe what you have been doing to express this value	Obstacles What is keeping you from better honoring this value?	Action You will take to increase score	Action Deadline
1)	▶	▶	▶	▶	▶
2)	▶	▶	▶	▶	▶
3)	▶	▶	▶	▶	▶
4)	▶	▶	▶	▶	▶
5)	▶	▶	▶	▶	▶
6)	▶	▶	▶	▶	▶
7)	▶	▶	▶	▶	▶
8)	▶	▶	▶	▶	▶

Adapted from: The Center for Ethical Leadership's Core Values Assessment (www.ethicalleadership.org) and Co-Active Coaching Values Clarification Exercise (www.thecoaches.com).

Transfer your core values to the upper-left segment of the Values-Interests-Strengths-Needs (VISN) Chart in Annex 3-2. Transfer your priority activities to the upper-right segment.

Annex 3-2. Values-Interests-Strengths-Needs (VISN) Chart

Separate annex documents available to facilitators upon request (LeadGrowShape@plei.org).

You'll be prompted when to fill this out (see Modules numbers below). Keep adjusting it as new revelations come to you.

Values Why you do things (meaning, purpose) [Modules 3 and 4]		Interests What activities bring you joy? What's really fun? [Module 14]
1.		1.
2.		2.
3.		3.
4.		4.
5.		5.
	Your Name	
Strengths What you're really good at doing [Modules 8 and 14]	Version Date:	Needs What does your involvement need to provide for you? (be selfish) [answer on your own]
1.		1.
2.		2.
3.		3.
4.		4.
5.		5.

Module « 4 »   MANAGING THE CLOCK: OPTIMIZING YOUR TIME

☞ Learning Objectives:

Objective 1. To identify strategies to better manage one's time.
Objective 2. To recognize the difference between scheduling one's priorities and prioritizing one's schedule.
Objective 3. To compare and contrast how the participants allocate their time with what they value.

In this Module, we explore your time. Time management is the art of controlling your own time and using it to your best advantage. This Module is about getting more things done that are aligned to your interests, talents, and values. Participants will apply their core values to direct finite time and energy toward activities that meet internal and external needs in a way that provides meaning and purpose. Meanwhile, do not forget other Modules where we explored how to prioritize doing the most important things, in contrast to doing just anything. Remember the chief lesson from Covey's "Big Rocks" story (from Module 3).

[*Optional*] The "Juggle of Life" examines factors that contribute to misalignment of priorities, and why we might engage these factors in our lives. Instead, we will discuss how to overcome challenges and increase one's opportunity for a more successful life.

4.1. Readings or activities before class:

Read and be prepared to discuss the text on time management that follows.

MASTERING TIME

Time is certainly the world's scarcest commodity. There are ways to organize your time that will make you more productive: group similar tasks, avoid duplicate tasks, handle a piece of paper only once. Does saving time interest you? Together, we will work on streamlining your approach to work and life.

Did you know the average leader works undisturbed about 9 minutes between interruptions? You can control time, just as you can budget money. Days and hours have a lot in common with dollars and cents. Initially, it may take some conscious effort. If you master your time, you can master your life.

Most pharmacists would rather be spending more of their time counseling patients and consulting with physicians. Would you rather be doing different things with your time, things that would make you happier and more professionally satisfied? You can.

Your use of time reflects your personality. Not every suggestion presented here will work for you. Use the ones which fit your personality and style. The object is to be both efficient and effective.

IT'S YOUR TIME

Take a look at your yesterday. Did you control your time? If not, who or what distracted you from your agenda? Your list probably includes your professors, your boss, customers, staff, spouse, family, and telephone callers, looking at Facebook posts, Twitter, Snapchat, Instagram, *et cetera*. Anyone or anything else?

Analyze the day, hour by hour. Then go back and break it down by categories of events and activities (e.g., commuting, reading reference books, answering telephone calls, writing and reading correspondence, filling prescriptions).

Schedule your time by your values [explored in the core-values exercise in Module 3]. Does how you spent your time yesterday reflect your own set of values? Was your use of time properly balanced, according to your own set of values? How can you control or minimize unwanted intrusions on your time?

Too involved in details? Write shorter correspondence, eliminate unimportant items, delegate as much of what is important as you can.

WHAT IS YOUR TIME WORTH?

Really... How much is an hour of your time worth? Work it out right now:

$_____ per hour = (hourly salary) X 1.3 (to account for benefits)

$_____ per hour = (monthly salary) / 21 workdays per month / _ hours per day *

$_____ per hour = (annual salary) / 240 workdays per year / _ hours per day *

    * include commuting time

You can make separate calculations according to your own situation: the value of an hour if a part-time job was full time, what your best salary ever translates to, what an hour will be worth after you graduate, *et cetera*. Use this value when weighing alternatives, when considering the purchase of labor-saving devices, and when billing for consultations.

DELEGATION

Do you delegate all you can? Delegation strengthens your communication skills, it helps build up involvement by your team in their tasks, and it frees you to accomplish more.

Failure to delegate may result from reluctance to train your teammates. Remember that training is an investment that will yield a harvest of extra time for you later. Some bosses fear that the staff will make mistakes. But if you view your role as that of the coach, you will realize how much more can be accomplished by a team. The coach must be clear on the game strategy. Teammates must be clear when executing plays. And the more the team practices, and the more demanding those practices are, the more proficient the team becomes.

Some leaders fear success by subordinates; those leaders fear losing their job, their esteem, or control of the work place. Actually, one's success reflects one's skills as a leader. And fear of success is part of a negative feedback loop. Design your team's accountability system so they report to you periodically on progress. That way you can intervene with help before the last minute, if needed. In most cases, you are not paid for how much effort you put into a job; you are paid for the results you accomplish.

When you delegate, be available to answer general questions and provide guidance, of course. State what you want accomplished, not how to do it. Find out whether the people to whom you will delegate have the right interests and talents to accomplish the work. Determine whether they have what they need to accomplish the work by asking directly. You will be amazed by your team's resourcefulness and ingenuity. Be prepared for the results to be a bit different than you may have done it yourself. Only correct the product if it is essential to success. Otherwise, you risk disengagement by your teammates and your future ability to delegate to others will be diminished.

Get things done through other people. Develop the art of giving the right person the right job. Delegating to an overqualified subordinate to assure the job is done right may lead to boredom and frustration. Help your teammates stretch, exercise new muscles, and gain new competencies.

Help your staff learn from mistakes, so they become better themselves.

FINDING TIME

When you use other people's ideas, you find extra time. By considering other people's experiences, you gain the benefit of their labor. In fact, you can use your own past activity. Save work you do, especially analyses and reports; you might be able to reuse the work that went into them later in a modified form.

ORGANIZING, SCHEDULING, PRIORITIZING

What is your system for scheduling projects? Do not spend a major portion of your time on scheduling itself, but do have a system that organizes your activity. Schedule the next day's activities each afternoon; this gives time for ideas to incubate subconsciously.

Schedule flexibly; interruptions happen no matter what you do. Anticipate the turmoil and be prepared to respond to it. If you lose control of your schedule, do not spend time worrying. Simply re-establish control at the earliest opportunity. When you prioritize your work, you already know where to apply your effort for the greatest return on investment.

Recognize that people tend to underestimate the time involved in what they enjoy doing and overestimate the time for what they dislike. Use gaps in the schedule to make telephone calls or draft quick messages. Consolidate similar tasks into groups: calls, messages, file searches, *et cetera*.

Do you have a filing system? Do you waste a lot of time retrieving addresses, articles, or reports? When handling paper or computer files, know what to keep, what to throw away. If you are hesitant to discard something, ask yourself how readily you can replace it if you change your mind later. If it will take a lot of work to replace it, keep it.

To organize projects, set up file folders for each day of the week (or month) and each of the succeeding months. Use these folders as "tickler" or "suspense" files, placing projects to be completed sometime in the future in the proper folder. As you plan your week, pull out all the projects from the folders and resort them by priority.

Why not do two things at once? We don't advocate multitasking, as multitasking does not equate to optimal productivity. We do suggest looking for opportunities to augment time already allocated.

- At the same time: delegate tasks before going on vacation. You will return to find preliminary reports waiting for you.
- At the same place: combine trips to meet several goals.
- While traveling: use travel time to read, listen to podcasts, do brain work (the initial sorting of facts).

Or write the summary report of a conference while on the way home.

KNOW WHEN TO SAY "NO"

Turn down assignments, when you can, if they are more appropriate for someone else, or if you lack the time, personnel, or other resources to do it properly. Reject requests that do not relate to your goals. Saying no at the right time can allow you to give proper attention to major projects, albeit at the expense of minor ones.

HOW TO SAY "NO"

Without the ability to say "no" to at least some of the external requests that come into your life, you will never be able to say "yes" to your internal desires to pursue activities aligned with your core values. Here's an exercise to help you become more comfortable in your ability to say "no."

Step 1: The first step in learning to say "no" is to understand the reason(s) WHY you might find it so hard to do so. In the space below, list the top reason(s) you find it hard to say "no." What do you fear might happen?

Step 2: Now ask yourself, what is the actual likelihood your biggest fears will be realized? Does the degree of probability justify the degree of fear you possess?

Step 3: In reality, it is less about the actual act of saying "no," and more about how you say it. See if you can come up with at least three different ways to say "no" that will make it even less likely that your worst fears will be realized:

If you are not sure how to effectively say "no," Celestine Chua of the Personal Excellence Blog

43

(http://personalexcellence.co) provides these seven simple ways for you to do so. Use the method most appropriate to your situation.

1. "I can't commit to this, because I have other priorities at the moment."

If you are too busy to engage in the request or offer, this will apply. Responding this way lets the person know your plate is full at the moment, so he/she should hold off now and for some time. If it makes it easier, you can also share what you are working on, so the person can better understand. If you think there is a good chance you do not have time but are not quite sure, tell the person you should check your schedule and get back to them. Just be sure you actually do get back to them.

2. "Now's not a good time, because I'm in the middle of something. How about we reconnect at «future time»?"

It is common to get requests for help while you are doing something else. This method is a great way to (temporarily) hold off the request. First, you let the person know now is not a good time. Secondly, you make known your desire to help by suggesting another time (at your convenience). This way, the person does not feel dismissed.

3. "I'd love to do this, but …"

This is a gentle way of breaking no to the other party. It is encouraging, as it lets the person know you like their idea. Of course, only say this if you really mean it. This strategy works in situations when someone makes you a great offer that you just cannot accept due to prior commitments (#1) or different needs (#5).

4. "Let me think about it first and I'll get back to you."

This is more like a "Maybe" than a straight out "No." If you are interested, but you do not want to say "yes" just yet, use this reply. Sometimes you will get a great offer that seems to meet your needs and values, but you may need to delay on committing to allow time to reflect. If the person is sincere about the request, he/she will be willing to wait a short while. Specify a date or time range (say, in 1 to 2 weeks) when the person can expect a reply.

If you are not interested in what the person has to offer at all, do not lead him/her on. Use methods #5, #6 or #7, which are definitive.

5. "This doesn't meet my needs now, but I'll keep you in mind."

If someone is pitching a deal or opportunity that just is not what you are looking for, let him/her know straight-out that it does not meet your needs. Otherwise, the discussion can drag on longer than it should. It helps let the person know there is nothing wrong about what he/she is offering, but that you are looking for something else. At the same time, by saying you will keep him/her in mind, it signals you are open to future opportunities. Add this part only if it is true.

6. "I'm not the best person to help you on this. You might try X…"

If you are being asked for help with something that you cannot contribute much to or do not have resources to help, let it be known they are asking the wrong person. If possible, refer them to an alternate they can follow-up on – whether it is someone you know, someone who might know someone else, or even a certain department. Make it a point to offer an alternate contact, so the person does not end up in a dead end. This way you help steer the person to the right place.

7. "No, I can't."

The simplest and most direct way to say no. We build up too many barriers in our mind to saying no. Often, these barriers are self-created and do not truly exist. Do not think so much about saying no and just say it outright. You will be surprised when the reception is not half as bad as what you imagined it might be.

BE GOOD TO YOURSELF

We will talk about stress elsewhere in this Workbook, but the key to peak performance is to take breaks periodically and relax. "Sharpen the saw," as Stephen Covey would say. Do the things that relax you: give yourself coffee breaks, close the door and put your feet up on the desk, browse through the library, walk to another part of the building, or do whatever refreshes your mind and prepares you to return to conquering the job.

Enjoy whatever you are doing. If you are not having fun, something needs to be changed.

Easy As A, B, C

Time-management expert Alan Lakein described an ABC method of designating priorities. He uses A designators for high value items, B for medium, and C for low value. Items should be further prioritized as A-1, A-2, B-1, B-2, *et cetera*. Evaluate each of your goals based on its payoff once completed. Do not consider how much time is involved, but rather the goal's impact. Then make a list of the tasks needed to accomplish these goals. After all, you cannot do a goal.

Set priorities according to your values, labeling the task based on the ABC system. Update the list daily, at the same time of the day. Keep only one list, not several partial lists. See which tasks can be delegated, then schedule your time based on the remaining tasks.

Lakein says 80% of everything in the world has a C priority. Focus on the other 20%, where the value is. Do not get bogged down in low-value activities. Spend your time going after grade-A customers, grade-A jobs, and grade-A projects.

The key to Lakein's system is the question: "What is the best use of my time right now?" Ask yourself this question frequently, several times a day. It will help get you back on track after interruptions.

Upgrade or downgrade tasks whenever appropriate. Get in the habit of asking yourself: "What will happen if I do not do that C task?" If the answer is nothing, do not do it. If your grade-C is your boss' grade-A, give it an aging period. If it does not go away, do it and get it over with.

Here's one of Lakein's ways to designate a task: if nobody ever asks about it, it is a C. If they write a follow-up letter, it is a B. If they telephone, it is an A. If they come in person, it is a crisis, an A+.

Lakein's final advice: do it now! Get it over with before it escalates. Do not procrastinate, it is not worth the guilt, anxiety, stress, overtime, or fatigue. When confronted with an A of overwhelming size, poke a hole in it – do some piece of it that can be resolved quickly. That trims the task a bit and makes you feel good about doing something. Take lots of little bites that move the task along. Once you gain momentum, block out a chunk of time and finish the project once and for all.

Time-Savers

Organization

List your goals and the tasks needed to attain them. Make a to-do list and prioritize it. Work on to-do list items, but resist the temptation to skip over difficult items. Concentrate on one thing at a time. Write down good ideas to pursue later.

Handle each piece of paper only once: file it, throw it away, answer it, or delegate it. It costs money to reply to a query, mostly labor (i.e., time). Shorten your answers. Use form letters or standard paragraphs (word processors make this easy). Stop reading junk mail or do it only once a week. Pick up the telephone and resolve questions right away.

To get started, begin with something easy, but make sure the hard ones still get done. Or start with a hard one, so you have the encouragement of getting it out of the way. Keep your desk top cleared for action, with the most important thing on top. Have a do-not-disturb period every day.

Schedule meetings just before lunch or quitting time. Participants will limit comments to what is important or what really matters to them. Eat just a light lunch, so you do not get sleepy.

Communication

Listen actively in every discussion. Ask questions. If someone else has the answer, you gain the time they used to develop the answer.

Telephone calls: group them. Plan before you call what you will say and what you will seek.

Personal Style

Stop trying to be a perfectionist; be realistic. Shoot for excellence, not perfection. Consider lowering your standards. Not every project deserves the finest. Put your waiting time to good use. Do not waste time feeling guilty or worried. Redirect that energy into active planning for the future.

When you find yourself procrastinating, ask yourself what you are avoiding or what you fear. Set deadlines for yourself and others. Stick to them flexibly. Get rid of busywork. It is not how much you are doing that is important, but rather how much you get done.

Decision-making principle: a clear statement of the problem is 50% of the solution.

Closure: know when to stop a task or conversation; do not overdo it.

Develop your planning skills so crises are avoided. Identify your prime time, the time of the day when you do your best work. Use this time for your most important projects. Spend 15 minutes a day thinking, just thinking. Use mistakes as a learning tool.

TIME-WASTERS

Here is a list of insidious time-wasters. Which ones are notorious for lurking around your desk?

Having no systematic approach. Waiting for decisions. Confused responsibilities. Lack of coordination or communication between teammates or sections. Lack of standards or procedures. Failure to have alternate plans. Attempting too much at once. Misplaced items. Lack of preparation. Doing everything yourself. Wasting other people's time. Excess socializing. Unmanageable distractions.

Take a look at your own day. What other time-wasters do you compete with?

DISCUSSION

These paragraphs have scratched the surface on time management and delegation strategies. We mean for this to be a thought-provoking Module, not an all-inclusive one. If we have raised questions in your mind about how to schedule or delegate more effectively, we have succeeded.

To a great extent, excellent pharmacists make excellent use of time. Plan today how you can become a better time manager.

So, what is the best use of your time right now?

4.2. Resources needed:

Consider your personal core values, such as those identified in Module 3.
Annex 4-1. Your Priorities to Balance
For "Juggle of Life:" Box of balls of different colors, shapes, weights, and sizes.

4.3. In-class activities:

"No matter how busy you are, you must take time to make the other person feel important." Mary Kay Ash

Step 1. Questions?
Step 2. Quote.
Step 3. Exercise.

JUGGLING MULTIPLE ACTIVITIES

a. When busy, people often refer to "juggling" activities. An accomplished juggler makes it look easy – smooth and rhythmic – as objects are caught and released and rotated in the air. But it is not easy for people not skilled in juggling, or when the number of objects grows unmanageable. Juggling may seem frenetic and anxiety provoking, particularly when objects are dropped.

b. Another way to think about managing objects is by thinking about a Ferris wheel. Look at the Ferris-wheel diagram below – a larger version appears in Annex 4-1. Rank your priorities by assigning the letters A through F to the most important priority activities in your life. If you have more or fewer than six main priorities, that is fine. Annotate the spaces as you wish.

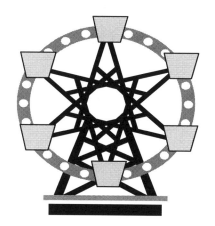

A. ✍ _____ ▦

B. ✍ _____ ▦

C. ✍ _____ ▦

D. ✍ _____ ▦

E. ✍ _____ ▦

F. ✍ _____ ▦

For each priority, define it. In other words, state what it means or why it is a priority. For example, if health is a priority, it may be because heart disease runs in your family. Or if family is important, it may be so because you were an only child and regretted not having siblings.

Step 4. Moving on, what does success or happiness looks like? Take 5 minutes to draw a picture or select a clip-art image, to create a graphical representation of your picture of success or happiness. Do not underestimate the power of images to convey meaning (see: television ads). A picture = 1,000 words.

Step 5. Imagine your life as a game in which five balls are in play. The balls are called WORK, FAMILY, HEALTH, FRIENDS, and INTEGRITY. It is an incredible expenditure of time and energy, but you keep all of them from dropping, because it is what is expected of you and you must not fail. Which of the five is rubber, which is glass, which is metal?

Once you can identify and comprehend the composition of each ball, you will have the beginnings of balance in your life – knowledge improves our ability to make decisions.

Note: Balance may not mean "equal attention." It means appropriate attention or appropriate emphasis.

Step 6. **Application to Pharmacy**:

a. Describe the priorities in your workplace or college setting. Focus on actual day-to-day activities people engage in. Who set the priorities?

> i. What is the contribution of each individual team member?
>
> ii. What role can each team member contribute towards identifying local priorities and the underlying rationale for them (i.e., their composition)?
>
> iii. Would it be important to know individual, personal priorities and the position that work holds, as if it were one of the juggled balls? Would it help to know whether WORK was rubber or glass? How?

Note: It is important to emphasize that we are not discussing "goal setting." Assume all <u>identified</u> priorities are important. Focus on identifying composition (e.g., rubber or glass), so we can best determine how to juggle them (as well as the consequences if something is dropped). The "goal" is to achieve a better balance of priorities.

b. Explore a pharmacy's organizational priorities further. Do they differ for each type of individual (professional *versus* nonprofessional; shift leader *versus* staff pharmacist)? Where does WORK fall in the hierarchy of balls that each juggles personally? How will knowing this information benefit the group's work?

> i. By doing so, it is possible that you can identify common priorities.
>
> ii. Also, you can better match tasks or responsibilities to individuals.
>
> iii. Further, you demonstrate that you care.

This last aspect cannot be underestimated. When individuals feel cared for, they are often willing to care for you, demonstrate respect for your knowledge and be motivated to tackle the work at hand. A spirit of collaboration is then possible, which can offset other threats or distractions.

Step 7. **Threats to Achieving Balance**

a. An obvious threat is one we have already covered – juggling things aimlessly as is expected or because we have not considered something different:

> i. A hierarchy of priorities for a given situation;
>
> ii. Alignment of personal priorities with those of our employer, our profession, *et cetera*.

What keeps us from looking at what we are juggling in greater depth? What keeps us from understanding what we are focused on and the rationale for doing so? In other words, what keeps us from achieving the first step towards establishing a balanced (and hopefully healthy) life?

b. Form up in groups of two to three people for 3 to 4 minutes to identify additional reasons.

c. Could an aimless juggle be related to a fear of failing or letting others down?

Step 8. [Optional] Refer to the "How to Say No" section of the pre-class reading. Using the pair-share technique, have one participant ask the other to perform a task. The listening participant uses one or more of the how-to methods to deflect the request. Practice four to six different requests each.

Step 9. [Optional] Priority, Balance, & Alignment: The "**Juggle of Life**"

a. Three volunteers stand across from each other about 4 to 5 feet apart, such that they form a triangle.

b. Discuss the way the volunteers managed the balls. In general, how did they do? If the volunteers chose to start again, is their approach to keeping the balls from dropping the same each time? What circumstances caused the balls to drop? What happened when the balls dropped? How did the individual volunteers react? If anyone choose to hold on to any of the balls (and not keep them in the air), make a mental note for later in the discussion. If the goal was to keep the balls in play without dropping them, how did the volunteers feel when they began to see balls drop?

c. Now, recall the goal of this activity (i.e., keeping the increasing number of balls of different shapes and sizes in play).

d. Why? For what purpose did the exercise serve and who decided? Did the volunteers ask or did they behave according to what was "expected of them"? Even if they had determined the purpose, would it have mattered much not knowing what each ball represented?

e. What are your priorities?

✎ _____ ⌨

f. They are important to me because:

✎ _____ ⌨

g. If I were to let one or more of these priorities drop, I would feel:

✎ _____ ⌨

4.4. Discussion questions:

Per facilitator

4.5. After-class assignments:

A. *Facilitator discretion: For those who find the exercise of inventorying how their time was spent enlightening, or for those who had a difficult time detailing how they spent their time, this optional activity may be fruitful.* Keep a digital camera with you for the next 7 days. Take a picture of each major activity each day. At the end of the week, make a simple collage of your life. Then reflect on how you spent your time.
  - How much time was spent on "important" things?
  - What would you do different next time (next week)?
B. Use your priority activities from the Ferris wheel to adjust the upper-right segment of the Values-Interests-Strengths-Needs (VISN) Chart in Annex 3-2. Adjust the values section based on any new insights you had.
C. Fulfill the before-class activities for the next Module assigned by your facilitator.

4.6. Bibliography, references, & resources:

Anonymous. Spend professional time differently, say pharmacists. *Am Pharm.* 1987;27:19.
Dobbins RV, King CM Jr. Revised classification and filing system for hospital pharmacy. *Hosp Pharm.* 1983;18:7-35.
Lakein A. *How to Get Control of Your Time and Your Life.* New York: Signet, 1973.
Scott DA. *How to Put More Time in Your Life.* New York: Signet, 1980.
Smith WE, Breslauer M. Follow-up file and system. *Hosp Pharm.* 1983;18:36.
Uris A. *The Executive Deskbook, 2nd ed.* New York: Van Nostrand-Reinhold Company, 1976.
White SJ. Managing the pharmacy manager. *Am J Hosp Pharm.* 1984;41:516-521.

Annex 4-1. Your Priorities to Balance

Separate annex documents available to facilitators upon request (LeadGrowShape@plei.org).

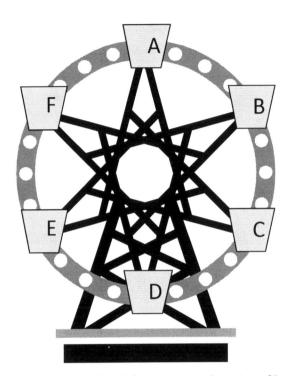

List six priorities in your life. For each, add a definition or explanation of how it came to be a priority.

A. ✎ _____ ▦

B. ✎ _____ ▦

C. ✎ _____ ▦

D. ✎ _____ ▦

E. ✎ _____ ▦

F. ✎ _____ ▦

Module « 5 »   LEADER LABORATORY

☞ Learning Objectives:

Objective 1. To provide experiential opportunities for participants to perform leading-by-doing.
Objective 2. To design a project, explain a vision to others, assemble a team, and execute that project.
Objective 3. To reflect on a leading-by-doing experience and gain insights by explaining it to others.

This Module puts leadership theory into practice. In short, participants are asked to "do leadership" or, more simply, to lead something. We call it Leadership-by-Doing. Participants can select from myriad options.

But before the immersion, participants learn the nomenclature for the medley of leadership styles (from authoritarian through *laissez-faire*, plus several other dimensions to boot). All the thought leaders are considered.

In the end, though, to lead is to do. Chemists must perform chemical reactions. And leaders must have their time in the barrel, to deal face-to-face with the people who would be persuaded to work together to accomplish a task. Fear not, it happens all the time. And we'll teach the timid some tricks to make it easy.

5.1. Readings or activities before class:

Read and be prepared to discuss the following text passage about leadership.
After reading, complete Annex 5-1: Leadership-Style Crossword Puzzle (or follow facilitator instructions).

A PRÉCIS* ON LEADERSHIP
* FANCY WORD FOR SUMMARY

Bill Zellmer pointed out that college and early pharmacy practice teaches that "success depends on independent hard work." Organization skills, human-resources and personnel-management skills, leadership and motivation skills only recently have been offered as formal programs in many colleges. Such skills were typically left to the curriculum of "The Big Game of Life" or the School of Hard Knocks.

Each time student pharmacists get involved in a professional program, they pick up valuable skills: patient counseling, resource management, project scheduling, budgeting, planning, and many others. Perhaps less obviously, the same can be said for social events, like planning a dinner-dance, a political campaign, or a charity drive. What better way is there to learn about motivation than to try to wake up college students early on a Saturday morning so they can perform blood-pressure screenings? Student activities certainly are a vehicle for leadership. But they are effective vehicles only if participants take advantage of the opportunities for leadership available to them.

WHAT IS THIS THING CALLED LEADERSHIP?

Human-resource experts generally agree that leadership is the activity of influencing others towards accomplishing a task. John W. Gardner, who directed the Leadership Studies Program, called leadership "the process of persuasion and example by which an individual (or leadership team) induces a group to take action...." Hersey & Blanchard noted that leadership, the process, is a function of the leader, the followers, and the situation.

Management, on the other hand, is defined differently by many writers. Hersey & Blanchard describe management as that subset of leadership emphasizing organizations; they call management "a special kind of leadership in which the achievement of organizational goals is paramount." Gardner and many others define managers as those holding directive posts in organizations; to them, managers preside over organization functions, allocate resources (including people's time), and set priorities.

Some writers consider pure leadership and pure management as two extremes of a single continuum. Winston Churchill is a historical example of a man who was both a good leader and a good manager; Golda Meir had a similar mix of leadership and management ability. My impression of Martin Luther King, Jr., is that he had strong leadership qualities, but I am unaware of his business-management skills. The "pure" manager might be exemplified by a taxi dispatcher, who can move people's bodies without moving their minds. Our own goal might be to improve our mix of both leadership behaviors and management skills.

Theories also abound about what motivates people. McGregor's Theory X and Theory Y describe two sets of managers: the first set (Theory X) assumes people to be fundamentally lazy, irresponsible, and resistant to change. Theory-Y managers believe work can be as natural as play and that people can be self-directed and creative at work if properly motivated. Individual styles generally fall in a continuum between these two poles. To an extent, these theories are self-fulfilling prophesies. The pharmacist who has little confidence in a new technician may find that the technician need not exert any energy to live up to the expectations held for him.

Maslow's theory of the hierarchy of needs (physiologic, safety, social, esteem, and self-actualization) holds that motivation comes from workers' unmet needs; and that satisfied needs are not motivators. Many pharmacists (certainly not all) are at the esteem phase of this model; support personnel frequently have unmet social and esteem needs.

Herzberg described two sets of factors in the work place, hygiene factors and motivators. His hygiene factors include pay, benefits, supervision, working conditions, and work relationships. When hygiene factors are adequate, they are not motivators; if they are inadequate, they are dissatisfiers. Motivators, to Herzberg, include achievement, recognition, pride in work, responsibility, and advancement. Applying this theory to a pharmacy may involve having adequate recognition programs for employees, delegation and diffusion of responsibility among the staff, and dual-tracked advancement plans for both aspiring practitioners and managers.

What motivates volunteer leaders? The most common answer is to return to the organization part of the benefits the leader received earlier. There are also personal benefits such as networking (e.g., contacts, visibility, insight). There may also be an altruistic desire to help colleagues reach their goals, and perhaps to serve the public through the activities of the organization.

Can you imagine ways to motivate those you associate with? One pharmacist might be positively motivated by being assigned responsibility for a project he or she enjoys, such as moderating a journal club. Others might not be influenced by getting more duties, but would respond to time off to attend to family events or professional meetings.

WHO'S A LEADER? AM I A LEADER?

Any time you try to influence someone else's behavior, you are a potential leader. That person can be a peer, a subordinate, or a superior. If your proposal for redesigning a pharmacy is adopted, you have led that portion of the project. Some lead in small ways, some in large. If you are looked to for the answers to a problem, you are a leader. The followers have decided it.

But what makes leaders special? Bennis and Nanus say its intensity of vision, an ability to communicate goals, conviction in beliefs, and positive self-regard. Gardner's years of analysis and synthesis suggest six respects by which leaders distinguish themselves:

- they think longer term,
- they grasp the relationship of their unit to larger entities,
- they influence constituents beyond their jurisdiction,

- they emphasize vision and values,
- they have the political skill to cope with conflicting requirements, and
- they think in terms of renewal.

How Can I Lead? It Depends...

There are other ways of modeling leadership. Some use simple categories, such as autocratic, participative, and *laissez faire*. Blanchard *et al.* are proponents of a situational-leadership model [explored in Module 15], which describes four types of leadership behavior, varying by the degree of task orientation and the degree of interpersonal relationship a situation entails. Blake and Mouton described a similar matrix with axes labeled as concern for people *versus* concern for task.

Wikipedia lists six categories under the heading "leadership style," but that is not a complete list. Other groups have used other terms to define specific styles of leadership. Here are thumbnail descriptions of several labeled styles, so you can compare and contrast them. As you read this list, think of individuals you have known in your life who might fit these descriptions. If you have trouble fitting someone into one of these categories, try to describe what is different in their style.

- **Authoritarian**: An authoritarian (or autocratic) leadership style emphasizes the distinction between the authoritarian leader and his or her followers. Direct supervision is key in maintaining their relationship and their environment. Authoritarian leadership styles typically follow the vision of those who are in control, offer little room for dialog, and claim the benefit of efficiency. Examples: a police officer directing traffic, a teacher ordering a student to do his or her assignment, and a supervisor instructing a subordinate to clean a workstation. Traits: sets goals individually, engages primarily in one-way and downward communication, controls discussion with followers, and dominate interaction.

- **Charismatic**: Charismatic leadership has a broad knowledge of a domain of expertise, has a self-promoting personality, exhibits great energy, and is willing to take risks and use irregular strategies to stimulate their followers to think independently.

- **Laissez-faire** (or free-rein): A laissez-faire leadership style occurs when the rights and power to make decisions is given fully to the worker. Laissez-faire leaders allow the group to have wide freedom to make decisions about their work. These followers are self-ruling, with the leader offering guidance and support as requested. The laissez-faire leader provides group members with materials needed to achieve their goals, but does not directly participate in decision-making unless followers request assistance.

- **Participative** (or democratic): With a participative leadership style, the leader shares the decision-making abilities with group members by promoting the interests of the group and by practicing social equality. The democratic aspects expect everyone should play a part in group decisions. Even so, the democratic style still requires guidance and control by a specific leader. Traits: Honest, inspiring, fair-minded, broad-minded. Regrettably, roles are unclear or time is short, democratic leadership can lead to communication failures and uncompleted projects. Democratic leadership works best when members are skilled and eager to participate.

- **Paternalistic**: A paternalistic leader acts as a father figure, by taking care of their subordinates as a parent would. This leader supplies ample concern for followers or workers, receiving in return the trust and loyalty of the group. Workers are expected to be committed to what the leader believes and not work independently. The relationship between these co-workers and leader can be very solid.

- **Servant**: Servant leadership is both a leadership philosophy and a set of leadership practices. Traditional leadership generally involves the accumulation and exercise of power from a position of stature. By comparison, the servant-leader shares power, puts the needs of others first and helps people develop and perform as highly as possible.

- **Situational**: Hersey & Blanchard's term for a matrixed response to task behavior and relationship behavior. See Module 15 and Annex 15-1 for details.

- **Transactional**: Transactional leaders motivate followers through a system of rewards and punishments. Two factors form the basis for this system: contingent reward and management-by-exception. Contingent reward involves material or psychological rewards for performance. With management-by-exception, the leader intervenes when subordinates do not perform acceptably and initiates corrective action. Transactional leaders focus on increasing the efficiency of established routines, more on existing rules than with making changes.
- **Transformational**: A transformational leader is not limited by his or her followers' perception, but rather works to change or transform the followers' needs and redirect their thinking. Leaders that follow the transformation style challenge and inspire followers with a sense of purpose and excitement. They also create a vision of what they aspire to be, and communicate this idea to others.

Your leadership style range or flexibility is the repertoire of styles you can employ. Some people are only able to act as coaches; they have no capacity, for example, to direct tasks.

Leadership-style adaptability is even more important to effectiveness than the breadth of one's repertoire. Adaptability is the ability to vary styles appropriately according to the demands of the situation.

In progressive organizations, it is common for staff to negotiate with supervisors on standards for performance appraisals, analogous to a management-by-objective (MBO) approach. Hersey & Blanchard suggest that it is not unreasonable to also negotiate a primary leadership style with your boss, coaching and supporting being common choices.

OPPORTUNITIES FOR LEADERSHIP IN PHARMACY

Many people consider leadership in pharmacy to be limited to the executive councils of the myriad associations with 3- and 4-letter acronyms. We certainly need leaders there, to help shape practice standards, health policy, and our legislative agenda. But the truth is that leaders are needed and are present all around us, in pharmacies of all sizes and types.

Leaders in pharmacy coach their colleagues in therapeutics and counseling. Leaders in pharmacy shape community pharmacy services, from multi-outlet chains to independent entrepreneurs. Pharmacy leaders organize teams to perform industrial and clinical research; and they develop and deliver outreaching pharmacy services in hospitals and institutions. Leaders in pharmacy influence patients to be more compliant in medication use. They also influence prescribers to select rational drug therapy. The scope of leadership in pharmacy ranges from national policy affecting millions to the one-to-one pharmacist-patient interaction commemorated in Norman Rockwell prints. Leadership is an essential part of excellent pharmacy.

LEADER DEVELOPMENT

Leadership can be developed through exposure to needs, where the leader-apprentice creates a project to meet the need. Or through exposure to problems, where the leader-student practices the search for resolution. In most cases, leadership development is a matter of exercising and marshaling skills we already have.

Gardner calls these experiences:

- Opportunities for participants to test their judgment under pressure, in the face of opposition, and in the fluid and swiftly changing circumstances so characteristic of action.
- Opportunities to exercise responsibility and perhaps to try out one or another of the skills required for leadership.
- Opportunities for participants to test and sharpen their intuitive gifts and to judge their impact on others.
- Exposure to the untidy world, where decisions must be made on inadequate information and the soundest argument does not always win, where problems do not get fully solved or, if solved, surface anew in another form.

That is why leadership, except as theory, cannot fully be taught on paper nor in a classroom. By definition, leadership involves both people and doing. The best way to develop effective leadership behavior is through practice and experience in the laboratory of life [hence Module 5]. Small organizations provide ample opportunity to develop leadership experience while working on the mission of the organization. Working your way up from project or committee chair to a junior officer to an executive officer is one good leadership-development path. In retrospect, this can be seen by reverse engineering the career steps of many accomplished pharmacy leaders.

Gardner continues: "Leaders have always been generalists. Tomorrow's leaders will very likely have begun life as trained specialists, but to mature as leaders they must sooner or later climb out of the trenches of specialization and rise above the boundaries that separate the various segments of society. Only as generalists can they cope with the diversity of problems and multiple constituencies that contemporary leaders face."

"Young potential leaders must be able to see how whole systems function, and how interaction with neighboring systems may be constructively managed. They must be exposed to experiences that broaden their horizons and introduce them to other worlds."

You are in the midst of this broadening now.

Here is a rule of thumb for enhancing leadership: practice. Repeated efforts, trial and error, and learning from "mistakes" help each of us become ever better. To a great extent, excellent pharmacists are excellent leaders and motivators. Plan today how you can become a better leader in pharmacy. In the meantime, take a glance from time to time at Appendix 7 and its pithy reflections on leaders and leadership.

5.2. Resources needed:

None other than this Module

5.3. In-class activities:

"Tell me and I forget. Teach me and I remember. Involve me and I learn." Benjamin Franklin

"Teaching about leadership is necessary to enable others to lead effectively,
*but it is not sufficient. Not sufficient in the sense that leadership requires **doing***
and leadership development therefore requires action-learning (or learning on the job)
to find one's voice, develop, and hone one's skills." Posner BZ. J Lead Educ. 2009;8(1):1-10.

Step 1. Questions?
Step 2. Quote.
Step 3. Project.

OPTIONS FOR YOUR INDIVIDUAL LEADERSHIP-BY-DOING PROJECT

a. Organize a (professional or service) project on campus or the surrounding community (e.g., CPR, first-aid certification, fund raising), involving a team of at least two other people.

- Assemblies, grand rounds, advocacy programs, legislative-process discussions, health fairs, clinical-skills competitions, networking within multi-campus organizations, business-plan competitions, interprofessional seminars, post-graduate roundtables, formulary-review competitions, community outreach, *et cetera*.

b. Learn a new hobby (e.g., musical instrument, golf) or learn a new skill (e.g., painting, plumbing), then teach another person the basics of that hobby or skill.

c. Go interview [suggestions appear in Module 22] at least two people who are "positionally successful" (e.g., a group president). Reverse engineer the steps each took to prepare for their current positions. Compare and contrast the leadership lessons they offer you.

- In other words, if the presidential domino was the most recent one to fall, what were the preceding dominos? What were the series of preparatory offices that the president held previously? Prepared to be president by previously serving as vice president, and that by serving as committee chair, and that by serving as committee member, *et cetera*.

d. Use the content of Module 25 to develop and implement a legislative advocacy program.

e. Lead two groups of people in a cross-cultural experience: Organize an event where Group A learns more about Culture B, and vice versa.

f. Use the content of Module 20 to develop and pitch a business case.

g. Lead a group through a face-to-face goal-setting or problem-solving or decision-making or conflict-settling exercise or write up a critique of officer performance or public meetings [see Modules 21, 29, 30, 31, 32, or 33].

h. If you want to make a name for yourself as an innovator, make a case for a different kind of project with your facilitator.

Some thoughts:

As you work to accomplish these projects and develop these skills, you will encounter trial and error in the same ways that developing leaders must learn to take on new projects, work with others, maximize successes, deal with mistakes, and apply new ideas towards personal growth.

A college group may be one of the hardest kinds of group to organize, insofar as it is an assembly of equals, of peers. Coercion rarely works because a college group is a volunteer organization and the leader is rarely able to exert the "stick" of withholding a paycheck, invoking penalties, denying a promotion, *et cetera*. This laboratory is a chance to try practicing your motivational and collaborative skills with your peers.

5.4. Discussion questions:

Per facilitator
Facilitator discretion: Use of Annex 5-1. Leadership-Style Crossword Puzzle

5.5. After-class assignments:

A. After completing one of the project ideas described above, write a __-page paper addressing these points:

  1. Describe the project you undertook.

  2. Describe your output or results.

  3. Now comment on the process of the project and the results of the project:
  ▷ Describe positive experiences; describe negative experiences.
  ▷ Describe any failures (or near-failures) you had and how you dealt with it.
  ▷ Do you like working in a group or team for a class project? Why or why not?
  ▷ What role do you typically take when working in a group or team? Why?
  ▷ What leadership styles or strategies did you experience in your project?
  ▷ What concerns did you have in organizing others to accomplish your task?
  ▷ How cohesive was the group you assembled? Why?
  ▷ What are the most important things you have learned from your experience in this course?
  ▷ How might what you have learned be useful to you in future experiences?
  ▷ What material from the Workbook or other sources was most useful to you in your project?

  4. Share any additional thoughts or comments relevant to your experience.

B. Fulfill the before-class activities for the next Module assigned by your facilitator.

5.6. Bibliography, references, & resources:

APhA Academy of Student Pharmacists, AACP Committee on Student Professionalism. Pharmacy Professionalism Toolkit for Students and Faculty, version 2.0, 2009. www.aacp.org/resources/studentaffairspersonnel/studentaffairspolicies/Documents/Version_2%200_Ph armacy_Professionalism_Toolkit_for_Students_and_Faculty.pdf

Bennis W, Nanus B. *Leadership: The Strategies for Taking Charge*. New York: Harper Row, 1985.

Boyd B, Williams J. Developing life-long learners through personal-growth projects. *J Lead Educ*. 2010;9(2):144-50. www.journalofleadershiped.org/attachments/article/148/Boyd_and_Williams.pdf

Chesnut R, Tran-Johnson J. Impact of a student leadership development program. *Am J Pharm Educ*. 2013 Dec 16;77(10):225. www.ncbi.nlm.nih.gov/pmc/articles/PMC3872944/pdf/ajpe7710225.pdf

Coers N, Lorensen M, Anderson JC II. Case study: Student perceptions of groups & teams in leadership Education. *J Lead Educ*. 2009;8(1):93-110. www.journalofleadershiped.org/attachments/article/203/JOLE_8_1_Coers_Lorensen_Anderson.pdf

Flashcards via Quizlet, https://quizlet.com/class/3716098/, Leadership Styles » 14 terms

Gardner JW. *Leadership Papers-1: The Nature of Leadership*. Independent Sector, Washington, DC, 1986.

Gardner JW. *Leadership Papers-7: Leadership Development*. Independent Sector, Washington, DC, 1987.

Hersey P, Blanchard KH. Management of Organizational Behavior: Utilizing Human Resources, 4th edition. Prentice-Hall, Inc., Englewood Cliffs, NJ; 1982.

Herzberg F. One more time: How do you motivate employees? *Harvard Business Review*. 1987;65(Sep-Oct):109-120.

McGregor D. *Leadership and Motivation*. Cambridge, Mass: MIT Press, 1966.

Ross LA, Janke KK, Boyle CJ, Gianutsos G, Lindsey CC, Moczygemba LR, Whalen K. Preparation of faculty members and students to be citizen leaders and pharmacy advocates. *Am J Pharm Educ*. 2013 Dec 16;77(10):220. www.ncbi.nlm.nih.gov/pmc/articles/PMC3872939/pdf/ajpe7710220.pdf

Zellmer WA. A good place to work. *Am J Hosp Pharm*. 1984;41:889.

Annex 5-1. Leadership-Style Crossword Puzzle

Separate annex documents available to facilitators upon request (LeadGrowShape@plei.org).

Across

7. Another name for authoritarian style
10. Another name for participative style
11. Another name for laissez-faire style
12. Matrixed response to task behavior and relationship behavior

Down

1. Leader works to change followers' needs and inspire followers with purpose
2. Leaders motivate followers through rewards and punishments, plus management-by-exception
3. Rights and power to make decisions given fully to worker
4. Shared decision-making; group practices social equality
5. Emphasizes distinction between authoritarian leader and followers. Direct supervision is key
6. Leader acts as parent, taking care of subordinates
8. Broad expertise, self-promoting persona, energetic, irregular strategies to stimulate independent thinking
9. Leader shares power, puts needs of others first, helps people develop

Module « **6** »   FAILURE: THE UNDERAPPRECIATED INSTRUCTOR

☞ Learning Objectives:

Objective 1. To identify one's priorities and align them with how we view facets of life (personal and professional), so that we can determine an optimal blend.

Objective 2. To recognize that everyone fails, and the importance of learning from failure to enable future success.

Objective 3. To recognize behaviors related to failure.

This Module helps participants examine their emotions and actions when faced with failure. Yet we are reassured that failure is the underappreciated instructor. How can that possibly be? Understanding your understanding of failure will help you see how your perceptions and reactions to the situations of daily living are shaped. This is so true of situations that challenge you and rock your spirit. These times (when failure takes hold) may inhibit or affect an individual's ability to lead a group or participate in a group.

At times, fear of failure may saddle a person or a group with retention of activities that no longer have meaning or purpose. Those activities may be retained to avoid change or criticism, even if the activities have lost relevance. Instead, we have the power to choose to retain or divest those activities, once we understand them.

Proactive consideration of failure allows participants an opportunity to determine areas that may require attention (and possibly change) to adequately prepare for future failure or, even better, the success and growth that can result. "Successful" failure means that we have learned and are enabled to advance.

6.1. Readings or activities before class:

Read the Hamilton quote below. What does this quote mean to you? How do you feel about investing time like this?

6.2. Resources needed:

Annex 6-1. Failure – The Underappreciated Instructor

6.3. In-class activities:

> *"People are training for success when they should be training for failure.*
> *Failure is far more common than success." J. Wallace Hamilton*

Step 1. Questions?
Step 2. Quote.
Step 3. Exercise.

Part I – Why People Fail: The Impact Of Failure On Groups

What Does Failure Mean to You?

a. What are your attitudes toward failure today?

✍ _____ ⌨

b. Think about a recent setback you experienced. How did it make you feel? What did you do about it?

✍ _____ ⌨

c. What has failure MEANT to a <u>group</u> you belong to?

✍ _____ ⌨

d. <u>Who</u> defines success or failure for that group?

✍ _____ ⌨

e. Think about a recent group setback and describe how the group felt.

✍ _____ ⌨

f. Is failure easier – or harder – in a group setting, where no one individual takes a risk?

✍ _____ ⌨

▶

g. What is your approach to failure? How do you deal with failure?

✍ _____ ⌨

Part II – The Monkeys

Step 4. The Monkeys, from *Failing Forward*, by John C. Maxwell.

"Four monkeys were placed in a room that had a tall pole in the center. Suspended from the top of that pole was a bunch of bananas. One of the hungry monkeys started climbing the pole to get something to eat, but just as he reached out to grab a banana, he was doused with a torrent of cold water. Squealing, he scampered down the pole and abandoned his attempt to feed himself. Each monkey made a similar attempt, and each one was drenched with cold water. After making several attempts, they finally gave up.

Then researchers removed one of the monkeys from the room and replaced him with a new monkey. As the newcomer began to climb the pole, the other three grabbed him and pulled him down to the ground. After trying to climb the pole several times and being dragged down by the others, he finally gave up and never attempted to climb the pole again.

The researchers replaced the original monkeys, one by one, and each time a new monkey was brought in, the others would drag him down before he could reach the bananas. In time, the room was filled with monkeys who had never received a cold shower. None of them would climb the pole, but not one of them knew why."

PART III – TEN REASONS PEOPLE FAIL

Step 5. Next, consider the list of Top Ten Reasons People Fail, and accompanying comments, as observed by John C. Maxwell (section B of Annex 6-1).

a. Your facilitator will read the reasons out loud. Consider each reason fully, both from the individual perspective and the group perspective. Use the table below to jot down any of the ten that strike you as meaningful.

If any reasons relevant to you are not read out, add your reason to the list.

Self (individual)	Group
▸	▸
▸	▸
▸	▸
▸	▸
▸	▸
▸	▸
▸	▸

"People are training for success when they should be training for failure.
Failure is far more common than success." – J. Wallace Hamilton

Often fear of failing or disappointing others compels us to work to "keep balls in the air" or "from dropping." Understanding why people fail and how people behave in response to failure permits you a chance to see whether any of these ideas apply to you. Considering your views on failure and examining how you behave in response to failure can help you to design strategies to prepare you to overcome challenges. Understanding what you think or feel about failure may help you make decisions pertaining to what you are juggling so that you can adjust accordingly to achieve a better balance. This is true personally and professionally.

6.4. Discussion questions:

Per facilitator …

In what ways is it important for a pharmacist to understand, prepare for, and learn from failure? Personally? Professionally?

6.5. After-class assignments:

A. While in a public setting (cafeteria, restaurant, campus, shopping center) or taking in the day's news, find examples of "successful" failure: failure that enables future growth. Do in groups, if you wish.
B. Fulfill the before-class activities for the next Module assigned by your facilitator.

61

6.6. Bibliography, references, & resources:

Flashcards via Quizlet, https://quizlet.com/class/3716098/, Reasons Why People Fail (Maxwell) » 10 terms
Harford T. *Adapt: Why All Success Begins with Failure*. New York: Farrar, Straus & Giroux, 2011.
Maxwell JC. *Failing Forward*. Nashville: Thomas Nelson Press, 2000.

Annex 6-1. Failure – The Underappreciated Instructor: A Summary

Separate annex documents available to facilitators upon request (LeadGrowShape@plei.org).

A. Some Common Approaches to Failure

- ▸ Blaming others
- ▸ Repeating the same mistakes
- ▸ Expecting never to fail again
- ▸ Expecting to continually fail
- ▸ Accepting tradition blindly
- ▸ Being limited by past mistakes
- ▸ Thinking "I am a failure"
- ▸ Quitting

B. Top Ten Reasons Why People Fail

Reason	Comment
1. Poor people skills (didn't assess needs)	Lack of understanding people; lack of knowledge of needs of others, inability to communicate and motivate others.
2. Negative attitude (lack of motivation)	Thwarts self-motivation and motivation for others; defeating, negative, distracting.
3. Bad fit (didn't assess needs)	Inability to find or create an environment that suits an individual's strengths and permits him/her to shine, mismatch knowledge and skills with goals or tasks.
4. Lack of focus (didn't assess needs)	Priorities all over the place. Risk of miscommunication and disconnect between people. Inefficient use of resources without accomplishment of goals or tasks.
5. Weak commitment (lack of motivation) (lack of leadership trait)	Threat to accomplishment; threat to motivation of others; falling short of doing your best.
6. Unwillingness to change	Inflexibility; taking need to change or improve personal and therefore resent and resist change; stuck on past; limit potential to start fresh and explore uncharted areas.
7. Taking shortcuts (assumptions)	Cutting corners can circumvent the lesson provided by the journey; unwilling to pay dues; sign of impatience, poor self-discipline and lack of self-respect or love.
8. Relying solely on talent	Can serve as a handicap; overlook the need to grow and develop.
9. Response to poor information	Inability to weed through information critical to successful decision-making. Victim of gossip or assumptions.
10. Lack of goals	Emptiness; absence of desire, direction, passion—may lead to a sense of aimlessness.

Adapted from: Maxwell JC. *Failing Forward*. Nashville: Thomas Nelson Press, 2000.

Module « 7 » WHY MATTERS: PASSION & MOTIVATION THAT UNDERGIRD LEADERS

☞ Learning Objectives:

Objective 1. To compare and contrast common ideas about being a leader *versus* the work of leadership.
Objective 2. To identify leadership challenges that have the potential to be demotivating.
Objective 3. To discuss the human tendency to collapse subjective interpretations onto objective facts, and how this tendency can affect motivation.
Objective 4. To discuss the importance of identifying and leveraging one's passion as a source of internal motivation to sustain leaders through challenging times.

Many people pursue leadership positions because they like the idea of being a leader (or receiving the esteem accorded to people in front). But once they become titled as a leader, they may realize that there is a big difference between imagining what it is like to be a leader and actually performing the work of a leader. This Module starts by contrasting the image of leader with the work of leader.

Leader positions can be fraught with frustrations and disappointments. Many people will question and disagree with a leader's vision. Those who agree may offer to help and not follow through. Challenges such as these can suck out enthusiasm, induce doubt, sap will and energy. This program will help participants identify their life's passions and leverage them as a source of limitless energy to drive leadership pursuits.

7.1. Readings or activities <u>before class</u>:

Emotional Intelligence: Try to locate this article without paying fees: Goleman D. What makes a leader? *Harvard Business Review* 1998;76:93-102. Instead of paying fees, use this option: en.wikipedia.org/wiki/Emotional_intelligence. Read one or the other and be prepared to discuss it. Be ready to discuss Daniel Goleman's five skills of emotional intelligence:

- **Self-awareness**: Knowing one's emotions, strengths, weaknesses, drives, values, and goals – and their effects on others
  ▷ Hallmarks: Self-confidence, realistic self-assessment, self-deprecating sense of humor
- **Self-regulation**: Controlling or redirecting disruptive emotions and impulses
  ▷ Hallmarks: Trustworthiness, integrity, comfort with ambiguity, openness to change
- **Motivation**: Being driven to achieve for the sake of achievement
  ▷ Hallmarks: Strong desire to achieve, optimism (even when facing failure), organizational commitment
- **Empathy**: Considering others' feelings, especially when making decisions
  ▷ Hallmarks: Expertise in building and retaining talent, cross-cultural sensitivity, service to clients and customers
- **Social skill**: Managing relationships to move people in desired directions
  ▷ Hallmarks: Effectiveness in leading change, persuasiveness, expertise in building and leading teams

Ask yourself: why these five and not others?

After reading, complete Annex 7-1: Motivation & Demotivation Crossword Puzzle (or follow facilitator instructions).

7.2. Resources needed:

None other than this Module

7.3. In-class activities:

"Motivation is a fire within. If someone else tries to light that fire under you,
chances are it will burn only briefly." Stephen R. Covey

Step 1. Questions?
Step 2. Quote.
Step 3. Exercise.

TAPPING INTO YOUR ULTIMATE ENERGY SOURCE

a. Compare and contrast the following photographs and reflect on the elements of each that relate to leadership. Write your notes in the space below:

b. Pair-share your thoughts on the following questions:

- ▸ Which photo better represents the average person's image of being a leader? In what way(s)?
- ▸ Which photo better represents the day-to-day work of being a leader? In what ways(s)?
- ▸ Which photo more closely matches your frame of mind when you decided to take a leadership role in an organization? Has your frame of mind changed since you made your decision? In what way(s)?

WHAT DEMOTIVATES A LEADER?

Step 4. Which aspects of the "work of leadership" do you find to be the most challenging and frustrating? List them in the space below and describe one specific leader experience that was especially challenging or frustrating to you:

Aspects: ✍ _____ ⌨

Your experience: ✍ _____ ⌨

a. Pair-share the following:
   ▷ Which aspects did you identify to be the most challenging and frustrating? Why do you think those aspects are so difficult for you?
   ▷ What is the experience like when you must confront and deal with those challenges and frustrations? Think about the specific example you listed above and describe what that experience did to your energy and motivation to continue leading others.
   ▷ What happens when you lose your motivation to lead? Where do you go (physically or emotionally)? Why? What is the impact on you? Your followers? The organization?

b. Identify a previous leadership experience that was especially demotivating to you (perhaps the one you wrote about above). Do your best to reflect on what ACTUALLY happened as if you were an uninterested observer looking at the experience from a short distance away. In the left-hand column below, list the OBJECTIVE facts associated with the circumstance. For example, let's say your experience relates to a meeting you called that was poorly attended. Your facts might be (1) I sent out an email about a meeting, and (2) 20% of the invitees showed up.

Objective Facts	Score	Subjective Interpretations	Score
▸		▸	
▸		▸	
▸		▸	
▸		▸	

	►		►	

c. Pair-share: Present the facts of your experience, and then on a scale of 1 (low) to 10 (high), rate how demotivating the experience feels to you based on the facts alone. (1 = not demotivated at all and 10 = completely demotivated)

d. Now, in the right-hand column above, list the subjective interpretation you made (if any) for the associated fact on the left. Here are some examples:

EXAMPLE 1:

Objective: I sent out an email about a meeting.

Subjective: Everyone knew about the meeting and they all had time to plan to attend, but nobody cared to come.

EXAMPLE 2:

Objective: 20% of the invitees showed up

Subjective: Nobody really cares about what we are doing. They all just joined to pad their CVs.

e. Pair-share:

▷ Present your subjective interpretations of the facts, and again rate your level of demotivation on a scale of 1 to 10. Did your rating go up, down or stay the same?

▷ Other than your motivation levels, what else might your subjective interpretations affect (negatively or positively)?

▷ Discuss the cost/benefit ratio of your interpretations. If the costs of your interpretations outweigh their benefits, why would you create them? Assuming you cannot stop creating them, what could you do to minimize their potential negative impacts?

Step 5.

PASSION: THE ULTIMATE SOURCE OF MOTIVATION

a. What are you MOST passionate about? If you could do only ONE thing for the rest of your life, what would it be? What do you enjoy doing so much, that a life without it would not be a life worth living? Enter your ideas in this space:

✍ _____ ⌨

b. Pair-share:

▷ What was your experience in trying to identify a single great passion and reduce it to writing?

▷ Maybe you were not able to come up with something. Why might that be? If you are willing, share your passion, and then describe how it has shaped your life decisions or events.

c. Finding your WHY:

▷ Simon Sinek famously told people and businesses around the world to "Start with Why." What would be the purpose(s) for beginning with that thought?

▷ Unfortunately, identifying your unique and compelling "WHY" may be easier said than done. Complete the following list of questions to see how your passions and personal "WHY" may already be showing up in your life.

d. WHAT IS MY WHY? Start by listing your top 4 WHATs ... things you do that you find to be especially enjoyable, engaging and meaningful. These must be activities you actually enjoy DOING (i.e., they cannot be things you just like the IDEA of doing).

e. Next, list your top 4 WHYs for the first WHAT. WHY specifically do you find this activity especially engaging, enjoyable or meaningful? The more specificity you can provide for this, the better.

f. Repeat this step of identifying the WHYs that correspond to each of your WHATs.

What #1 _____ ▣

    Why #1-1 _____ ▣

    Why #1-2 _____ ▣

    Why #1-3 _____ ▣

    Why #1-4 _____ ▣

What #2 _____ ▣

    Why #2-1 _____ ▣

    Why #2-2 _____ ▣

    Why #2-3 _____ ▣

    Why #2-4 _____ ▣

What #3 _____ ▣

    Why #3-1 _____ ▣

    Why #3-2 _____ ▣

    Why #3-3 _____ ▣

    Why #3-4 _____ ▣

What #4 _____ ▣

    Why #4-1 _____ ▣

    Why #4-2 _____ ▣

    Why #4-3 _____ ▣

    Why #4-4 _____ ▣

Step 6. Review all the WHYs you identified for your four favorite activities. List any recurring terms or themes below:

✎ _____ ⌨

a. Pair-share:

    i. Was it difficult for you to identify your WHYs, or to even identify four enjoyable, engaging and meaningful activities in the first place?

    ii. Were you surprised by any of your WHYs or common themes?

    iii. Do one or more of your WHYs contain the kernel of a passion so strong that it would compel you forward in life despite significant challenge and adversity?

    iv. Where do your WHYs fit in your career plan? In 5 to 10 years, do you see yourself being paid to do a job that lets you pursue your passions? If not, why not? What might you do to change that?

    v. Imagine you are performing an activity for your organization that you love to do because it aligns with one or more of your passions. What would that activity be?

b. In the space below, write down three commitments for pursuing a passion of yours over the next year in a way that serves your organization.

By _____ (date) I commit to: ✎ _____ ⌨

By _____ (date) I commit to: ✎ _____ ⌨

By _____ (date) I commit to: ✎ _____ ⌨

Step 7.

STOCKING YOUR SHELVES

Lack of awareness about ourselves (such as sources of motivation) can affect our ability to lead. Group development is at risk; growth can be stunted. Self-love or motivation provides degrees of independence and strength. They guard against "taking things personally." Moreover, they can preserve an individual's spirit. We create a living "hell" by making assumptions and taking things personally. Taking things personally is the start of a cycle that includes ineffective leadership.

Below are some ideas you can use to promote a source of support for yourself.

Investment into Your Motivational Well

Suggested Ideas	Your Ideas
Investing resources to enhance current knowledge and skills	▶
Investigating new areas of interest (e.g., pottery, art class, exercise)	▶
Providing service to others (e.g., providing pet therapy, visiting hospice patients)	▶
Reading books on leadership, team building and relationships, biographies	▶
Engaging in open and honest communication	▶

Looking to see how others conduct themselves and pick out what might work for you	▸
Attending an immersion leadership course	▸
Developing or strengthening spirituality	▸

7.4. Discussion questions:

Per facilitator …
How do motivation and demotivation enter the life and career of a pharmacist?

Match the term with the correct definition:

1. Empathy	__	a. Being driven to achieve for the sake of achievement
2. Motivation	__	b. Considering others' feelings, especially when making decisions
3. Self-awareness	__	c. Controlling or redirecting disruptive emotions and impulses2
4. Self-regulation	—	d. Knowing one's emotions, strengths, weaknesses, drives, values, and goals – and their effects on others1
5. Social skill	__	e. Managing relationships to move people in desired directions5

7.5. After-class assignments:

A. Each time you hear someone else use the word "motivation," think about which of your WHYs is most active at that time.
B. Fulfill the commitments you made for pursuing a passion of yours.
C. Fulfill the before-class activities for the next Module assigned by your facilitator.

7.6. Bibliography, references, & resources:

Flashcards via Quizlet, https://quizlet.com/class/3716098/, Emotional Intelligence (Goleman, *etc.*) » 7 terms
Goleman D. What makes a leader? *Harvard Business Review* 1998;76:93-102.
Rickert DR, Smith RE, Worthen DB. The 'seven habits': Building pharmacist leaders. *Am Pharm.* 1992 Aug;32(8):48-52.
Sinek S. *Start with Why: How Great Leaders Inspire Everyone to Take Action.* New York: Portfolio Press, 2011. www.startwithwhy.com

Annex 7-1. Motivation / Demotivation Crossword Puzzle

Separate annex documents available to facilitators upon request (LeadGrowShape@plei.org).

Across

1. Considering others' feelings
3. Lack of interest in and enthusiasm about work
5. Strong and barely controllable emotion
7. Controlling or redirecting disruptive emotions and impulses

Down

2. Being driven to achieve for the sake of achievement
4. Managing relationships to move people in desired direction
6. Knowing one's emotions, strengths, weaknesses – and their effects on others

Module « **8** »   KNOWING ME, KNOWING YOU

☞ Learning Objectives:

Objective 1. To provide insights into various dimensions of human personality and styles of interacting with others.

Objective 2. To discuss how one's personal characteristics can be applied within a pharmacy practice.

Objective 3. To discuss how one's personal characteristics can be applied within one's personal life.

Objective 4. To list complementary strengths required for high-performing teams.

In this Module, we leave the hard work to others (StrengthsFinder®, Myers-Briggs, *et cetera*). Our job is to help participants understand what those categories or colors mean, how to apply the findings to everyday life. We have a bit of experience at that.

At its core, leadership involves understanding human nature. The fancy computer interfaces of many of these behavioral inventories or psychological instruments or leadership tools, or whatever you want to call them, derive from the insights of Carl Jung from the 1920s. That's almost a century ago but, don't forget, people are people. Some things never change.

8.1. Readings or activities before class:

Complete the evaluation or data-entry process for the personality inventory directed by your facilitator before coming to class. Read and be prepared to discuss any reports you receive.

8.2. Resources needed:

Self-assessment instruments licensed by the school of pharmacy or host university.

8.3. In-class activities:

"Your vision will become clear only when you can look into your own heart.
Who looks outside, dreams; who looks inside, awakes." Carl Jung

Step 1. Questions?
Step 2. Quote.
Step 3. Findings.
Note: many of these instruments derive in varying degrees from Carl G. Jung's *Psychological Types*, developed in the 1920s.

a. **StrengthsFinder**, www.strengthsfinder.com/home.aspx, https://www.gallupstrengthscenter.com/?gclid=CN_xrYCSh8wCFcYfhgodFlcOaQ. StrengthsFinder 2.0 is an online assessment, where participants respond to 177 stimuli. Each item lists a pair of potential self-descriptors. This input yields a report of the five strongest of several themes (signature themes), which are grouped into four domains:

Executing: Achiever, arranger, belief, consistency, deliberative, discipline, focus, responsibility, restorative

Influencing: Activator, command, communication, competition, maximizer, self-assurance, significance, WOO (winning others over)

Relationship-Building: Adaptability, connectedness, developer, empathy, harmony, includer, individualization, positivity, relator

Strategic Thinking: Analytical, context, futuristic, ideation, input, intellection, learner, strategic

Application: Janke KK, Traynor AP, Sorensen TD. Refinement of strengths instruction in a pharmacy curriculum over eight years. *Am J Pharm Educ*. 2011 Apr 11;75(3):45.

b. **Myers-Briggs Type Inventory** (MBTI), www.myersbriggs.org. The MBTI identifies one of 16 personality types, based on four domains.

Favorite world: A preference to focus on the outer world or on one's own inner world: Extraversion (E) or Introversion (I).

Information: A preference to focus on the basic information one takes in or on interpreting and adding meaning: Sensing (S) or Intuition (N).

Decisions: When making decisions, a preference to first look at logic and consistency (Thinking, T) or to first look at the people and special circumstances (Feeling, F)?

Structure: In dealing with the outside world, a preference to get things decided (Judging, J) or to staying open to new information and options (Perceiving, P)?

c. **Insights Discovery**, https://www.insights.com/564/insights-discovery.html. After a 20-minute online evaluation, the participant receives a profile describing strengths and weaknesses, communication style, approach to problems and value to a team. The profile outlines that person's unique "color mix:"

Sunshine Yellow (sociable, dynamic, demonstrative, enthusiastic, persuasive),

Cool Blue (cautious, precise, deliberate, questioning, formal),

Earth Green (caring, encouraging, sharing, patient, relaxed), and

Fiery Red (competitive, demanding, determined, strong-willed, purposeful).

d. **Lumina Spark**, https://www.luminalearning.com. The Lumina Spark portrait also assesses eight psychological aspects and 24 behavioral traits based on the participant's response to statements and Jungian principles. The portrait describes one of four archetypes:

Commanding Archetype (Red)

Conscientious Archetype (Blue)

Inspiring Archetype (Yellow)

Empowering Archetype (Blue)

These dimensions are linked with personality types:

Extraversion E+ or Introversion E-

People Focused A+ or Outcome Focused A-

Big Picture Thinking O+ or Down to Earth O-

Discipline Driven C+ or Inspiration Driven C-

Hot Reactor N+ or Cool Reactor N-

The Lumina Spark approach holds that these five factors are not bimodal, but rather form a normal distribution (i.e., an individual can possess both introverted and extraverted qualities). Within each of the five factors are sub-factors that Lumina calls "qualities." This approach does not require a calculation based on judging and perceiving scores, instead using the degree of preference an individual has for a factor as determined by the strength of their score in it.

e. Kouzes & Posner's **Student Leadership Practices Inventory** (LPI, studentleadershipchallenge.com/userfiles/faq_slpi.pdf). The two-part Student LPI has been validated among fraternity chapter presidents, sorority chapter president, dormitory resident assistants and multiple other college student groups (Posner, 2004; Posner, 2012). The Student LPI uses both Self and Observer questionnaires for the student leader and people who have observed the student in action. Each survey features 30 statements based on the Five Practices of Exemplary Leadership to evaluate the frequency with which students engage in behaviors associated with each practice.

Model the Way

Inspire a Shared Vision

Challenge the Process

Enable Others to Act

Encourage the Heart

Kouzes JM, Posner BZ. *The Student Leadership Challenge: Five Practices for Exemplary Leaders.* San Francisco: Jossey-Bass, 2008.

f. **Birkman Method®** (birkman.com) derives from theories of Roger W. Birkman from the 1940s, who believed that personality and social perception differences were likely to emerge more clearly in a questionnaire measuring both perceptions of self and perceptions of others. Today, its reports feature colors, symbols, quadrants, and scales to help interpret complex personality traits. The Birkman Method questionnaire allows online assessment, using 298 questions (250 true/false and 48 multiple-choice questions). The survey requires an average 30 minutes to complete. Scale development resulted in:

Ten scales describing occupational preferences (Interests),

Eleven scales describing more effective behaviors 5 (Usual behaviors),

Eleven scales describing interpersonal and environmental preferences or expectations (Needs), and

Eleven scales to describe less than effective behaviors (Stress behaviors).

g. **Values in Action** Inventory of Strengths, www.viacharacter.org. The Values in Action (VIA) Inventory of Strengths (VIA-IS) assesses an individual's character strengths. Christopher Peterson and Martin Seligman created this instrument to operationalize their Character Strengths and Virtues (CSV) Handbook and classify positive human strengths. The VIA-IS uses 240 items to measure 24 character strengths in 30 to 40 minutes. The results rank the participant's strengths from 1 to 24, with the top four to seven strengths considered "signature strengths." In this system, six categories of strength are considered:

Wisdom and Knowledge: creativity, curiosity, judgment, love of learning, perspective

Courage: bravery, perseverance, honesty, zest

Humanity: love, kindness, social intelligence

Justice: teamwork, fairness, leadership

Temperance: forgiveness, humility, prudence, self-regulation

Transcendence: appreciation of beauty and excellence, gratitude, hope, humor, spirituality

h. **MindTime** maps (www.mindtimemaps.com) help groups develop a greater awareness of how thinking is shaping and driving people's roles, decisions, attitudes, and sentiments. A simple 2-minute quiz locates people in the "world of thinking.™" Participants choose from a menu of pre-prepared surveys on topics such as brand allegiance, innovation, leadership, and happiness. These results are shown as correlations between thinking archetypes and participant's responses.

8.4. Discussion questions:

Per facilitator
Based on the instrument used, refer to the interpretation key.
  ▸ In which domains or archetypes do you "show up," based on your top themes or types?
  ▸ Reflect on various teams and groups you affiliate with. Based on your results, what do you contribute to the group? What themes or types would need to be contributed by other group members?
  ▸ Do you believe you are part of well-rounded teams? If not, what domain(s) might be missing?
  ▸ How might you personally make accommodations for your any current "deficits"?
  ▸ What might you do to create more well-rounded leadership teams in the future?

8.5. After-class assignments:

A. Each time you hear someone else say the word "style," think about your behavioral styles you just learned about. Consider how to use your styles like an artist's palette of colors, to paint your future.
B. Transfer your strengths from the leadership-style inventory to the lower-left segment of the Values-Interests-Strengths-Needs (VISN) Chart in Annex 3-2. Adjust any other entries that need to be updated.
C. Fulfill the before-class activities for the next Module assigned by your facilitator.

8.6. Bibliography, references, & resources:

Janke KK, Traynor AP, Sorensen TD. Refinement of strengths instruction in a pharmacy curriculum over eight years. *Am J Pharm Educ.* 2011 Apr 11;75(3):45. www.ncbi.nlm.nih.gov/pmc/articles/PMC3109799/

Posner BZ. A leadership development instrument for students: Updated. *J College Student Development* 2004;45(4):443-56.

Posner BZ. Effectively measuring student leadership. *Admin Sci* 2012;2:221-34.

Traynor AP, Janke KK, Sorensen TD. Using personal strengths with intention in pharmacy: Implications for pharmacists, managers, and leaders. *Ann Pharmacother.* 2010 Feb;44(2):367-76.

Module « 9 »   SECURING YOUR LEADERSHIP OXYGEN MASK

☞ Learning Objectives:

Objective 1. To identify preceding events that contribute your position on a leadership path.
Objective 2. To differentiate player roles from victim roles.
Objective 3. To understand how different leadership qualities and approaches can lead to disempowerment and victimhood for all involved, instead of success.

When you think about yourself, are you on a leadership path or meandering through the wilderness? Are you reacting to external stimuli or grabbing a machete and forging your own trail?

This Module shows the interplay between mind (vision), spirit (values), heart (compassion), and body (discipline) for an individual seeking to find his or her own voice. Comparably, considering groups seeking excellence, mind-spirit-body-heart manifest as pathfinding-modeling-aligning-empowering.

Human interactions are remarkable, miraculous, inspiring, impressive, you name it. Jump on board, this leadership stuff is a trip.

9.1. Readings or activities before class:

Reflect on how intentional or unintentional your path toward leadership has been to date. Think also about what you can do NOW to become more intentional in determining your own pathway.

- ▸ Do you believe you were born to lead?
- ▸ Did you wake up one day and say "I am a leader!"?
- ▸ Describe your leadership path: Purposeful, intentional, haphazard, serendipitous, _____?
- ▸ Where did your leadership path begin?
- ▸ Did you succeed at one thing, and thenceforth people started labeling you a leader?
- ▸ Would you say that your parents were leaders?
- ▸ Was your path borne out of necessity?
- ▸ Maybe no one else would fill a leader position and you took it on by default?
  ▷Or maybe you said "yes" once, and now people come to you repeatedly.
- ▸ After all we have talked about so far, would you still assert: "Nope, I'm not a leader"?

Write down notes on these points to discuss in class:

✍ _____   ⌨

9.2. Resources needed:

None other than this Module

9.3. In-class activities:

"Happiness grows less from the passive experience of desirable circumstances
than from involvement in valued activities
and progress towards one's goals." David Myers & Ed Diener

Step 1. Questions?
Step 2. Quote.
Step 3. Exercise.

EVERYTHING BEGINS & ENDS WITH YOU

Anyone who has flown on an airplane has heard the instruction to "...secure your own (oxygen) mask first..." and, only then, help someone else in need. The importance of ensuring our own safety during an aviation emergency is easily understood, yet many people live their daily life disregarding their own needs or security. Such practices can jeopardize one's own health and well-being, as well as the well-being of others nearby, far more frequently than any airplane mishap.

Leaders must realize the importance of self-centeredness and self-care, and how these two are completely different than egocentricity and self-gain.

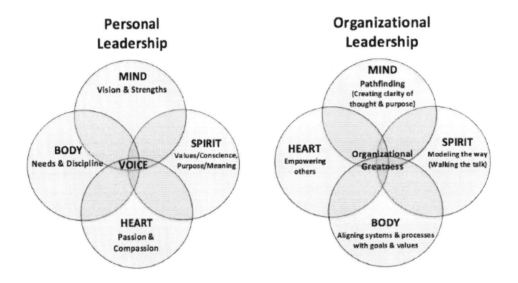

Step 4.

LIES, DAMNED LIES, VICTIMHOOD, & PERSONAL DEVELOPMENT

a. List a handful of "truths" that you were taught as a child (or young adult) that you have subsequently found to be untrue (or much more complicated than originally discussed). Why do you think these were told to you the way they were?

b. Popcorn your answers back to the facilitator.

c. How did these affect you back then – and how might they continue affecting you now? Has your relationship with the "liar" been altered in any way because of the event? Why or why not?

✎ _____ ⌨

d. Pick one example that really stands out to you for some reason and share it with someone you have not spoken with yet.

✎ _____ ⌨

e. Discuss as a group how similar phenomena happen in college or business settings – and how they may relate to personal development.

f. Listen for how these same, seemingly unkind (if not unethical?) practices may serve alternate purposes when the "big picture" is taken.

g. Listen for differences in the way people look at life. Do they blame others for what happens in their lives, or do they look for how they can shape the situation, regardless of the cause? Ponder the differences between victims, villains, and players (or actors) (adapted from Patterson *et al., Crucial Conversations*).

Victim stories: "It's Not My Fault." Too often ignores the role you played in the problem. Exaggerates innocence. Backward looking.

Villain stories: "It's All Your Fault." Too often turns decent humans into villains and focuses only on the role others play in the problem. Ignores the role you play(ed). Overemphasizes other person's guilt or stupidity. Backward looking.

Helpless stories: "There's nothing else I can do." Looking forward to explain why you cannot change your situation. Often arise from villain stories and cedes control to others by reinforcing powerlessness.

Antidotes:

Turn victims into **actors** or **players**. Don't pretend not to notice your role in the problem, or to refuse to assume responsibility. When you might claim "I didn't do anything," that constitutes your part.

Turn villains into humans. Ask why would a reasonable person do what this person is doing? Assume positive intent and seek to understand.

Turn the helpless into the **able**. Consider what you really want, then act accordingly. Even if you have little control over creating the situation, how can you control your response to it?

Now, back to our situation: Listen for differences between people who look at life through the eyes of a "victim" *versus* those who look at life through the eyes of a "player" (or actor). Listen for such differences.

✎ _____ ⌨

h. Reflect how our early experiences with "liars" might set up a default victim setting deep within our brains. Explore, specifically, how this might manifest by subconscious beliefs and actions.

✎ _____ ⌨

i. Discuss your thoughts with someone – really listen, and empathize, if this is an unsettling realization for them!

j. Listen to how common victimhood may be in our personal and professional lives. Imagine what might be done to help those who habitually place blame externally shift toward identifying their role in any given situation and what they can contribute. Another way to look at this is to help someone determine why they would relinquish that which is in their control? This can help turn victims into players.

Step 5.

POWERSTRIP *VERSUS* POWERTRIPS – SAME LETTERS, DIFFERENT OUTCOME?

a. Reflect on a time when you assumed you knew something was a certain way, only to find out later that it was much different than you had thought:

✍ _____ ⌨

b. Meet someone you do not know and share the details. How did this affect you at the time – or did you even notice your incorrect assessment of the person or situation? How does this realization affect your thinking or actions now?

✍ _____ ⌨

c. Listen to how frequent (or rare) incorrect assumptions dictate the process and outcomes of life situations – paying attention if any single part is unaffected (and why):

d. Pick one example that really stands out to you for some reason and share it with someone you have not spoken with yet.

✍ _____ ⌨

e. Go back to the earlier definition(s) of leadership [see Module 5] and list as many "personal attributes" of leadership you can think of – i.e., what does a leader "look like" and how do they "act" differently than other people:

✍ _____ ⌨

f. Combine your list with another person's to craft an even more comprehensive list. After compiling your combined list, try to think of even more attributes, thinking of even the subtlest examples.

✍ _____ ⌨

g. Listen for what the collective group came up with, adding anything you and your partner missed.

✍ _____ ⌨

h. Circle or highlight ALL attributes of the master list that you feel are transcendent leadership qualities, in other words, those attributes that work perfectly well in ALL situations. Make sure that these work well NOT just for the leader, but for the people they are interacting with and trying to develop over time.

i. Engage in a discussion on whether there are transcendent leadership qualities, noting if any or all of these are, actually, "qualified."

NOTES: ✍ _____ ⌨

j. Note any of the master list of qualities that you feel may be "self-limiting" for either the leader or the people with whom they are interacting. In other words, the quality may serve a short-term purpose, but is not self-sustaining or would lead to a different outcome.

NOTES: ✍ _____ ⌨

k. Engage in a discussion around this, noting how your understanding or your view of the quality may now be changed.

NOTES: ✍ _____ ⌨

Step 6.

WHAT GOES AROUND, COMES AROUND (EVENTUALLY)

a. Take a few moments to reflect on the "Personal Leadership" graphic at the start of this Module (adapted from Covey's *First Things First*) – looking intensely at the four overlapping circles of mind, spirit, heart and body. List a few ways that each of them are vitally important to the "wholeness" of a leader. For example, how does a leader's _____ make or break their effectiveness?

NOTES: ✍ _____ ⌨

b. Of these circles, is there any area for which your view has changed because of your own life experiences? For example, did you think a leader had to be charismatic at all times to rally followers, only to find out that charisma is a fleeting and superficial quality?

✍ _____ ⌨

c. Discuss with a new friend your thoughts. Note, specifically, how the example you discuss has a ripple effect on the other circles.

✍ _____ ⌨

d. After coming together as a larger group, engage in a discussion about how, and possibly why, we have been taught to think certain things about leadership, and how we might go about combating the myths, fallacies, or disempowering approaches of our past.

NOTES: ✍ _____ ⌨

e. Take a moment to reflect how you have cultivated the maintenance or development of your own mind, spirit, body and heart – both within and outside of your career or schooling. What is your therapy and who in your life is involved, if anyone?

✍ _____ ⌨

f. Meet someone you have not previously spoken with and share one of your therapies.

g. Participate in a group discussion reflecting how important it is to take time to "cultivate" your entire leadership garden: using mental and physical activities akin to watering, weeding, pruning every aspect. Covey used the analogy of taking time for "sharpening the saw."

NOTES: ✍ _____ ⌨

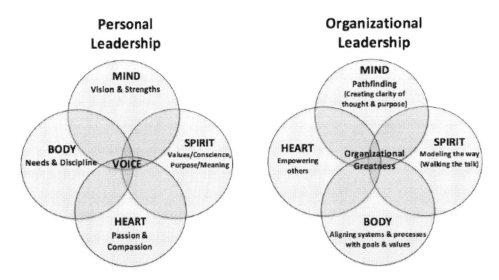

9.4. Discussion questions:

Name some examples of pharmacists encountering victims or players.
In what kinds of settings might pharmacists perceive themselves as victims or players?

9.5. After-class assignments:

A. While in a public setting (cafeteria, restaurant, campus, shopping center), watch the people around you and find one who is taking control of a situation (by retaining control, identifying their own role or contributing to the evolving situation), and selecting a specific path among multiple options. Do in groups, if you wish.
B. Fulfill the before-class activities for the next Module assigned by your facilitator.

9.6. Bibliography, references, & resources:

Covey SR. *First Things First*. New York: Free Press, 1996.
Flashcards via Quizlet, https://quizlet.com/class/3716098/, Crucial Conversations (Patterson) » 6 terms
Patterson K, Grenny J, McMilan R, Switzler A. *Crucial Conversations: Tools for Talking When Stakes Are High, 2nd ed*. New York: McGraw-Hill, 2012:116-125.

Module « **10** »   MAKING THE MOST OF EARS: LISTENING WELL

☞ Learning Objectives:

Objective 1. To identify key skills in effective listening.
Objective 2. To illustrate how difficult the act of listening can be.
Objective 3. To identify tools for active listening.

This Module is all about listening. ♪ If you spend all your time talking, how will you ever know if your message has been received? And how will you ever receive the messages of others?

Listening is the key and you can only listen once you stop talking. You can only listen well with practice and a high degree of self-awareness. Even then, you need to concentrate on what the other person is saying, not on what you will say next. Read on to focus upon your listening skills.

10.1. Readings or activities <u>before class</u>:

Read and be prepared to discuss the following text passage about listening skills.
After reading, complete Annex 10-1: Listening Crossword Puzzle (or follow facilitator instructions).

Listening is important in the business world. Good listening skills can improve customer satisfaction, enhance productivity and reduce mistakes, and increase information sharing that leads to more creative and innovative work. In healthcare, better listening helps prevent medication errors.

Effective listening is a foundation for positive human relationships. Listening skills increases your number of friends and social networks, and enhances self-esteem and confidence.

Effective listening is not a passive activity. To be a good communicator, one must actively listen for what the other person has to say and actively work to understand what he or she wants.

Listening requires focus. Good listeners pay attention, are patient, and keep open minds. They concentrate on receiving all the information the other person is transmitting, verbally and nonverbally. Effective listeners take responsibility to assure they are interpreting the speaker's message as intended by the speaker. To increase your listening skills:

<u>Pay attention</u>: Communicate readiness to listen through eye contact and posture. Eye contact makes the other person feel important. Glance away occasionally, so he or she does not feel threatened. Listen for key ideas and feelings, rather than specific words. Listen to how the message is said, as well as what is said. Listen also for what is not said; is a fact or feeling conspicuous by its absence? Pick a place and time conducive to listening; anticipate and prevent interruptions. Communicate acceptance through empathetic responses. Observe the speaker's nonverbal behavior and consider its contribution to the message. Ask the speaker to clarify words or statements you do not understand. Mentally question whether you are hearing accurate information, from objective sources, that tell the whole story.

<u>Be patient</u>: Let the speaker know that time is available to discuss the issue. Be aware of your own nonverbal cues. Do not drum your fingers, fidget, or otherwise communicate impatience or boredom. Avoid

interrupting the speaker. Trying to complete the speaker's sentences for him or her is especially disruptive. Avoid prying questions. Allow time for feelings to be volunteered. Sharing feelings is risky; it makes each of us vulnerable. It may take several sessions on the same topic to air all the facts.

Keep an open mind: Suspend judgments and decisions until the speaker finishes. Do not interrupt to correct an error in the speaker's delivery nor if you disagree with a statement. Control your responses to emotion-laden words or phrases. Avoid one-upmanship (e.g., my scar is longer than yours). Do not be prejudiced by the speaker's appearance or mannerisms. As you listen, try to understand things from the speaker's point of view. Try to discover his or her desired outcome. Listening does not mean problem solving. You cannot solve others' problems for them, and you might be able to help them to sort out their facts and feelings, provide a little insight, and enable them to decide things for themselves.

If it is appropriate for you to evaluate the speaker's remarks, let him or her know that your reaction is your interpretation. Start by saying, "From what you've said, I think the problem involves ... "

You will have plenty of time to reflect upon content and to search for meaning. Our rate of speech is roughly 100-150 words per minute, while the rate of thought (and thus listening) is about 400-500 words per minute.

TOOLS OF ACTIVE LISTENING

Empathetic responses: "I see," "uh-huh," "go on," a nod of the head. "Tell me more…" Use these to establish rapport, to encourage the speaker, or to convey acceptance.

Restatement: Repetition of part of the speaker's own words to show receipt of message. "I've had this rash for three days." "For three days?" Use to encourage the speaker to explore other aspects of the issue.

Paraphrasing: Restating in your own words your interpretation of the speaker's message. "So, you believe you shouldn't take medication if you do not feel sick." Use to confirm understanding, to help speaker evaluate his or her own feelings about an issue, or to help a speaker reach his own solution to a problem.

Summation: To condense large portions of discussion and to highlight key ideas. "I understand your comments to mean…," "The things most important to you include…," "So, you're treating mainly gram-negative bacteria….," "Where is that emotion coming from?" Use to focus the discussion, to confirm understanding, to guide the speaker to a new idea, or to get agreement to close the discussion.

Listening is a building block of success. One of the most important things we give each other is attention.

TEN PRINCIPLES OF LISTENING

Good listeners notice not only to what is being said, but also to what is left unsaid or only partially said. Effective listening finds inconsistencies between verbal and non-verbal messages.

1. **Stop Talking**. Do not interrupt. Do not talk over the other person. Do not finish their sentences for them.
2. **Prepare Yourself to Listen**. Relax. Focus on the speaker. Put other things out of your mind. Concentrate on the messages being communicated.
3. **Put the Speaker at Ease**. Help the speaker to feel free to speak. Think of their needs and concerns. Nod or use other gestures to encourage them to continue. Maintain eye contact, but do not stare.
4. **Remove Distractions**. Focus on what is being said. Avoid unnecessary interruptions.
5. **Empathize**. Try to understand the other person's point of view. Let go of preconceived ideas. If the speaker says something that you disagree with, corral those thoughts and do not let them interfere with the speaker's line of reasoning. Do not impose your "solutions."
6. **Be Patient**. A pause, even a long pause, does not necessarily mean that the speaker has finished. Be patient and let the speaker continue in their own time. Honor the speaker's need for time to formulate what to say. Occasionally, you might as a clarifying question: "Back up a second. I didn't understand what you just said about…" Ask questions only to ensure understanding.
7. **Avoid Personal Prejudice**. Be impartial. Do not become irritated. Do not let the person's habits distract you from what is being said by the person (the message transmitted). Focus on what is being said and try to ignore styles of delivery.
8. **Listen to the Tone**. Volume and tone both add to what someone is saying. Let these help you to

understand the points of emphasis in what is said.

9. <u>**Listen for Ideas, Not Just Words**</u>. You need to get the whole picture, not just bits and pieces. One of the purposes of listening is to link together pieces of information to reveal the ideas of others.

10. <u>**Wait and Watch for Non-Verbal Communication**</u>. We do not just listen with our ears, but also with our eyes. Even so, do not jump to conclusions about what you see and hear. Always seek clarification, to ensure that your understanding is correct.

Eventually, it will be the other's turn to listen, and you would want reciprocal respect as he or she listens to you. You might start by asking: "Would you like to hear my ideas?"

Adapted from: SkillsYouNeed.com, www.skillsyouneed.com/ips/listening-skills.html#ixzz45oizBzmc, May 2016.

10.2. Resources needed:

None other than this Module

10.3. In-class activities:

"If we were supposed to talk more than we listen, we would have two tongues and one ear." Mark Twain

Step 1. Questions?
Step 2. Quote.
Step 3. Exercise.

STORY-TELLER—LISTENER—OBSERVER TRIAD

a. First, recall a time when you were completely engrossed in an activity. It could be a professional activity or a personal one. Consider the following as you attempt to recall the activity as completely as possible: Where were you? How did you get there? How did you begin the activity? What were you thinking when you began? How long did the activity last? What did you feel like when you were done? Take about 5 minutes to remember.

b. Divide into groups of three people. Designate an initial Story-teller, Listener and Observer.

c. Review the three roles. Story-Teller is to describe the experience to Listener about being completely engrossed in an activity. Story-Teller must NOT engage the Observer. Listener is to say NOTHING during the exchange and must continue looking intensely into Story-Teller's eyes the whole time–no looking away or at any other part of Story-Teller's face [yes, we know this differs from the tips above]. Observer is to take specific notes about what he/she saw/heard from both Story-Teller and Listener. A depiction appears below.

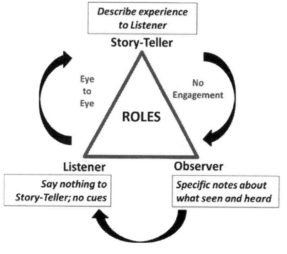

d. Switch roles, rotating to the left. Do NOT pause to discuss. Proceed. Switch. Repeat one more time, so that each person experiences each role once.

e. Each Observer records below what happens while watching the exchange between Story-Teller and Listener. Record any additional information or feelings about observations. Prepare for discussion amongst the participants of each triad (and not as a big group).

Notes as Observer: ✍ _____ ⌨

f. Engage in a discussion of what happened between the roles in the triad, starting from the perspective of Story-Teller: What language did Story-Teller use (objective *versus* subjective, factual *versus* emotive, detailed *versus* vague, personal *versus* impersonal, optimistic *versus* pessimistic, *et cetera*)?

✍ _____ ⌨

g. What did Story-Teller think of the avocal Listener?

✍ _____ ⌨

h. How did being in the company of an avocal listener feel to Story-Teller? ...to Listener? Was this experience shared with Story-Teller, even though Story-Teller was focused only on sharing?

✍ _____ ⌨

i. Now from Listener's perspective: How did it feel to be a pure Listener? What did you notice about the experience? How difficult was it to only use your ears? How was it to not be able to provide feedback or convey your level of interest? Does nodding or offering an "uh-huh" mean that you are interested and engaged in listening to another? Can it also act as a verbal façade behind which to hide?

✍ _____ ⌨

j. How did knowing there was an external Observer affect either the Story-Teller or the Listener and their experience during the activity?

Notes: ✍ _____ ⌨

10.4. Discussion questions:

Would it be possible to have deeper levels of listening if you can declare your intention at the outset (i.e., I am going to listen to you intensely and will limit my input to you), so that the Story-Teller would have a deeper understanding from where you are coming and experience greater ease to allow the story to come across more fully?

This exercise is intended to help you pay attention to YOU in each role. It is not easy to introduce an increased level of consciousness if you are not accustomed. It is also intended for you to consider what you do when you listen and to challenge whether it is authentic. If you nod or say "uh huh," is it because you are genuinely interested in the story or are you on autopilot and accustomed to respond this way out of habit or to mask your disinterest and/or discomfort?

Recall the tools of active listening from the pre-class readings. Active listeners use techniques such as restatement, paraphrasing, summation, and questions to manage the course of the conversation.

This is part of the hard work of listening. Practice is essential! Sharing your intention is required! Utilizing any listening technique or tool must occur with authenticity to be effective.

How many ways do pharmacists use listening skills?

10.5. After-class assignments:

A. Review the Ten Principles of Listening and consider how well you engage in each by taking an honest assessment of yourself. Take a risk and share your assessment with someone you trust and determine whether they agree with you. If not, find out why?

B. Practice these listening techniques you learned in this Module in your everyday life. Listening is a building block of success. One of the most important things we give each other is attention.

C. Fulfill the before-class activities for the next Module assigned by your facilitator.

10.6. Bibliography, references, & resources:

Bookbinder LJ. Empathy, Listening Skills & Relationships. http://learninginaction.com/PDF/ELSR.pdf.

Flashcards via Quizlet, https://quizlet.com/class/3716098/, Listening Principles & Tools » 16 terms; Listening-Skills Lexicon » 9 terms

Oliver CH. Communication awareness: Rx for embarrassing situations. *Am Pharm.* 1982;22: 533-535.

Polanski RE, Polanski VG. Environment for communication. *Am Pharm.* 1982;22:545-546.

SkillsYouNeed.com, www.skillsyouneed.com/ips/listening-skills.html#ixzz45oizBzmc, May 2016.

Witte KW, Bober KF. Developing a patient-education program in the community pharmacy. *Am Pharm.* 1982;22:540-544.

Zellmer WA. Let's talk. *Am J Hosp Pharm.* 1987;44:1323.

Annex 10-1. Listening Crossword Puzzle

Separate annex documents available to facilitators upon request (LeadGrowShape@plei.org).

Across

2. Suspend judgment and decisions
5. Repetition of speaker's own words
6. Stating in your words your interpretation
8. Allow time to discuss issue
9. Feeling free to speak

Down

1. Condensing large passages into key ideas
3. Unnecessary interruptions
4. I see, go on
7. Focus with eye contact and posture

Module « **11** » HOW DO I OCCUR?

☞ Learning Objectives:

Objective 1. To compare and contrast one's self-image with the image perceived by others.
Objective 2. To identify (mis)alignments between personal values and behaviors.
Objective 3. To list three behaviors to start or stop doing to better align their internal values with external perceptions.

This Module starts with an extensive out-of-class interview exercise. It can do much more than tell you whether your actions and behaviors are aligned with your values. The "How Do I Occur?" exercise can be a powerful tool to uncover your "blind spots," by having objective third-parties help you see beyond difficult circumstances.

Determining how you occur to others is risky. This is not an easy exercise. When you begin the exercise, prepare to resist taking what you hear as a personal assault on your character, if what you learn seems negative. If what you learn seems positive, resist taking what you hear as permission to allow your ego to inflate. In other words, set your mind to that of an objective learner of how others perceive you (rightly or wrongly).

11.1. Readings or activities before class:

Conduct the in-depth out-of-class "How Do I Occur" interview with at least one person, explained below.

While it may be hard to believe, many of the things in life that cause us the most frustration and anger are often merely reflections of behaviors and attitudes that WE put out into the world. For example, consider:

▸ The leader who complains nobody else will contribute, and is such a control freak she never allows anyone else to do anything.
▸ The parent who is angry that he must do everything for his daughter, yet seldom invests the time to teach her what she should do, how to do it, and why.
▸ The man who is angry that his girlfriends keep leaving him, and does not realize his insecure and overbearing nature is what keeps pushing them away.

The amazing thing is that when we are in the midst of these vicious cycles, the ways in which we contribute to them are invisible to us. Before we know it, we are caught in recurring patterns of pain and misery, and cannot figure out why "bad things keep happening to me."

The mind's ability to find external causes for problems is incredibly powerful. The person who was just fired from their fourth consecutive job by yet another "bad boss" simply cannot see that the only constant in all those situations was herself!

A. Identify at least one, preferably three, people from your personal and professional lives who know you to varying degrees, with whom you can have an honest, non-judgmental, non-confrontational conversation.

B. Invite each of them to schedule a 20- to 30-minute interview with you to help you complete an important assignment for this awesome leadership program you are doing. Tell them that you are inviting them

89

specifically, because <u>you believe they can be totally honest with you</u>, and that you trust they can provide valued feedback in a constructive and non-judgmental way.

C. At the beginning of the interview, refresh your interviewee's memory about the purpose of this exercise, and tell them you really desire and <u>value their honesty and candor</u>, which should be constructive and non-judgmental. Let them know that you want to hear their honest perceptions, and that you promise not to get offended or upset because you are really committed to furthering your self-awareness and improvement.

NOTE: It is critically important for you to remember as you listen to the person's responses that there are no right or wrong answers, just their perceptions (i.e., how you occur to them). And while you may not like, or may disagree with some perceptions, it is important that you do not do anything to dispute or and counter them during the interview. You will get nothing from becoming defensive. Their perceptions are their perceptions and they are completely REAL – even if they are grounded in their own subjective "stories." Just focus on writing down their exact words.

Ask the following questions. You can pick and choose from, or customize, the list to fit your needs, interests, and relationship with your interviewee. Do not shy away from something though, just because it may be uncomfortable.

1. What kind of first impression do I give off? What kinds of things do I say or do to give that impression?

✎ _____ ⌨

2. After their initial response, ask them to talk about the little things, if they did not already do so ... things like facial expressions, speaking too much or little, tone of voice, eye-rolling, frequent or loud sighing, being distracted by your smartphone, even bad breath or body odors!

✎ _____ ⌨

3. When my name comes up in conversation with other people, what is the context?

✎ _____ ⌨

4. When you think of me, what is the first thing that comes to mind?

✎ _____ ⌨

5. What do I do that drives you nuts?

✎ _____ ⌨

6. What kinds of things can I be truly counted on to do?

✎ _____ ⌨

7. What kinds of things would you probably NOT count on me to do?

✎ _____ ⌨

8. In what kinds of circumstances or situations am I good to have around?

✍ _____ ⌨

9. In what kinds of circumstances or situations would it be best to have me working on other things?

✍ _____ ⌨

10. In what kinds of situations do I "come alive" and breathe life into others?

✍ _____ ⌨

11. In what kinds of situations do I disengage, shut down, or suck vibrancy out of others?

✍ _____ ⌨

12. If you had to describe me to a potential employer in 30 seconds or less, what would you say?

✍ _____ ⌨

13. If you had to describe me to a prospective spouse in 30 seconds or less, what would you say?

✍ _____ ⌨

D. Repeat this interview with two other people. You may want to open a word-processing document to take the notes more easily.

11.2. Resources needed:

Optional: Annex 11-1. Johari Window

11.3. In-class activities:

> *"At the center of your being you have the answer;*
> *you know who you are and you know what you want."* Lao Tzu

Step 1. Questions?
Step 2. Quote.
Step 3. Discuss exercise.

a. Most importantly, consider how "what YOU put out in the world" affects "what the WORLD gives to you." Of all your thoughts and behaviors, which ones might be attracting the "good" people, experiences and opportunities in your life? Conversely, which ones might be attracting all the "bad" people and experiences, or your lack of opportunity? You might be surprised to see how much of what the world does to (or for) you is really a product of your own doing or thinking.

✍ _____ ⌨

b. How hard was it to conduct the interview and to listen to the feedback without responding? Were blind spots revealed to you? Was there alignment between what you believe to project and how you occur? What themes emerged, if any?

✎ _____ ⌨

IMPORTANT NOTE: This exercise is not intended to suggest that you are a bad person or doing things wrong! It does not intend to suggest that you need to make radical changes based upon what you learn. The exercise is intended to increase your awareness of what you contribute to the way in which you occur to others. It allows you an opportunity to assess whether the results you do garner are ones you desire. It shines the light on the fact that you are in control and can make choices (adjustments) if what you contribute is not serving you well.

Of course, your choices may not change how you are perceived, if other people are not able or willing to engage with you to improve their understanding of you (*versus* only relying upon the "the story they have written" based upon their observations).

11.4. Discussion questions:

Per facilitator ...
How might you go about determining how patients perceive their pharmacist(s)?

11.5. After-class assignments:

A. Given what you now know of how you personally occur to others, think about your best friends. Are there things you might or should tell them, that would help them grow? Would they be willing to accept your input without harming your relationship?
B. Fulfill the before-class activities for the next Module assigned by your facilitator.
C. Conduct the Johari Window exercise described in Annex 11-1.

11.6. Bibliography, references, & resources:

Flashcards via Quizlet, https://quizlet.com/class/3716098/, Johari Window » 4 terms
Handy C. *21 Ideas for Managers: Practical Wisdom for Managing Your Company and Yourself.* San Francisco: Jossey-Bass, 2000.
Luft J, Ingham H. The Johari window, a graphic model of interpersonal awareness. *Proceedings of the Western Training Laboratory in Group Development.* Los Angeles: University of California, Los Angeles, 1955.

Annex 11-1. Johari Window

Separate annex documents available to facilitators upon request (LeadGrowShape@plei.org).

The Johari Window is a technique used to help people better understand their relationship with themselves and others. It was created by psychologists Joseph Luft and Harrington Ingham (Joe + Harry = Johari) in 1955. During the exercise, participants receive a list of adjectives, out of which they pick 10 to 12 that they feel describe their own personality. Second, people who know the participant are given the same list, and each pick an equal number of adjectives that describe the subject. These adjectives are then inserted into a grid known as the Johari Window.

Two axes are used to create a grid of four cells, or four panes of a window. One axis involves whether the attributes of the adjective are known to the participant or not. The other axis addresses whether the attributes of the adjective are known to others or not. Each of the four quadrants is given a distinct name, as explained below.

	Known to self	Not known to self
Known to others	Open, Arena	Blind spot
Not known to others	Hidden, Façade	Unknown

Open or Arena: Adjectives selected by both the participant and peers. This quadrant represents traits of the subjects that both they themselves and peers are aware of.

Hidden or Façade: Adjectives selected only by subjects, but not by their peers. These represent acknowledged information that peers are unaware of. The participant can choose to disclose this information or not.

Blind Spot: Adjectives not selected by participants, but only by peers. These represent information that the participant is not aware of, but others are. Others can decide whether and how to inform the individual about these "blind spots."

Unknown: Adjectives not selected by either subjects or their peers. These represent the participant's behaviors or motives that were not recognized by anyone participating. This may be because they do not apply or because there is collective ignorance of the existence of these traits.

Participants may want to consider expanding their Open (Arena) quadrant, resulting in greater knowledge of oneself. Voluntary disclosure of Hidden quadrant information may result in greater interpersonal intimacy and friendship.

The following 57 adjectives are used as possible descriptions of the participant. Obviously, the selection of the observer will influence the likelihood that certain adjectives will be selected. For example, selection of class mates or work partners may decrease the likelihood that a family-oriented adjective is selected. Conversely, selecting family members or social acquaintance may decrease the likelihood of selecting work-oriented adjectives.

able	accepting	adaptable	bold	black
brave	calm	caring	cheerful	clever
complex	confident	dependable	dignified	empathetic
energetic	extroverted	friendly	giving	happy
helpful	idealistic	independent	ingenious	intelligent
introverted	kind	knowledgeable	logical	loving
mature	modest	nervous	observant	organized
patient	powerful	proud	quiet	reflective
relaxed	religious	responsive	searching	self-assertive
self-conscious	sensible	sentimental	shy	silly
spontaneous	sympathetic	tense	trustworthy	warm
wise	witty			

Source: Luft J, Ingham H. The Johari window, a graphic model of interpersonal awareness. *Proceedings of the Western Training Laboratory in Group Development.* Los Angeles: University of California, Los Angeles, 1955.

Module « **12** »   WHAT KIND OF PROFESSIONAL CAN I BE?

☞ Learning Objectives:

Objective 1. To assess the meaning and relevance of the Oath of a Pharmacist.
Objective 2. To assess the meaning and relevance of the Code of Ethics for Pharmacists.
Objective 3. To define characteristics of a profession and traits of a professional.

Pharmacy is a profession. Pharmacists are professionals. What do those words really mean?

This Module explores definitions, oaths, pledges, codes, ethics and more. Don't take lightly what it means to be a pharmacist, because the public expects your behavior to be exemplary, trustworthy, serving, covenantal, ethically sound, and much more. Are you up to it?

If you thought it was about a certain number of dollars per hour, you should think again.

We explore you and what your future might look like. Well, to tell the truth, you have multiple alternate futures. Which will you choose? Which will you build?

12.1. Readings or activities <u>before class</u>:

A. Review the following nomenclature (from various sources):
- ▸ <u>Profession</u>: a vocation requiring knowledge of some department of learning or science; an occupation that involves prolonged training and a formal qualification; a type of job that requires special education, training, or skill. Classically, the purpose of a profession is to supply disinterested objective counsel and service to others, for a direct and definite compensation, wholly apart from expectation of other business gain.
- ▸ <u>Professional</u>: a person engaged or qualified in a profession.
- ▸ <u>Covenant</u>: an agreement, usually formal, between two or more persons to do or not do something specified.
- ▸ <u>Trust</u>: an agreement, usually formal, between two or more persons to do or not do something specified; the obligation or responsibility imposed on a person in whom confidence or authority is placed.

B. Read and be prepared to discuss the Oath of a Pharmacist, the commentary about it, and the Pledge of Professionalism (Appendix 3).
C. Read and be prepared to discuss the Code of Ethics for Pharmacists (Appendix 4; in Canada, read provincial code of ethics).
D. After readings, complete Annex 12-1: Professionalism Crossword Puzzle (or follow facilitator instructions).

12.2. Resources needed:

Appendix 3: Oath of a Pharmacist and Pledge of Professionalism
Appendix 4: Code of Ethics for Pharmacists [in Canada, refer to provincial code of ethics]

Optional: Your school's honor code.

12.3. In-class activities:

"Now more than ever, student pharmacists are able to be at the forefront of patient care." APhA-ASP/AACP, 2009

Step 1. Questions?
Step 2. Quote.
Step 3. Exercise.

TABLE 12-1: APhA-ASP/AACP-COD TASK FORCE ON PROFESSIONALISM DEFINITIONS

Characteristics of a <u>Profession</u>:

1. Prolonged specialized training in a body of abstract knowledge
2. A service orientation
3. An ideology based on the original faith professed by members
4. An ethic that is binding on the practitioners
5. A body of knowledge unique to the members
6. A set of skills which form the technique of the profession
7. A guild of those entitled to practice the profession
8. Authority granted by society in the form of licensure or certification
9. A recognized setting where the profession is practiced
10. A theory of societal benefits derived from the ideology

If you were a Hollywood movie producer, what story concept could you use to bring these characteristics to life? What setting (e.g., contemporary, Western, sci fi)?

TABLE 12-2: APhA-ASP/AACP-COD TASK FORCE ON PROFESSIONALISM DEFINITIONS

Traits of a <u>Professional</u>

1. Knowledge and skills of a profession
2. Commitment to self-improvement of skills and knowledge
3. Service orientation
4. Pride in the profession
5. Covenantal relationship with the client
6. Creativity and innovation
7. Conscience and trustworthiness
8. Accountability for his/her work
9. Ethically sound decision making
10. Leadership

Source: Benner J, Beardsley R, APhA-ASP/AACP-COD Task Force. White Paper on Pharmacy Student Professionalism. *JAPhA*. 2000; 40(1):96-102.
www.aacp.org/resources/studentaffairspersonnel/studentaffairspolicies/Documents/1999WhitePaperProfessionalism.pdf

If you were a Hollywood movie producer, what instructions would you give the screen writers, to bring these traits to life? What actors or actresses come to mind?

Step 4. Oath of a Pharmacist and Pledge of Professionalism (Appendix 3).

Step 5. Code of Ethics for Pharmacists (Appendix 4).

Step 6. [Optional]: Your school's honor code.

12.4. Discussion questions:

Per facilitator

12.5. After-class assignments:

A. While in a public setting, watch the people around you and find someone who provides disinterested objective counsel or service, someone who operates in or creates instantaneously a position of trust, someone who in that instant has created a covenantal relationship. Keep your eyes wide open: it could be a fast-food clerk who is helping an intellectually disabled customer. Do in groups, if you wish.
B. Fulfill the before-class activities for the next Module assigned by your facilitator.

12.6. Bibliography, references, & resources:

APhA Academy of Student Pharmacists, AACP Committee on Student Professionalism. Pharmacy Professionalism Toolkit for Students and Faculty, version 2.0, 2009. www.aacp.org/resources/studentaffairspersonnel/studentaffairspolicies/Documents/Version_2%200_Ph armacy_Professionalism_Toolkit_for_Students_and_Faculty.pdf

ASHP Council on Pharmacy Management. ASHP statement on leadership as a professional obligation. *Am J Health-Syst Pharm*. 2011 Dec 1;68(23):2293-5.

Benner J, Beardsley R, APhA-ASP/AACP-COD Task Force. White Paper on Pharmacy Student Professionalism. *JAPhA*. 2000; 40(1):96-102.

Boyle CJ, Beardsley RS, Morgan JA, Rodriguez de Bittner M. Professionalism: A determining factor in experiential learning. *Am J Pharm Educ*. 2007 Apr 15;71(2):31. www.ncbi.nlm.nih.gov/pmc/articles/PMC1858614/pdf/ajpe31.pdf

Brown D, Ferrill MJ. The taxonomy of professionalism: Reframing the academic pursuit of professional development. *Am J Pharm Educ*. 2009 July 10; 73(4):68. www.ncbi.nlm.nih.gov/pmc/articles/PMC2720364/pdf/ajpe68.pdf

Flashcards via Quizlet, https://quizlet.com/class/3716098/, Professionalism » 11 terms

Sorensen TD, Traynor AP, Janke KK. Inviting scholarship in leadership in pharmacy. *Innov Pharm*. 2010;1(1): Article 1. pubs.lib.umn.edu/innovations/vol1/iss1/1.

Yanicak A, Mohorn PL, Monterroyo P, Furgiuele G, Waddington L, Bookstaver PB. Public perception of pharmacists: Film and television portrayals from 1970 to 2013. *JAPhA*. 2015 Nov-Dec;55(6):578-86.

Annex 12-1. Professionalism Crossword Puzzle

Separate annex documents available to facilitators upon request (LeadGrowShape@plei.org).

Across

2. Solemn promise regarding one's future behavior
3. Philosophy distinguishing between right and wrong human actions
8. Person qualified in a profession
9. Set of standards set forth by an authority
10. Esteem, high regard, privilege

Down

1. Set of principles affirming a form of conduct
4. Obligation on a person in whom confidence placed
5. A group entitled to practice a profession
6. Vocation requiring knowledge and qualification
7. Agreement to do something specified
8. Solemn promise or vow

Module « **13** »   WHAT IS LEADERSHIP?

☞ Learning Objectives:

Objective 1. To assess one's personal degree of leadership skills and leadership qualities.
Objective 2. To identify facts and myths about leadership.
Objective 3. To contrast varying beliefs and orientations of administrators, managers, and leaders.

What are the essential criteria for an exemplary leader? This Module explores what each participants' own feelings about leadership are, how they rate themselves as leaders, and where they feel they should concentrate for personal leadership development.

This Module also addresses the distinctions between leadership, management, and motivation; opportunities for leadership in the profession of pharmacy; and specific ways leadership can be developed. If you thought leadership = influence (as we said back in Module 1), well, that's true. But leadership is a matter of biology, which is so much more complicated than chemistry. So, it's a bit more complicated than that simple equation. Fear not, we'll explain.

13.1. Readings or activities <u>before class</u>:

A. Complete Annex 13-1. Personal Leadership Assessment.
B. Complete Annex 13-2. Facts & Myths.

13.2. Resources needed:

A. Annex 13-1. Personal Leadership Assessment.
B. Annex 13-2. Facts & Myths.
C. Annex 13-3. Primary Orientation of Administrators, Managers, & Leaders.

13.3. In-class activities:

> *"There are two ways of being creative. One can sing and dance.*
> *Or one can create an environment in which singers and dancers flourish." Warren Bennis*
> *"Leaders are people who do the right thing;*
> *managers are people who do things right." Warren Bennis*

Step 1. Questions?
Step 2. Quotes.
Step 3. Self-Assessment.
Step 4. Exercise.

FACTS & MYTHS

Discuss Annex 13-2.

13.4. Discussion questions:

Per facilitator ...

Per Annex 13-2, share ideas about how you have seen various facts (or myths) come true in a pharmacy.

Per Annex 13-3, categorize (anonymously) some pharmacists (or other professionals) you have known as administrators *versus* managers *versus* leaders (recognizing that the same people can exhibit different characteristics in different circumstances)

If you had a blank slate, what criteria would you use to select your peers for recognition with membership in Phi Lambda Sigma Pharmacy Leadership Society? Compare and contrast how your criteria compare with the actual criteria (www.philambdasigma.org)?

13.5. After-class assignments:

A. Review the matrix in Annex 13-3: Primary Orientation of Administrators, Managers, & Leaders. Think of three to five supervisors you know or have had. From your experience, categorize each as an administrator, a manager, or a leader.

B. Fulfill the before-class activities for the next Module assigned by your facilitator.

13.6. Bibliography, references, & resources:

Bennis W, Nanus B. *Leadership: The Strategies for Taking Charge*. New York: Harper Row, 1985.

Blanchard K, Johnson S. *The One-Minute Manager*. New York: William Morrow, 1982.

Blanchard K, Ziganni P, Ziganni D. *Leadership and the One-Minute Manager*. New York: William Collins, 1985.

Cohen A. Tips to improve the manager/leader's performance. *Hospital Topics*. 1985;63(Jan-Feb):38-40.

Dorn RC. Measure your leadership knowledge. *Leadership 1984*, pp. A47-A49.

Gardner JW. *Leadership Papers-1: The Nature of Leadership*. Independent Sector, Washington, DC, 1986.

Gardner JW. *Leadership Papers-7: Leadership Development*. Independent Sector, Washington, DC, 1987.

Hersey P, Blanchard KH. *Management of Organizational Behavior: Utilizing Human Resources, 4th ed*. Prentice-Hall, Inc., Englewood Cliffs, NJ; 1982.

Herzberg F. One more time: How do you motivate employees? *Harvard Business Review*. 1987;65(Sep-Oct):109-120.

McConkey DD. Are you an administrator, a manager, or a leader? *Business Horizons* 1989(Sep-Oct):15-21.

McGregor D. *Leadership and Motivation*. Cambridge, Mass: MIT Press, 1966.

Peters T, Austin N. *A Passion for Excellence: The Leadership Difference*. New York: Random House, 1985.

White SJ, Generali JA. Motivating pharmacy employees. *Am J Hosp Pharm*. 1984;41:1361-6.

Zaleznik A. Managers and leaders: Are they different? *Harvard Business Review* 1977;55:67-78.

Zellmer WA. A good place to work. *Am J Hosp Pharm*. 1984;41:889.

Annex 13-1. Personal Leadership Assessment

Separate annex documents available to facilitators upon request (LeadGrowShape@plei.org).

A. Rank yourself on how well you exhibit these leadership *qualities:*

Quality	Low				High
1. Self-confidence	1	2	3	4	5
2. Respect for and confidence in others	1	2	3	4	5
3. Ability to empower or challenge others	1	2	3	4	5
4. Fairness, being equitable	1	2	3	4	5
5. Ability to work with people at any level	1	2	3	4	5
6. Ability to communicate with others	1	2	3	4	5
7. Expertise, knowledge within a subject	1	2	3	4	5
8. Ethical behavior	1	2	3	4	5
9. Creativity	1	2	3	4	5
10. Willingness to take a calculated risk	1	2	3	4	5
Sum of scores:			►		
Mean score (sum ÷ 10):			►		

B. How well do you translate your leadership talents into action? Rank yourself on how well you use these leadership *skills*:

Skill	Low				High
1. Delegate	1	2	3	4	5
2. Motivate, inspire	1	2	3	4	5
3. Coach, counsel, develop	1	2	3	4	5
4. Encourage teamwork	1	2	3	4	5
5. Serve as a model	1	2	3	4	5
6. Discover/create new opportunities/goals	1	2	3	4	5
Sum of scores:			►		
Mean score (sum ÷ 6):			►		

Note: This instrument has not been psychometrically validated. The scores are suitable for introspection only.

C. From the items in the boxes above, list three aspects of your leadership *capacity (qualities)* you would like to improve. Then list three aspects of your leadership *skills (behavior)* you would like to improve:

Capacity/Qualities:

a. _____ b. _____ c. _____ ⌨

Skills/Behavior:

a. _____ b. _____ c. _____ ⌨

Annex 13-2. Leadership Facts & Myths

Separate annex documents available to facilitators upon request (LeadGrowShape@plei.org).

This survey gauges your opinions about leadership. Circle or highlight "true" or "false" to these questions. Think about various aspects of leadership and personnel management.

True False	1. Most leaders find that most of their problems involve administrative or technical issues where they lack expertise.
True False	2. Most leaders are knowledgeable and skillful about delegating tasks.
True False	3. Good leaders are able to structure their days to allow time for reflection on key association issues.
True False	4. Most of a leader's information comes from the organization's hierarchy or its profession.
True False	5. Almost any outstanding strength a leader possesses can also be a liability.
True False	6. Boundless self-confidence is critical to being a successful leader.
True False	7. An organization's past leaders are the most important source of information about serving a successful term.
True False	8. There is little that can be learned from working with a leader who is not doing a good job.
True False	9. On-the-job failures play an important role in learning about leadership.
True False	10. To get the job done, leaders must be able to stand alone and avoid depending on other members.
True False	11. There is only one pathway to the top positions in our organization.
True False	12. Leaders empower associates to make a significant contribution and to be challenged in their work.
True False	13. Intermediate positions (such as committee chair) contribute little to the development of the skills needed by the top volunteer in an organization.
True False	14. To lead an organization to success, the volunteer leader must emphasize financial goals above all else.
True False	15. The most successful organization leaders are those who create an environment in which others in the organization can be successful and feel fulfilled.
True False	16. Most highly successful leaders believe that their role is to be efficient managers of the organization and concentrate on doing things right.
True False	17. Most successful organization leaders want to be in charge and enjoy having decision-making responsibility.
True False	18. To reach the top in most organizations, a leader must be able to get along well with all kinds of people.
True False	19. In most organizations, one big mistake will prevent a member from ever reaching the top position.

True False	20. Part of a leader's job is to define what his or her organization stands for and what its guiding values should be.

Adapted from: Dorn RC. Measure your leadership knowledge. *Leadership 1984*, pp. A47-A49.

I answered ___ questions "correctly" on (date) _____ 🖼

[Hint: take the test again in a few weeks, and see how you improve.]

21. Pick some peers in a student group you belong to who you consider good examples of leadership. Why did you choose them?

✎ _____ ⌨

22. How many leaders can there be in one student group? How many should there be?

✎ _____ ⌨

23. What are the differences between leading a fraternity or sorority, leading a squad of soldiers, and leading the staff members of a pharmacy?

✎ _____ ⌨

24. What is your personal definition of leadership?

✎ _____ ⌨

25. Are leadership and management the same thing?

✎ _____ ⌨

Annex 13-3. Primary Orientation of Administrators, Managers, & Leaders: A Summary

Separate annex documents available to facilitators upon request (LeadGrowShape@plei.org).

For pondering...

	Administrator	Manager	Leader
Primary Driver:	Power	Mixture of power and achievement	Achievement
Authority:	Emphasizes formal authority and power	Authority goes with the position	Maximum use of informal authority
People:	Emphasis on controls and time spent	Emphasizes team effort	Lead by example
Basis of Loyalty:	Demand it	Earn it	Willingly given by subordinate
Subordinate Loyalty:	Is to the policy	Mixed between the policy and the manager	Is to the leader
Subordinate Initiative:	Poor, follow the leader and policy	Prepares and follows a plan	Forces people to take responsibility and exercise it
Decision-Making Basis:	The decision is made by the policy/procedure	Stick with policy except where exceptions are fully justified	Special circumstances require different decisions
Time Frame for Thinking:	Short-range, month to month, year to year	Medium-range, 2-4 years	Strategic, 5-10 years
Strategic Orientation:	Internal	Internal except when major external events intervene	External
Change:	Maintain status quo, don't rock the boat or make waves	Changes made if major problems dictate or when pressure builds up	Change is encouraged continuously
Big *versus* Small Picture:	Concentrates on details	Details as they fit into a system	Concepts and a big picture
Handling Mistakes:	Protect my rear and offer excuses, pin the guilty	Emphasize why it happened, not who caused it	Learn from them, don't dwell on them once solved
Approach to Problems:	Avoid	Solve as they develop — reactive	Problems are normal part of the job—proactive
Conflict:	Avoid	Address if they become major	They will occur—concentrates on resolving them to improve

Risk Taking:	Avoid	Accepts minimal risk	Encourages planned risk taking
Information Sharing:	Little	Need-to-know basis	Open and frank
Using Information:	Overwhelmed by too much	Uses what is required for decisions, for what is being done (reactive)	Highly selective, determines which is significant and what should be done (proactive)
Communicating:	Top down and internal	Seeks organized methods	Promotes two-way communication and external communication
Delegation:	Has limited authority so is limited delegator	Delegates clear-cut authority to match responsibility	Delegates extensively with minimal controls
Planning Approach:	Knee-jerk reactions, short range	Long and short range	Concentrates on strategies and the long range
Clock Watching or Hours Worked:	9 to 5	As required by workload	Results are the important thing, not the hours
Results *versus* Potential:	Works below potential	Strives to achieve potential	Achieves full potential
Team Building:	Clones	Based on the skills required by the job	Picks people with complementary skills

Adapted from: McConkey DD. Are you an administrator, a manager, or a leader? *Business Horizons* 1989(Sep-Oct):15-21.

Module « **14** »   FORMING & SUSTAINING EFFECTIVE TEAMS

☞ Learning Objectives:

Objective 1. To discuss how individuals organize into groups or teams.

Objective 2. To discuss the merits of Cog's ladder as a model for group development, and applications in college life and pharmacy practice settings.

Objective 3. To discuss Tuckman's stages of group development [storming-norming-forming-performing], and applications in college life and pharmacy practice settings.

Objective 4. To describe Csíkszentmihályi's concept that (mis)matching tasks and strengths can have on individuals and groups.

Objective 5. To discuss the idea of "flow" & its application to selecting pursuits, and delegating tasks.

You know from biology classes that individual organisms wiggle and move and have various degrees of action. And when more than one of them come together, when the organisms form a pride or a pod or a litter or a colony, the complexity and the output increases geometrically (heck, exponentially).

So it is with humans. When humans form teams, they can accomplish... anything... or nothing. Those other animals are, oh, so predictably productive. Why is it so complex with humans? What helps human teams succeed? How are human teams best nurtured?

To illustrate how a leader can maximize and sustain group performance, we introduce you to the concept of "flow." Flow promotes the happiness and fulfillment of members. What is "flow"? It is not about giving up anything to get along (i.e., "going with the flow" or "giving up to get along"). Instead, "flow" occurs when a person's skills are perfectly matched to a set of chosen or assigned challenges.

To illustrate how a leader can maximize and sustain group performance, we introduce you to the concept of "flow." Flow promotes the happiness and fulfillment of members. What is "flow"? It is not about giving up anything to get along (i.e., "going with the flow" or "giving up to get along"). Instead, "flow" occurs when a person's skills are perfectly matched to a set of chosen or assigned challenges.

Mihaly Csíkszentmihályi developed the psychological concept of "flow," a highly focused mental state. Csíkszentmihályi once said: "Repression is not the way to virtue. When people restrain themselves out of fear, their lives are by necessity diminished. Only through freely chosen discipline can life be enjoyed and still kept within the bounds of reason."

Csíkszentmihályi contends that people are happiest when they are in a state of flow—a state of concentration or absorption with an activity and situation. Nothing else seems to matter. They are said to be "in the zone" or "in the groove." Flow is an optimal state of intrinsic motivation, involving great engagement, fulfillment, and skill. Intrinsic motivation leads to goal-seeking, enjoyment of challenges, and increased happiness.

With these insights, this Module helps introduce leaders to identifying the situations of their individual members. From there, leaders can help individual members align to the needs and activities of the group.

Even though flow is a phenomenon of an individual, it contributes to group dynamics (and hence accomplishments). The potential power of teams is unleashed when each individual has his or her own skills and challenges aligned, and are thus in flow. Each individual flow state needs to be complementary to the flow states of the others – they can be overlapping, but that is not necessary if the team's work needs them to be different.

Leaders can use the concepts in the flow pie as a diagnostic tool, to assess why certain members of the team may be disengaged. For example, if someone on the team is bored, the leader may want to increase the level of challenge, or give them a different challenge that is better matched with that person's skill level.

14.1. Readings or activities <u>before class:</u>

Read and be prepared to discuss the detailed descriptions of Cog's Ladder and Tuckman's Stages of Group Development. Compare and contrast the two models of group development.

After reading, complete Annex 14-3: Group-Development Crossword Puzzle (or follow facilitator instructions).

COG'S LADDER FOR GROUP DEVELOPMENT

<u>Stage 1:</u> **Polite** (often when groups first come together)

a. getting acquainted

b. low-risk information sharing

c. cliques form

d. high need for group approval

<u>Stage 2:</u> **Why We're Here** (often when group first addresses a task)

a. goals and objectives clarified

b. cliques wield influence

c. hidden agendas form

d. some risks and commitments

<u>Stage 3:</u> **Bid for Power** (perhaps when individuals hold different opinions)

a. competition

b. conflict

c. cliques wield power and control

d. need for group approval declines

e. risk taking is high

<u>Stage 4:</u> **Constructive** (may become evident in subsequent exercises)

a. attitude of active listening

b. cliques begin to dissolve

c. progress towards goals

d. creativity is high

e. group cooperation

<u>Stage 5:</u> **Esprit** (may be evident on last day, after goal(s) achieved)

a. high group morale

b. intense loyalty

c. high individuality and creativity

d. cliques are absent

e. closed membership

f. synergy

Progression:

a. Movement from Stage 1 to 2 (from Polite to Why) may occur by the simple suggestion of one member.

b. Movement from Stage 3 to 4 (from Bid for Power to Constructive) requires the ability to listen.

c. Movement from Stage 3 to 4 can be blocked by one competitive member or subgroup.

d. Movement from Stage 4 to 5 (from Constructive to Esprit) requires unanimous agreement.

e. The group proceeds through these stages only to the extent that members are willing to grow.

Sacrifices:

a. Movement from Stage 1 to 2 (from Polite to Why) requires each member to relinquish the comfort of nonthreatening topics and risk the possibility of conflict.

b. Movement from Stage 2 to 3 (from Why to Bid) may require members to commit to a group purpose they do not agree with fully. Members must also risk personal attacks.

c. Movement from Stage 3 to 4 (from Bid to Constructive) requires members to stop defending their own views and risk the possibility of being wrong.

d. Movement from Stage 4 to 5 (from Constructive to Esprit) demands that members trust each other.

What stage is your group in?

✎ _____ ⌨

Cog's Ladder: Optional Quiz

1. The first stage in Cog's ladder of group development is:

    a. Polite

    b. Why We're Here

    c. Bid for Power

    d. Constructive

    e. Esprit

2. A competitive stage characterized by conflicts, cliques, and high risk taking is the _____ stage.

    a. Polite

    b. Why We're Here

    c. Bid for Power

    d. Constructive

    e. Esprit

3. A stage characterized by high morale, intense loyalty, and synergy is the _____ stage.

    a. Polite

    b. Why We're Here

    c. Bid for Power

    d. Constructive

    e. Esprit

4. A stage characterized by search for goals and objectives, formation of hidden agendas, and a low level of risk and commitment is the _____ stage.

    a. Polite

    b. Why We're Here

    c. Bid for Power

    d. Constructive

    e. Esprit

TUCKMAN'S STAGES OF GROUP DEVELOPMENT

Bruce Tuckman proposed four stages for group development in 1965, labeled:

Forming – Storming – Norming – Performing

Tuckman considered each phase to be necessary and inevitable for the team to grow, face up to challenges, tackle problems, find solutions, plan work, and deliver results.

- **Forming**: The team assembles and learns about opportunities and challenges. Members agree on goals and begin tasks to achieve the goals. Team members initially may behave independently. They may be motivated, but are often relatively uninformed about the team. Team members are usually well behaved, but focused on themselves. Mature team members begin to model appropriate behavior even at this early phase.

- **Storming**: Next, participants form opinions about the character and integrity of other participants. They may voice these opinions if they find someone shirking responsibility or attempting to dominate. Sometimes participants question the actions or decision of the leader as the tasks grow harder. Disagreements and personality clashes must be resolved before the team can progress beyond this stage. Some teams may re-enter this stage if new disputes arise. To advance, emphasize tolerance of each team member and their differences.

- **Norming**: Resolving disagreements and personality clashes from the "storming" stage can result in greater intimacy, allowing a spirit of co-operation to emerge. Sharing a common goal helps. Team members begin to accept and tolerate the whims and idiosyncrasies of other team members. Risk may arise if members become so focused on preventing conflict that they hesitate to share controversial ideas.

- **Performing**: Once group norms and roles are established, group members can focus on achieving common goals. Members in this stage are motivated and knowledgeable. The team members are now competent, autonomous and able to handle decision making without supervision. Dissent is expected and allowed, if it is channeled through processes acceptable to the team.

Even high-performing teams can revert to earlier stages under certain circumstances. Many long-standing teams go through these cycles multiple times as they react to new members, new goals, new environmental conditions, or new leaders.

Later scholars have added other stages to this scheme, preserving the rhyming theme with terms such as adjourning (or mourning), renorming, and transforming.

14.2. Resources needed:

Print off a paper copy of Annex 14-1 and Annex 14-2 before coming to class.
Annex 14-1. Insert Pieces for Challenge-Skill-Task Wheel (Part 1)
Annex 14-2. Challenge-Skill-Task Wheel (Part 2)
Part II requires the answers to the personality inventory taken in Module 8 or outside this course.
Facilitator discretion: Use of Annex 14-3. Group-Development Crossword Puzzle

14.3. In-class activities:

> *"Individual commitment to a group effort--that is what makes a team work, a company work,*
> *a society work, a civilization work." Vince Lombardi*

> *"Remember, teamwork begins by building trust.*
> *And the only way to do that is to overcome our need for invulnerability." Patrick Lencioni*

"Flow experiences lead to higher levels of happiness by transforming the formula of 'no pain, no gain' to 'present gain, future gain.'" Tal Ben-Shahar

Step 1. Questions?
Step 2. Quote.
Step 3. Exercise.

T-E-A-M-W-O-R-K

a. Look at the word T-E-A-M-W-O-R-K [on flip chart, white board, computer screen]. Privately, write down as many words as you can by using those eight letters. You have 3 minutes. Please be silent, to preserve the "magic" of the exercise.

✎ _____ ⌨

b. Is it absolutely true that, to achieve greatness, you need others?

✎ _____ ⌨

c. Can something of significant value be achieved by a lone individual? Explain.

✎ _____ ⌨

Alex Haley, author of *Roots*, was asked the meaning of a photo showing a turtle on top of a post. He replied that the turtle certainly did not get there alone. Remember all the people who have helped you to get where you are today: parents, teachers, *et cetera*. Each who has invested in you is part of your team.

Explore the significance of having a team *versus* individual efforts with these questions:

d. What advantages/disadvantages can be gained by having more members on your team?

✎ _____ ⌨

e. What do you consider the #1 reason why people may hesitant before joining a team?

✎ _____ ⌨

f. How can this hesitation be dealt with or eliminated?

✎ _____ ⌨

g. In what ways does a group you belong to currently operate as a team?

✎ _____ ⌨

h. In what ways could it use better teamwork to accomplish more?

✎ _____ ⌨

You may have heard this saying before: TEAM stands for Together Each Achieves More.

It is important for leaders of teams to understand the benefits of overcoming the difficulties of teamwork for the team to reach its full potential. Too often, leaders decide that it is easier to just do the work themselves. If so, the full potential of the team is not realized and the leader may become overstretched (e.g., overworked, overwhelmed, frustrated). Opportunities for group cohesion and development are wasted. This is when Leadership-by-Doing begins to fall short.

STRENGTHS & FLOW: LEVERAGING YOUR UNIQUE GIFTS

Great leaders seem to have a magical ability to get more from their teams than is humanly possible. Many leaders believe the key to such performance lies in charismatic inspiration, or draconian punishment or reward systems. While those strategies may work for a time, they alone can never produce sustained "superhuman" performance. This program will illustrate the importance of identifying peoples' strengths and aligning them with appropriate tasks matched in both type and complexity.

Step 4. Finding Flow: Appreciating the Effect of (Mis)Matched Tasks

a. Use the space below to describe an instance when you had to work on something unsatisfying. Something you dreaded the thought of even starting, and once you started, could not wait to be finished.

✏ _____ ⌨

b. Pair-share with your partner what that experience was like:
  ▷ What was the impact on you? On the other members of your team? On your desire to continue working with that team or organization?
  ▷ How successful were you in the task?
  ▷ On a scale of 1 (low) to 10 (high), how would you rate the level of value you contributed to the organization while performing this task?

c. Use the space below to describe an instance where you worked on something that was completely engaging. Something you could not wait to start doing, and once you started, was done before you knew it.

✏ _____ ⌨

d. Pair-share with your partner what that experience was like:
  ▷ What was the impact on you? On the other members of your team? On your desire to continue working with that team or organization?
  ▷ How successful were you in the task?
  ▷ On a scale of 1 (low) to 10 (high), how would you rate the level of value you contributed to the organization while performing this task?

e. Pair-share with your partner what you believe made those two experiences so different. As you share, jot down as many distinguishing factors as you can in the space below:

✏ _____ ⌨

FLOW PIE

Step 5. Flow Pie Exercise.
  a. Identify several people nearby and arrange yourselves in a group of 5 to 8 participants.
  b. Annex 14-1 contains several pie pieces. Each person in your group is to cut out the pie pieces from

their Annex.

    c. First, consider each axis and each of the emotional states.

        i. What types of emotional effects might be seen at different positions?

        ii. What types of physical effects might be seen at different positions?

        iii. What would be the "ideal" mixture of emotional and physical effects – and why?

    d. Next, have each group member work INDIVIDUALLY to arrange the pieces in the correct places in Annex 14-2.

    e. Once everyone is finished, compare notes. Learn from each other to develop a consensus order for the pieces and arrange them accordingly. Select one person from your group to justify your final arrangement.

It is desirable to be in a position of high skills and a highly challenging activity. That position is called "Flow," where high challenge and high skill meet. Flow is the best match of skills to the challenge. This information can be used to understand where a person exists in terms of feelings and behaviors and how they may relate to skill *versus* challenge levels.

A 45-degree angle across the graph from bottom left to upper right can indicate the "Flow" line. With intention, a person can be focused upon goal(s), but still stretched incrementally so as to attain the "next level." Move up on the challenge axis to match moving to the left on the skill axis, so that 45-degree angle is maintained – this is optimal. A little stretch is good (simulating) without being overwhelming. The leader can support the person to find a match of skill and challenge. Note, however, that Flow does not mean "an easy road" or giving in to "go with the flow." Flow depends upon structured and engaging activities.

Mismatches can lead to several emotional and physical problems, as you can see in various combinations of other levels of skill and other levels of challenge. Another way to think about mismatches can be illustrated by the following: "Do you like the thought of «INSERT IDEA»?" *versus* "Do you like «INSERT IDEA»?" – a small shift in words, but it can be pivotal.

Step 6.

WHAT ARE YOUR STRENGTHS AND HOW ARE YOU USING THEM?

    a. Briefly, refer to your results from the personality-inventory assessment [from Module 8]. Share your top strengths with your partner and listen carefully to their traits, and then reflect on the following questions and pair-share your observations:

    b. How did your results match up with what you previously believed your strengths to be? Were there any surprises? If so, why do you think that might be?

    c. As we go through life, we develop relationships with various authority figures (parents, teachers, bosses, *et cetera*) who may come to believe they truly know us. Can you find any incongruence between your top strengths and what one or more authority figures believed your strengths to be? If so, how could that incongruence have developed and what has been its impact on you and your relationship with them?

    d. How about your peers and close friends? Do you believe they would agree with your top strengths? Why or why not? Does it matter to you whether they agree? Why or why not?

    e. Reflect again on your top strengths and pair-share your observations on the following questions:

        i. To what degree are you able to leverage each of your strengths in your activities with your student group? How about school, work, family and friends?

        ii. What activities are you spending a lot of time on that do not leverage any of your strengths? What is the effect of that on you, your team and the organization you work for? How might you bring your strengths into play? What is a practical first commitment you can make to initiate that?

iii. What are some things you would like to do (that you are not doing now) that would engage your strengths? What is holding you back from doing that? What is a practical first commitment you can make to get past those obstacles?

iv. How well do you think your strengths align with your career goals? Do you see yourself being able to leverage them in the day-to-day activities of that job? If not, what is a practical first step you can make to identify alternate careers that may better align with your strengths?

Step 7. List three commitments you will make to increase the amount of time spent on activities that solidly align with your strengths, and then share them with a partner:

By _____ (date) I commit to: ✍ _____ ⌨

By _____ (date) I commit to: ✍ _____ ⌨

By _____ (date) I commit to: ✍ _____ ⌨

Step 8. Reflect on the weaknesses you acknowledge and pair-share your observations on the following questions:

a. Do you tend to spend more time thinking about and improving your weaknesses or your strengths? Why? What is the impact of that?

b. If you were delegated a task that you know is not well aligned with your strengths, how would you do?

c. If you had to appoint a committee to accomplish a given task, how would you approach that given what you know about strengths and flow?

Notes: ✍ _____ ⌨

Step 9. Building Effective Leadership Teams. In your group, reflect on the following questions as they relate to your top personality-inventory themes. [recall Module 8]
[Adapted from: http://businessjournal.gallup.com/content/113338/what-makes-great-leadership-team.aspx]

a. In which domains do you "show up"?

b. Reflect on your various work teams. Do you believe you are part of well-rounded teams, as described above? If not, what domain(s) do you believe are missing?

c. How might you make accommodations for your any current deficits?

d. What might you do to create more well-rounded leadership teams in the future?

Using strengths information can help you to form teams, as can understanding what makes an optimal match between skills and challenge presented by activities. Recall the signature themes described by your personality-inventory rubrics (Module 8).

14.4. Discussion questions:

Per facilitator …

Share ideas about how you have seen various pharmacy teams exhibit the characteristics of Cog's ladder or Tuckman's stages of team dynamics.

Facilitator discretion: Use of Annex 14-3. Group-Development Crossword Puzzle

14.5. After-class assignments:

A. The next time you are with members of a group you belong to, assess that group in terms of Cog's Ladder and Tuckman's stages. What can you do to nudge them into the next stage?
B. Use the interests (activities) and strengths you identified in this Module to adjust the upper-right and lower-left segments of the Values-Interests-Strengths-Needs (VISN) Chart in Annex 3-2. Adjust the values section based on any new reflections you have had.
C. Fulfill the commitments you made for scheduling your priorities.
D. Fulfill the before-class activities for the next Module assigned by your facilitator.

14.6. Bibliography, references, & resources:

Antonakis J, Fenley M, Liechti S. Learning charisma: Transform yourself into the person others want to follow. *Harvard Bus Rev* 2012;90:127-30.

Ben-Shahar T. *Being Happy: You Don't Have to Be Perfect to Lead a Richer, Happier Life* (2010); originally published in hardcover as T*he Pursuit of Perfect: How to Stop Chasing Perfection and Start Living a Richer, Happier Life*. New York: McGraw Hill Professional, 2009.

Ben-Shahar T. *Happier: Learn the Secrets to Daily Joy & Lasting Fulfillment.* McGraw Hill Professional, 2007.

Charrier GO. Cog's ladder: A model of group development. *Advanced Management Journal* 1972;37(1):30-7.

Csíkszentmihályi M. *Finding Flow: The Psychology of Engagement with Everyday Life.* New York: Basic Books, 1996.

Csíkszentmihályi M. *Flow: The Psychology of Optimal Experience.* New York: Harper & Row, 1990.

Flashcards via Quizlet, https://quizlet.com/class/3716098/, Challenge-Skill-Task Wheel (Flow Pie, Csíkszentmihályi) » 8 terms; Group-Development Lexicon » 9 terms

Langer EJ. *Mindfulness.* Reading, MA: Addison Wesley, 1989.

Myers D, Diener E. Who is happy? *Psychol Sci* 1995;6:10-17.
www.echocredits.org/downloads/2794689/Who.is.Happy.pdf

Rath T. *StrengthsFinder 2.0.* New York: Gallup Press, 2007.

Seligman MEP. *Flourish: A Visionary New Understanding of Happiness & Well-being.* New York: Free Press, 2011.

Tuckman B. Developmental sequence in small groups. *Psychological Bulletin* 1965;63 (6): 384–99.

White SJ, Generali JA. Motivating pharmacy employees. *Am J Hosp Pharm* 1984;41:1361-6.

Annex 14-1. Insert Pieces for Challenge-Skill-Task Wheel (Part 1)

Separate annex documents available to facilitators upon request (LeadGrowShape@plei.org).

Cut out the pie pieces, discarding the center.
Following your facilitator's instructions, place each piece into its proper place on Annex 14-2.

Adapted from: Csíkszentmihályi M. *Flow: The Psychology of Optimal Experience*. New York: Harper & Row, 1990.

This page intentionally blank.

Annex 14-2. Challenge-Skill-Task Wheel (Part 2)

Separate annex documents available to facilitators upon request (LeadGrowShape@plei.org).

Note the two axes: Skill *versus* challenge (complexity).
Place each piece from Annex 14-1 into its proper place here on Annex 14-2.

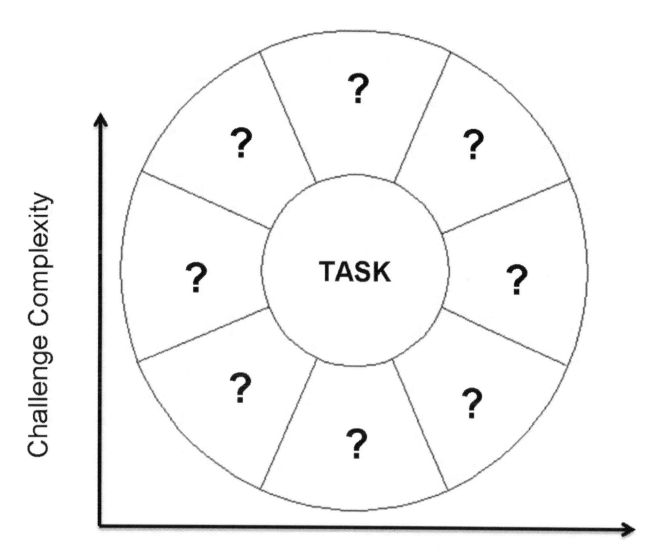

Adapted from: Csíkszentmihályi M. *Flow: The Psychology of Optimal Experience*. New York: Harper & Row, 1990.

Annex 14-3. Group-Development Crossword Puzzle

Separate annex documents available to facilitators upon request (LeadGrowShape@plei.org).

Across

4. Competition, conflict, cliques wield power and control
7. Team assembles, relatively uninformed about team, learns about opportunities and challenges
8. High group morale, loyalty, synergy
9. Participants form opinions about others, question the leader, disagreements and personality clashes

Down

1. Group norms and roles established, focus on achieving common goals
2. Active listening, cliques begin to dissolve, progress towards goals
3. Resolving disagreements and personality clashes, greater co-operation, tolerate whims of team members
5. Goals and objectives clarified, hidden agendas form
6. Low-risk information sharing

Module « 15 »   SITUATIONAL LEADERSHIP

☞ Learning Objectives:

Objective 1. To explore differing styles of leadership and circumstances when each may be appropriate.
Objective 2. To describe varying dimensions of leaders and their followers.
Objective 3. To help explore how to develop a repertoire of leadership skills and their application.

This Module considers various styles of leadership. Specifically, we address Hersey & Blanchard's Situational-Leadership Model, which addresses task behavior in light of relationship behavior. We pursue this model as depicted in popular entertainment (movie segments via YouTube and other Internet sites), as well as scenarios we are more likely to encounter in our present and future lives.

15.1. Readings or activities before class:

Rereading the leadership-style definitions in Module 5, section 5.1, may be helpful.
Read and be prepared to discuss the text for this Module, especially the nomenclature of Hersey & Blanchard's Situational-Leadership Model, summarized in Annex 15-1.
After reading, complete Annex 15-2. Situational-Leadership Crossword Puzzle.

15.2. Resources needed:

A. Internet access to play the video clips
B. Annex 15-1. Situational Leadership Model

15.3. In-class activities:

"Life is a balanced system of learning and evolution.
Whether pleasure or pain; every situation in your life serves a purpose.
It is up to us to recognize what that purpose could be." Steve Maraboli

Step 1. Questions?
Step 2. Quote.
Step 3. Exercise.

SITUATIONAL LEADERSHIP

General George S. Patton, Jr., and Martin Luther King, Jr., were both leaders, yet their approaches differed substantially. How can it be that they were each effective leaders, if they used such different styles?

Alternately, how did Franklin Roosevelt, Adolf Hitler, and Joseph Stalin vary in leading their nations through difficult times of economic trouble and war in the 1930s? This Module aims to explore differing styles of leadership and the circumstances under which each is optimal.

Step 4. Exercise:

SCENARIOS CALLING FOR SITUATIONAL LEADERSHIP

Scenario #1. Fund-raising for travel to Midyear Regional Meeting netted a lot of money. The problem is that so many members worked hard to raise the money, anticipating that most of the hard workers would be subsidized to attend. As the date gets nearer and people's plans and schedules change, only a subset of the members will be able to go. The problem is how to use the funds to the best advantage of the chapter and not allow those who cannot go feel neglected. You are a member of the group's executive committee. What do you recommend be done? Do you subsidize each traveler equally or according to their past or future likelihood to contributing to the chapter? Or do you set some of the money aside for other uses?

_____

Scenario #2. Problems among executive committee: One of the checks written by the chapter treasurer bounced, and an officer failed to submit a report to HQ on time for the second time this semester. Those two officers are present in today's executive committee meeting. How should we deal with these problems?

_____

Scenario #3. One of your classmates behaves in a way that makes many of your mutual friends believe he is an alcoholic. Another classmate is widely believed to periodically sell marijuana to other students. What are the responsibilities of student leaders in regards to these two students? Do leaders' responsibilities vary for these two forms of substance abuse?

_____

Scenario #4. You are a member of the executive committee of your student group. One of the younger students was appointed chair of the professional-projects committee. She comes to you complaining that only 50% of the people who volunteered for the committee have shown up for the last two meetings. And she is having problems getting people to show up for the monthly blood-pressure screening sessions at an alumnus' pharmacy. What is the problem? What do you recommend the chairperson do?

_____

Scenario #5. Attendance at group meetings is declining. Commuters complain if meetings are held in the evenings; P3s complain if they are held on weekends; others complain about other times. You are on the group's executive committee. What is the problem? What do you recommend be done?

_____

Scenario #6. A group of about six members declines to attend meetings or participate in social or professional events. Rumor has reached you, as an executive-committee member, that they do not plan to pay their dues next semester. What is the problem? What do you recommend be done?

_____

Scenario #7. People invited to pledge a fraternity or sorority decline for these reasons: "I just don't have enough time due to my academic pressures. I noticed a rivalry between the fraternities and, because I have friends in each group, I don't want to align with one group for fear of losing my friends in the other group. Besides, all I ever see your group do is party." This is not an isolated feeling. What is the problem? What should be done?

✍ _____ ▦

Scenario #8. The ultimate and fundamental problem facing executive committees is the motivation of individual members to contribute to group goals. How will you create an environment that encourages camaraderie and contributions to the team? What specifically will you as leaders do?

✍ _____ ▦

Have you considered:
- ▸ level of individual or group commitment to the task to be accomplished?
- ▸ supporters and opponents of the proposed course of action?
- ▸ what leadership principles are being applied?
- ▸ what do we intend to do if the first strategy is not successful?
- ▸ what additional information is needed before a decision can be reached or implemented?

15.4. Discussion questions:

Per facilitator …
Should a pharmacist avoid exhibiting any of the leadership behaviors in Hersey & Blanchard's model?

Situational Leadership: Optional Quiz
1. The two dimensions of Situational Leadership are:
   a. task and relationship
   b. task and behavior
   c. delegation and task
   d. situation and relationship
2. The S-2 (selling) quadrant is characterized by:
   a. high task behavior and high relationship behavior
   b. high task behavior and low relationship behavior
   c. low task behavior and low relationship behavior
   d. low behavior and high relationship behavior
3. The optimal relationship between a pharmacy director and a project leader is:
   a. Telling
   b. Selling
   c. Participating
   d. Delegating
4. Delegating does NOT involve which of the following behaviors?
   a. Observing
   b. Monitoring
   c. Fulfilling
   d. Establishing

5. The relationship between a pharmacy preceptor and an intern is often characterized by:
    a. high task behavior and high relationship behavior
    b. high task behavior and low relationship behavior
    c. low task behavior and low relationship behavior
    d. low behavior and high relationship behavior
6. The extent to which the leader engages in defining roles is:
    a. Relationship behavior
    b. Task behavior
7. The extent to which a leader engages in two-way (or multi-way) communication is:
    a. Relationship behavior
    b. Task behavior
8. The necessary knowledge, experience, and skill is known as:
    a. Ability
    b. Willingness
9. The necessary confidence, commitment, motivation is known as:
    a. Ability
    b. Willingness
10. Pharmacists should adopt one primary leadership style.
    a. True
    b. False

15.5. After-class assignments:

A. While sitting in a public setting (cafeteria, restaurant, campus, mall), watch the people around you and assign them to one of the four situational-leadership roles: Telling, Selling, Participating, Delegating. Do in groups, if you wish.
B. Fulfill the before-class activities for the next Module assigned by your facilitator.

15.6. Bibliography, references, & resources:

Flashcards via Quizlet, https://quizlet.com/class/3716098/, Situational-Leadership Model (Hersey & Blanchard) » 8 terms

Graham TS, Sincoff MZ, Baker B, Ackermann JC. Reel leadership: Hollywood takes the leadership challenge. *J Lead Educ.* 2003;2(2):37-45. www.journalofleadershiped.org/

Hersey H, Blanchard KH. *Management of Organizational Behavior: Utilizing Human Resources,* 4th ed. Englewood cliffs, NJ: Prentice-Hall, Inc., 1982.

Scott M, Weeks PP. Using film to teach authentic leadership. *J Lead Educ.* 2016;15(1):140-9. www.journalofleadershiped.org/attachments/article/419/v15i1scott0423.pdf

Waller DJ, Smith SR, Warnock JT. Situational theory of leadership. *Am J Hosp Pharm.* 1989;466:2336-41.

Williams JR. Pirates and power: What Captain Jack Sparrow, his friends, and his foes can teach us about power bases. *J Lead Studies.* 2011;5(2):60-68. www.journalofleadershiped.org/

Acknowledgement: To our good friend Richard A. Marasco, PharmD, who used movie segments with us in 1992 to exemplify leadership styles.

Annex 15-1. Situational-Leadership Model: A Summary

Separate annex documents available to facilitators upon request (LeadGrowShape@plei.org).

Task Behavior – the extent to which the leader engages in defining roles, telling what, how, when, where and if more than one person, who is to do what; goal-setting, organizing, establishing time lines, directing, controlling.

Relationship Behavior – the extent to which a leader engages in two-way (or multi-way) communicating, listening, facilitating behaviors, socio-emotional support: giving support, communicating, facilitating interactions, active listening, providing feedback.

Ability – the necessary knowledge, experience and skill.

Willingness – the necessary confidence, commitment, motivation.

S1: **Telling** – characterized by one-way communication in which the leader defines the roles of the individual or group and provides the what, how, why, when and where to do the task. Provides specific instructions and closely supervises performance. This style is appropriate where accomplishing the task is paramount and interrelations between boss and worker are of low consequence, such as a worker's first exposure to a task. Telling, guiding, directing, establishing.

S2: **Selling** – while the leader is still providing direction, he or she is now using two-way communication and providing the socio-emotional support that will allow the individual or group being influenced to buy into the process. Leader-made decision with dialogue or explanation. Explain your decisions and provide opportunity for clarification. Interactions between pharmacists and pharmacy technicians often fall in this category. Selling, explaining, clarifying, coaching, persuading.

S3: **Participating** – this is how shared decision-making about aspects of how the task is accomplished and the leader is providing fewer task behaviors while maintaining high relationship behavior. Leader/follower-made decision or follower-made decision with encouragement from leader. Share ideas and facilitate decision-making. Pharmacist-pharmacist relations are often of this type, in progressive work environments. Participating, encouraging, collaborating, committing.

S4: **Delegating** – the leader is still involved in decisions; however, the process and responsibility has been passed to the individual or group. The leader stays involved to monitor progress. Follower-made decision. Turn over responsibilities for decisions and implementation. Often seen in the relations between administrator and pharmacy director. Delegating, observing, monitoring, fulfilling.

D1. Unable and willing or insecure
D2. Unable but willing or confident
D3. Able but unwilling or insecure
D4. Able and willing or confident

Adapted from: Hersey H, Blanchard KH. *Management of Organizational Behavior: Utilizing Human Resources, 4th ed.* Englewood Cliffs: Prentice-Hall, Inc., 1982; https://en.wikipedia.org/wiki/Situational_leadership_theory

SITUATIONAL-LEADERSHIP MATRIX

HIGH **Relationship Behavior or Supportive Behavior** **LOW**	High Relationship & Low Task Behavior S3 — PARTICIPATING a – Group officer to Project Leader b – Member to novice (developmental) c – President to committee chair d – Instructor to inexperienced group	High Task & High Relationship Behavior S2 — SELLING a – Pharmacist to experienced technician b – Member to novice (teaching mode) c – Preceptor to intern
	Low Task & Low Relationship Behavior S4 — DELEGATING a – Hospital administrator to pharmacy director b – Advisor to experienced student group c – President to vice presidents	High Task & Low Relationship Behavior S1 — TELLING a – Pharmacist to inexperienced technician b – Member to novice (hazing, demanding) c – Professor to lecture hall d – Military basic training
	Low **Task Behavior** or	**Directive Behavior** High

D4. Able and willing or confident	D3. Able but unwilling or insecure	D2. Unable but willing or confident	D1. Unable and willing or insecure
High	Follower Readiness or Maturity		Low
Low	Direction by Leader		High

Adapted from: Hersey H, Blanchard KH. *Management of Organizational Behavior: Utilizing Human Resources, 4th ed.* Englewood Cliffs: Prentice-Hall, Inc., 1982; https://en.wikipedia.org/wiki/Situational_leadership_theory

Annex 15-2. Situational-Leadership Crossword Puzzle

Separate annex documents available to facilitators upon request (LeadGrowShape@plei.org).

Across

6. Behavior with two-way communication
7. Leader provides direction using two-way communication, decisions explained
8. Leader defines roles and details tasks

Down

1. Shared decision-making about how task is to be accomplished
2. Leader still involved, but passes process and responsibility to group
3. Necessary knowledge, experience and skill
4. Necessary confidence, commitment, motivation
5. Behavior where leader defines roles and time lines

Annex 15-3. Links to Video Clips

Separate annex documents available to facilitators upon request (LeadGrowShape@plei.org).

Links to Video Clips on Leadership:

Play several of these movie segments. After each one, ask where in the Situational Leadership matrix the leadership behavior would best fit. Be tolerant of more than one interpretation. Use your discretion according to local cultural norms; feel free to substitute other relevant clips.

While you watch any accompanying advertisements, consider "elevator speeches" and how to get your point across in 30 seconds or less.

URLs of leadership styles appear below:

Young Frankenstein [1974, Gruskoff/Venture Films, Crossbow Productions, Jouer Limited], put the candle back: https://www.youtube.com/watch?v=-ktmN0wvHQs

Dr. No [1963, MGM Studios], James Bond gets his Walther PPK: https://www.youtube.com/watch?v=tU98uP7pXA8

Beverly Hills Cop 2 [1987, Paramount Studios], Rosewood, get some wheels: https://www.youtube.com/watch?v=vKXi87tGxrA

Apollo 13 [2008, NBC Universal], We have a new mission: https://www.youtube.com/watch?v=gmLgi5mdTVo

Apollo 13 [2008, NBC Universal], not on my watch: www.wingclips.com/movie-clips/apollo-13/not-on-my-watch

The Martian [2015, 20th Century Fox], we're scrubbed: https://www.youtube.com/watch?v=Nz1swYRjEus

The Help [2011, Walt Disney Studios], agrees to interview, hire a maid: https://www.youtube.com/watch?v=XSisiUcnsQk

The Help [2011, Walt Disney Studios], Skeeter needs Aibileen's help: https://www.youtube.com/watch?v=07cCq_wcj0M

Julie & Julia [2009, Sony Pictures], both women, courage of your convictions: https://www.youtube.com/watch?v=DUhgY4ohhQA&index=4&list=PL8E802028E912CABD

Made in Dagenham: The Musical [2010, Sony Pictures], strike: https://www.youtube.com/watch?v=c-T5AbIof0g

Freedom Writers [2013, Warner Brothers], the showdown: https://www.youtube.com/watch?v=HU_BueZZNd8

Freedom Writers [2013, Warner Brothers], Holocaust and then Miep Gies (I am not a hero): www.wingclips.com/movie-clips/freedom-writers/you-are-heroes and then https://www.youtube.com/watch?v=AjGIJPE8B8I

Steel Magnolias [1989, TriStar Pictures], too much insulin: https://www.youtube.com/watch?v=ybbS5_qlkaQ

Hunger Games [2012, Lionsgate], rule change: https://www.youtube.com/watch?v=mgr2tLYYha4

Morning Glory [2010, Paramount], first day overload: www.wingclips.com/movie-clips/morning-glory/first-day-overload

Courageous [2011, Sony Pictures], better fathers: www.wingclips.com/movie-clips/courageous/better-father

Battle Los Angeles [2011, Columbia Pictures], back to battle (silent leadership): www.wingclips.com/movie-clips/battle-los-angeles/back-to-battle

Glory [1989, TriStar Pictures], tear it up: www.wingclips.com/movie-clips/glory/tear-it-up

Gandhi [1982, Sony Pictures], fighting without violence: www.wingclips.com/movie-clips/gandhi/fighting-without-violence

2012 [2009, Columbia Pictures], open the gates: www.wingclips.com/movie-clips/2012/open-the-gates

Coming Jan 2017: *Hidden Figures* [20th Century Fox], African-American women at NASA

Good Witch [2010s, Hallmark Channel]: various episodes: www.hallmarkchannel.com/good-witch

Module « **16** »   CAN WE, WILL WE, PULL ON THE SAME ROPE?

☞ Learning Objectives:

Objective 1. To describe diverging characteristics of four conversation styles, in the manner of Ford & Ford.
Objective 2. To employ conversation strategies to help develop a shared vision, to create clarity about the proposed future and help followers understand what it means for them and the role they can play in creating it.
Objective 3. To differentiate when an Initiative Conversation or Understanding Conversation is appropriate.

Have you ever been excited about a project or an idea, but you couldn't get other people near you as excited as you were? It can be frustrating to see something clearly and not have others see what you see.

That's where vision comes in. When a group refers to its vision, it means a shared understanding of what the group wants to accomplish in the future. The key word there is "shared."

Groups are collections of individuals. Groups cannot see, per se. It is the individuals in the groups who can understand what might happen in the future. If the individuals envision different futures, especially if those visions are drastically different, the group may not be able to achieve much of anything.

Given this backdrop, this Module begins our journey into individual visions, herding cats, and getting multiple individuals to envision the same, shared vision for a group.

16.1. Readings or activities <u>before class</u>:

Read Annex 16-1. Summary of Ford's Four Conversations.
Read and be prepared to discuss the text for this Module.
After reading, complete Annex 16-2. Four Conversations Unscramble.

16.2. Resources needed:

Annex 16-1. Summary of Ford's Four Conversations

16.3. In-class activities:

"A leader is one who knows the way, goes the way, and shows the way." John C. Maxwell
"He who thinks he leads, but has no followers, is only taking a walk." John C. Maxwell

Step 1. Questions?
Step 2. Quotes.
Step 3. Exercise.

CLARITY OF THOUGHT & PURPOSE

Identify a time where you were working with a group whose vision or goal was not clear. Explain the situation to your partner and discuss the following:

    a. What was the group's level of energy or motivation?

    b. How well did the members of the group work together?

    c. Did participation within or among the group change over time? How?

    d. How successful was the group? If they ended up successful, to what do you attribute their success?

Step 4. **Initiative Conversations**

    a. Think about a time when you saw or heard a leader clearly communicate an inspiring new goal or future. Your example could be from a personal experience or perhaps a famous speech. Write the name of the leader below and describe the new goal or future they were proposing.

    ✍ _____ ▦

    b. Pair-share your example with your partner. Once both of you have shared, discuss the common elements of each communication that made them so effective, and list those "key ingredients" below.

    c. Assemble into a group of ~5 individuals and cluster around a group member's internet connected smart phone or tablet. Open a browser and visit http://goo.gl/Sz90tl to watch an excerpt of a famous "initiative conversation." If for whatever reason your group is not able to watch or hear the video, have someone in your group read the excerpt of John F. Kennedy's "moon shot" speech to the U.S. Congress, located at the end of this Module.

    d. As a group, identify "key ingredients" from the speech and list as many as you can in the space below:

    ✍ _____ ▦

    e. Create YOUR OWN initiative statement. Reflect on the work we have done so far and identify a new goal or future that meets your group's need and lies within the intersection of your values, passions and strengths. In the space below, write an initiative statement that includes all the key ingredients.

    ✍ _____ ▦

    f. Turn to your partner and determine which of you will present their initiative statement first. Have that person deliver their statement BUT DO NOT DISCUSS IT YET. After the presentation, have the presenter ask the listener the following questions:

        i. Were all the key ingredients clearly present? If not, what was missing?

        ii. Which ingredients (if any) need to be clarified?

        iii. Was the level of detail too great, too little, or just right?

        iv. Was the delivery enlivening, engaging and compelling? If not, how could it be improved?

        v. How long did it take? 30 seconds or less? That would make it a good "elevator speech."

Once all those questions have been answered, switch roles with your partner and repeat the process.

    g. As pairs, or as a group, discuss the following:

        i. What part of creating and delivering your initiative statement was most challenging? Why?

        ii. How do you determine which individuals or groups need to hear your initiative statement? How do you decide the best way to communicate it to them? (e.g., verbal conversation, email, phone, PowerPoint presentation, written proposal, *et cetera*).

        iii. What would you do if you delivered your statement to someone and they did not like it? How likely is it that will happen?

iv. Is it possible to have too many Initiative Conversations? What risks might there be with starting too many new initiatives? Do you know anyone who does that? How do they occur to you?

v. Does the creation and communication of an incredible idea guarantee that people will act to make it real? Why?

Step 5. **Understanding Conversations**

a. When you created your initiative statement, you gave some thought to WHO would have to be involved to turn it into a reality. In the space below, make a comprehensive list of those individuals or groups.

b. Review your WHOs with your partner and have them ask you the following questions. When you are done, reverse roles and repeat.

i. Which of those individuals or groups is most integral to the realization of your goal or vision? Why?

ii. Which is most likely to be receptive to it? Why?

iii. Which is most likely to be unreceptive? Why?

iv. What individual or group is not on your list, but should be?

v. Which individual or group should you approach first to have an in-depth conversation about your initiative statement? Why?

c. In the space below, identify which group or individual you will approach first, and make a list of the goals you would like to achieve as a result of your conversation.

d. Share your list of goals with your partner. Did they have any goals in their list that would be good to add to yours? If so, write them in the space above.

e. Practice having an Understanding Conversation with your partner. First, tell them a little about the individual or group they will be role-playing. Give them some insight into what parts of your initiative statement they might question or be excited or concerned about. Then begin by reviewing your initiative statement and respond to the questions they ask. Once you are done, reverse roles and repeat.

f. As you have likely figured out, people tend to respond when you present them with a stimulus. In the space below, list some responses you are likely to encounter during an Understanding Conversation that may be difficult to manage.

g. Now pair-share your list and work with your partner to identify strategies for managing those difficulties. Document your strategies in the space above.

h. Discuss as a group what happens when an Understanding Conversation goes incredibly well.

i. Let's say the individual or group completely understands you vision or goal and your plan for achieving it. Can you assume they are on board and are willing to help? Why?

ii. What about when an individual or group demonstrates understanding AND excitement about your vision or goal and plan? Will that necessarily translate into productive action? Why?

16.4. Discussion questions:

Per facilitator …

Under what kinds of circumstances should pharmacists work to develop a shared vision?

Match the term with the correct definition:

1. UNDERSTANDING	__	a. Conversation when you need to delegate a task
2. INITIATIVE	__	b. Conversation to wrap up open or unresolved items
3. PERFORMANCE	__	c. Conversation to increase ownership and engagement
4. CLOSURE	—	d. Conversation to share new ideas or goals with people who can make them real

16.5. After-class assignments:

A. Reread Annex 16-1 on the four conversation types. The next time you hear one of these words, «initiative» or «understanding», apply what you've learned to that conversation.

B. For each group you belong to, go to their websites and print off their missions, visions, and values. Compare them. What surprises you? Do you see mismatches between stated expectations and reality?

C. Fulfill the before-class activities for the next Module assigned by your facilitator.

16.6. Bibliography, references, & resources:

Flashcards via Quizlet, https://quizlet.com/class/3716098/, Fords' Four Conversations » 4 terms; What to Cover » 8 terms; When to Use Which » 7 terms

Ford J, Ford L. *The Four Conversations: Daily Communication That Gets Results*. Oakland, CA: Berrett-Koehler Publishers, 2009. www.bkconnection.com

See also Module Z

JOHN F. KENNEDY'S "MOON SHOT" SPEECH TO U.S. CONGRESS, 25 MAY 1961

"These are extraordinary times. And we face an extraordinary challenge. Our strength as well as our convictions have imposed upon this nation the role of leader in freedom's cause…

…if we are to win the battle that is now going on around the world between freedom and tyranny, the dramatic achievements in space which occurred in recent weeks should have made clear to us all, as did the Sputnik in 1957, the impact of this adventure on the minds of men everywhere, who are attempting to make a determination of which road they should take. Since early in my term, our efforts in space have been under review. With the advice of the Vice President, who is Chairman of the National Space Council, we have examined where we are strong and where we are not, where we may succeed and where we may not. Now it is time to take longer strides—time for a great new American enterprise—time for this nation to take a clearly leading role in space achievement, which in many ways may hold the key to our future on earth.

I believe we possess all the resources and talents necessary. But the facts of the matter are that we have never made the national decisions or marshaled the national resources required for such leadership. We have never specified long-range goals on an urgent time schedule, or managed our resources and our time so as to insure their fulfillment.

I therefore ask the Congress, above and beyond the increases I have earlier requested for space activities, to provide the funds which are needed to meet the following national goals:

First, I believe that this nation should commit itself to achieving the goal, before this decade is out, of landing a man on the moon and returning him safely to the earth. No single space project in this period will be more impressive to mankind, or more important for the long-range exploration of space; and none will be so difficult or expensive to accomplish.

In conclusion, let me emphasize one point. It is not a pleasure for any President of the United States, as I am sure it was not a pleasure for my predecessors, to come before the Congress and ask for new appropriations which place burdens on our people. I came to this conclusion with some reluctance. But in my judgment, this is a most serious time in the life of our country and in the life of freedom around the globe, and it is the obligation, I believe, of the President of the United States to at least make his recommendations to the Members of the Congress, so that they can reach their own conclusions with that judgment before them. You must decide yourselves, as I have decided, and I am confident that whether you finally decide in the way that I have decided or not, that your judgment—as my judgment—is reached on what is in the best interests of our country."

Annex 16-1. Summary of Ford's Four Conversations

Separate annex documents available to facilitators upon request (LeadGrowShape@plei.org).

INITIATIVE CONVERSATION (IC)

When or Why to Use It: Share new ideas, goals, visions and futures with people who can participate in making them real. Note similarities to a business case, discussed in Module 20.

What to Cover:

- INITIATIVE STATEMENT:
  - ▷ WHAT future are you proposing? Be compelling.
  - ▷ WHEN are you proposing to have it done?
  - ▷ WHY it matters.
- TACTICAL CONSIDERATIONS:
  - ▷ HOW it will get done.
  - ▷ WHERE are the resources.
  - ▷ WHO needs to be involved.

Common Mistakes:

- Getting too caught up in the HOW, WHERE and WHEN. Be prepared to provide general answers to these questions, but save details for an Understanding Conversation, UC.
- Not being positive, enlivening and engaging.
- Using them too often without follow-through.
- Letting a few people who do not buy into your vision shut you down. If you believe in your vision, keep looking for others who share it. You might reply to an objection with: "That's an important consideration I'm still thinking through. What thoughts do you have?"

UNDERSTANDING CONVERSATION (UC)

When or Why to Use It:

- To increase ownership, buy-in and engagement.
- To create clarity about the future and what it means to "them" (and what it does NOT mean).
- To help people understand where THEY fit in.
- To help YOU improve your plan (especially the HOW, WHERE & WHO).

What to Cover & How to Say It:

- Keep your initiative statement at the forefront – especially the WHY. Underscore the value of your idea and the consequences of not achieving it.
- Discuss concerns and information gaps you learn by researching your target audience.
- Make it a CONVERSATION that helps people create their OWN entry into the proposal.
- Give people challenges and ask for solutions.

Common Mistakes:

- Getting derailed by unproductive (victim) conversations. Put those issues in the parking lot!
- Focusing too much on people who "just don't get it." Move on to the next person. If you are in a group, invite them to meet with you one-on-one later.
- Assuming that understanding or excitement equals acceptance and commitment.
- Expecting that understanding will itself generate action.

- Not thinking an Understanding Conversation is important.

PERFORMANCE CONVERSATION (PC)

When to Use: Every time you need to delegate a task.

What to Cover:

- It is not a PC if it does not end with a specific request and promise for:
  - ▷ WHAT will be done and WHEN the results will be reported or delivered. Set your follower up for success by:
  - ▷ Ensuring they understand WHY it is important and HOW they will to get it done.
  - ▷ Helping them identify and access WHO else may need to be involved and WHERE the necessary resources can be accessed.

Common Mistakes:

- Not being properly prepared or committed YOURSELF.
- Making demands, instead of having a conversation.
- Overlooking the HOW, WHERE, WHO and especially WHY.
- Not requiring an explicit "yes" (promise) or "no" answer.
- Accepting a "yes" from the wrong person. Sometimes the "right" answer from a given person is "no." In that case, find the "right" person to ask.

CLOSURE CONVERSATION (CC)

When to Use:

- Bring closure to open or unresolved items.
- Could be promises that were never fulfilled, actions or statements that were perceived as inappropriate, *et cetera*.
- Restart something that has become bogged down.
- Celebrate and acknowledge accomplishments.

What It Can Cover: The Four As:

- Acknowledge the issue and its impact.
- Apologize for mistakes and misunderstandings.
- Amend broken agreements – 4 Rs: Recognize, Report, Repair, Recommit.
- Appreciate others.

Common Mistakes:

- Failing to LISTEN.
- Insincerity.
- Losing sight of why we were even doing this (i.e., the WHAT, WHEN, WHY).

Adapted from: Ford J, Ford L. *The Four Conversations: Daily Communication That Gets Results*. Oakland, CA: Berrett-Koehler Publishers, 2009. www.bkconnection.com

Annex 16-2. Ford's Four Conversations Unscramble

Separate annex documents available to facilitators upon request (LeadGrowShape@plei.org).

CC = Closure Conversation
IC = Initiative Conversation
PC = Performance Conversation
UC = Understanding Conversation

When or Why to Use It	Enter IC, UC, PC, or CC
Bring closure to open or unresolved items	▶
Celebrate or acknowledge accomplishments	▶
Create clarity about future and what it means to them	▶
Each time you need to delegate a task	▶
Increase ownership and engagement	▶
Restart something that has bogged down	▶
Share new ideas or goals with people who can participate	▶

What to Cover	Enter IC, UC, PC, or CC
Acknowledge the issue and its impact	▶
Consequences of not achieving your idea	▶
Promise for what will be done, by when	▶
Repair broken agreements	▶
Specific request	▶
Value of your idea	▶
What future are you proposing?	▶
Why it matters...	▶

Common Mistakes	Enter IC, UC, PC, or CC
Accepting a 'yes' from the wrong person	▶
Assuming that excitement equals commitment	▶
Failing to listen	▶
Getting derailed by unproductive (victim) conversations	▶
Getting too caught up in how, where, and when	▶
Insincerity	▶
Letting people buy into your vision shut you down	▶
Making demands, instead of having a conversation	▶
Not requiring an explicit yes (promise) or no	▶

Module « 17 »   MISSION, VALUES, VISION

☞ Learning Objectives:

Objective 1. To differentiate between the meanings of mission, values, and vision.
Objective 2. To describe the effect of branding on products and people.
Objective 3. To describe how they would like their group to be perceived in the eyes of external stakeholders.
Objective 4. To identify the actions and behaviors of a "model" (exemplary) member.

Mission, Values, Vision: For some people in corporate America, they roll off the tongue too easily. Obligatory mission-writing sessions are, too often, hardly worth the time invested.

Even so, the essence of leadership is to inspire people to go where they have never gone before. Explaining your vision is crucial, if I am to get on your bus, rather than someone else's. How can we assure team alignment, if we can't agree on a common mission? I have one set of values – are your values similar?

The key is to approach these kinds of exercises honestly and with fresh eyes. Will we remember that, at its core, a volunteer organization is a group of individuals who willingly come together to pursue a common goal? Is it true that their common goal can be best achieved by working together (*versus* alone)? Often, what brings and holds these individuals together is a leader who can communicate a compelling vision of a better tomorrow.

This Module will help teach participants to effectively communicate a vision, and assist interested individuals in identifying their desired role in creating the new future.

A brand is the common name for what you understand about a thing. The Ford® Mustang brand. The Tim Hortons® brand. The Heinz® Ketchup brand. The Molson® brand. The iPhone® brand. The Cirque du Soleil® brand. A brand evokes sights, sounds, smells, touch, even tastes and smells.

You and I each have our own brands. My brand might be boring. But if I wanted to attract others to join me in a joint effort, I really should work on my brand image, if I want to convey the relevance of my mission, the vibrancy of my cause, the nobility of my effort.

17.1. Readings or activities <u>before class</u>:

Nomenclature (in order of precedence):

<u>Mission</u>: A group's reason to exist. The mission statement supports the vision and serves to communicate purpose and direction to members and outsiders. Objectives, goals, strategies, executions and tactics are used to achieve the mission.

<u>Values</u>: What the group believes in and how it will behave. Values guide decision-making and establish a standard that actions can be assessed against.

<u>Vision</u>: What we want to be. Describes the group as it would appear in a future successful state. A vision statement should challenge and inspire group members.

<u>Strategy</u>: The choice among several options of what our competitive game plan will be. A thoughtfully constructed plan or method or action that will be employed to achieve the result. Basic Elements: Objective (ends), Scope (domain), Advantage (means).

Objective: Synonymous with goal. The ends toward which effort and action are directed or coordinated. These ends are subordinate to the mission.

Tactics: Devices or actions taken to achieve a larger purpose. Narrow approaches to implement the strategy for reaching your goal.

Brand: The unique design, sign, symbol, and words used create an image that identifies a product and differentiates it from competitors. This image may be associated with a (favorable or unfavorable) level of credibility, quality, and satisfaction in the consumer's mind.

After reading, complete Annex 17-1: Mission-Values-Vision Crossword Puzzle (or follow facilitator instructions).

Read more: http://www.businessdictionary.com/definition/brand.html

17.2. Resources needed:

None other than this Module

17.3. In-class activities:

"All organizations are perfectly aligned to get the results they get." Arthur W. Jones

"What was it about my leadership that created this outcome?" Michael Hyatt

Step 1. Questions?
Step 2. Quotes.
Step 3. Exercise.

MATCHING WHAT YOU DO WITH WHAT YOU WANT

According to Jim Collins, leaders spend way too much time drafting, wordsmithing, and redrafting vision statements, mission statements, and values statements; and way too little time aligning their organizations with the values and visions already in place. This exercise will help participants identify misalignments in their own organization, and provide insight into the consequences of such misalignments and how they may be resolved.

Step 4. What Is Your Brand? Are Your Programs, Activities & Outcomes Aligned with It?

a. In the space below, describe the "brand" your group would like to convey to the outside world. In other words, how does your group want to be perceived by the community, university administration, faculty, and prospective employers? How would you like those groups to distinguish your group from all the other college organizations?

✎ _____ ⌨

b. In the space below, list three group activities, programs or outcomes that you believe clearly communicate this brand to the external world.

✎ _____ ⌨

c. Describe your desired brand to your partner, along with your supportive programs, activities or outcomes. Then discuss the following:

i. Was it easy or difficult to identify a distinguishing "brand" for your group? Why? Do you believe

137

most of the other members of your group would agree with the brand you identified? Why?

    ii. Was it easy to identify programs, activities or outcomes that clearly support your brand? What are some ways your group might increase the number or impact of such programs, activities or outcomes?

    iii. To what extent is your brand aligned with the mission, vision and values communicated by the national office? (See attachment). If your brand is not aligned with your group's core ideology, where did it come from and what are the implications?

d. Now reflect on how your group really "occurs" to external audiences? Think about all the public venues where members represent the group (formally or otherwise). What about all the images and messages communicated online, in newsletters, *et cetera*? In the space below, identify at least three ways in which your group or its members communicate messages that are out of alignment with your desired brand identity:

e. Share your observations with your partner and discuss the following:

    i. What purpose is served by communicating those misaligned messages?

    ii. What are the costs of those misalignments? To the group? To its members?

    iii. Can you identify a "root cause" for the misalignments? Are they perhaps the result of some specific group system or process (formal or otherwise)? If so, how might the system or process be tweaked to create a better alignment with your desired brand?

f. What are two practical commitments you can make to help your group better align its systems, processes and outcomes with your desired brand identity?

By _____ (date), I will: ✍ _____ ⌨

By _____ (date), I will: ✍ _____ ⌨

Step 5. **Alignment Begins Within**

a. Using EXACTLY SIX WORDS, describe what you believe is your group's vision of a "model" (exemplary) member:

✍ _____ ⌨

b. Share your six words with your partner and discuss the following:

    i. If all your peers back home were asked to rate their level of agreement with these six words on a scale of 1 (low) to 10 (high), what do you think the average rating would be?

    ii. How do you feel about that average? Would you like it to be higher? Why?

    iii. What do you think might be some benefits of a high score?

    iv. What do you think might be some costs of a low score?

c. In the space below, create a list of experiences, programs or activities peers are exposed to which you believe (1) communicate the importance of embodying those six words, and (2) provide the encouragement, support and incentive to do so. Then make a list of group experiences, programs or activities that promote or incentivize conflicting values or behaviors.

SUPPORTING: ✍_____ ⌨

CONFLICTING: ✍_____ ⌨

d. Share your lists with your partner, then pair-share on the following:

    i. What are some things your group might do to increase the number or impact of programs like those listed on the left?

    ii. What is the cost to the group of maintaining the programs and activities listed on the right? Are there ways to resolve the misalignments? If not, could or should those activities be discontinued?

e. What are two practical commitments you can make to help your group better communicate, encourage and support the behaviors and actions it wants to see from members?

By _____ (date), I will: ✍_____ ⌨

By _____ (date), I will: ✍_____ ⌨

17.4. Discussion questions:

Per facilitator …
What kinds of missions, values, and visions are appropriate for a pharmacy?
Facilitator discretion: Use of Annex 17-1. Mission-Values-Vision Crossword Puzzle

17.5. After-class assignments:

A. Write a six-word description of your engagement with each group you belong to. For which do you feel satisfaction? What is the emotion for the others?

B. Fulfill your commitment to help your group improve its alignment, communication, encouragement and support behaviors.

C. Fulfill the before-class activities for the next Module assigned by your facilitator.

17.6. Bibliography, references, & resources:

Business Dictionary. www.businessdictionary.com/

Collis DJ, Rukstad MG. Can you say what your strategy is? *Harvard Business Review* 2008;(Apr):92-90.

Developing Governance Group. DIY Committee Guide: Vision, mission and values. www.diycommitteeguide.org/resource/vision-mission-and-values

Flashcards via Quizlet, https://quizlet.com/class/3716098/, Mission, Values, Vision » 8 terms

Kenny G. Your company's purpose is not its vision, mission, or values. *Harvard Business Review* 2014;(Sep 3). https://hbr.org/2014/09/your-companys-purpose-is-not-its-vision-mission-or-values

Taylor NF. What is a mission statement? Business News Daily 2015 Jan 7, www.businessnewsdaily.com/3783-mission-statement.html

Annex 17-1. Mission-Values-Vision Crossword Puzzle

Separate annex documents available to facilitators upon request (LeadGrowShape@plei.org).

Across

1. Describes the group as it would appear in a future successful state
5. Narrow approaches to implement the strategy for reaching your goal
6. Choice among several options of the plan or action to achieve the result
7. Synonymous with objective

Down

1. What the group believes in and how it will behave
2. Ends toward which effort and action are directed or coordinated
3. Unique design, symbol, or words that identifies a product and differentiates it
4. Group's reason to exist, communicates purpose and direction

Module « **18** » CAN WE, WILL WE, PULL IN THE SAME DIRECTION?

☞ Learning Objectives:

Objective 1. To employ conversation strategies to create clarity about the proposed future and help followers understand what it means for them and the role they can play in creating it.

Objective 2. To differentiate when Performance Conversations or Closure Conversations are appropriate.

Objective 3. To list the steps required to help followers provide agreed upon deliverables by specified deadlines.

Even when followers understand and believe in a leader's goal or vision, significant effort must be made to enable their maximum contribution to its pursuit. This Module will help participants with skills to empower team members to complete tasks, and create a culture of mutual trust and accountability.

This Module builds on Module 16, where we introduced four types of conversation, to empower participants with understanding four different modes of communication. These four different kinds of conversation match who-what-when-where-why with the various degrees of readiness of human audiences to hear what a human speaker might say. Module 16 focused on two of the four conversations, initiative and understanding. In this Module, we harness the other two types of conversation: performance and closure.

It's gotta be in some radio manual somewhere: Make sure your audience has their receiver turned on before you exert energy in transmitting your message. Oh, and the two of you need to be on the same frequency.

18.1. Readings or activities before class:

A. View the Paper Chain Video #1 from TeamSTEPPS®, produced by the Agency for Healthcare Quality & Research:
www.ahrq.gov/professionals/education/curriculum-tools/teamstepps/officebasedcare/videos/paper-chains.html

1. What lessons for everyday life did you observe?

✍ _____ ⌨

2. What might you have offered, that the people in the video did not mention?

✍ _____ ⌨

B. View the Paper Chain Video #2 from TeamSTEPPS®, produced by the Agency for Healthcare Quality & Research:
www.ahrq.gov/professionals/education/curriculum-tools/teamstepps/officebasedcare/videos/paper-chain2.html

1. What lessons for everyday life did you observe?

2. What might you have offered, that the people in the video did not mention?

18.2. Resources needed:

Annex 16-1. Summary of Ford's Four Conversations
Annex 16-2. Four Conversations Unscramble

18.3. In-class activities:

> *"Accountability is the essence of possessing and maintaining integrity and in restoring integrity where there are repairable fractures."* Nancy A. Alvarez

> *"Success in life is directly proportional to the number of difficult conversations you are willing to have."* Tim Ferriss

Step 1. Questions?
Step 2. Quote.
Step 3. Exercise.

COACHING, ACCOUNTABILITY, INTEGRITY & ACKNOWLEDGEMENT

a. Reflect on a time when you led a group of individuals to organize and execute a given task or event. Pair-share the following:

   i. On a scale of 1 (low) to 10 (high), how would you rate the average level of contribution among all your team members?

   ii. On average, how well did the work of your team members meet your needs in terms of quality?

   iii. On average, how well did the work of your team members meet your needs in terms of timeliness?

   iv. What do you feel you did particularly well to maximize their contributions?

   v. What do you feel you could have done differently to maximize your team members' contributions?

b. **Performance Conversations**. In the space below, write a list of "key ingredients" you believe are "must have" elements of delegation or "performance" conversations.

c. Pair-share your list of key ingredients. Add any additional elements you did not previously include in the space above.

d. Once the entire group has a common understanding of Performance Conversation key ingredients, discuss the potential for Performance Conversations to slip into the realm of "micro-management." What might a person do to avoid this trap? What other common mistakes might leaders fall into during Performance Conversations?

e. In the space below, identify an individual with whom you need to have a Performance Conversation.

143

This could be related to the new goal or vision you previously identified, or something you are working on in your group back home. Once you have identified the individual, spend a few minutes outlining the key points of your Performance Conversation.

✍ _____ ⌨

Step 4. Practice a Performance Conversation with your partner. First provide your partner with a little background information about the conversation you will deliver and the individual they will be role-playing. Give them a sense of that individual's personality so they can be an effective practice partner for you. For example, would the role require that your partner respond "yes" to your request without putting much thought into what is really going to be required of them? Or maybe the role will require your partner to challenge you and question the appropriateness or necessity of the task.

a. Once you are done practicing the conversation, ask your partner the following questions. Once you have received answers to all the questions, reverse roles and repeat.

   i. Did I communicate a clear deliverable (WHAT), deadline (WHEN) and purpose (WHY)?

   ii. Was it conveyed as an unambiguous request?

   iii. Did I elicit a clear "yes" or "no" answer to my request?

   iv. Did I effectively coach you through the identification of the major HOWs, WHEREs and WHOs, without coming off as a micro-managing, control freak?

   v. Did I clearly offer assistance to help connect resources and remove obstacles?

   vi. Did I clearly communicate a productive follow-up plan to assess progress or completion?

b. Now that you possess an understanding of the importance and power of Performance Conversations, identify three people with whom you can commit to having such a conversation. Document your commitment in the space below:

By _____ (date), I will have a performance conversation with ✍ _____ ⌨

about: ✍ _____ ⌨

By _____ (date), I will have a performance conversation with ✍ _____ ⌨

about: ✍ _____ ⌨

By _____ (date), I will have a performance conversation with ✍ _____ ⌨

about: ✍ _____ ⌨

c. Ever hear a great idea for something you should do? According to the American Society for Training & Development (ASTD), there is only a 10% chance you will actually do it just because you heard it. Continuing this line of thought:

   ‣ If you consciously decide to do something, your chances increase to 25%.

   ‣ If you set a deadline for doing something, your probability increases to 40%.

   ‣ By creating a plan for doing something, your odds climb to 50%.

   ‣ By committing to someone else that you are going to do something, your chances rise to 65%.

While 65% is much better than 10%, you cannot really count on something that only has a 2-in-3 chance of success. Fortunately, ASTD offers a simple tool that can increase the odds to near perfect: an accountability appointment. The simple act of forcing yourself to report back to someone about whether you have done something you said you would do raises the chances of actually doing it to 95%. Given that, pair-share your commitments from Step 7 above, and discuss setting mutual accountability appointments with your partner that can occur well beyond the time you are together now!

Step 5. Closure Conversations: Restoring Integrity

a. Identify a time when you were working with one or more individuals in a meeting or on a task, when something someone said, did, or did not do significantly damaged the morale of the group. Describe the situation to your partner and pair-share on the following:

    i. What was the immediate impact on the team's level of "empowerment" (energy, productivity and commitment)?

    ii. What, if anything, was done to re-empower the team?

    iii. If something was done, did it help? Why?

    iv. If nothing was done, why not? What was the long-term impact on the group? Did the issue (and associated awkwardness) eventually resolve itself, or did it lead to other problems? Explain.

b. When humans work together, it is an eventual certainty that one person will feel "wronged" by the actions or statements of another. This can be especially common in groups where individuals habitually confuse their subjective interpretations with the objective facts, and fail to check in to gain understanding or clarify the actual intent.

For the purposes of this lesson however, it does not matter whether the wound is real or perceived; whether it was intentional or accidental. What matters is that it is experienced, and that the experience has an impact not just on the wounded person, but also on the team as a whole.

We call such instances "breakdowns in integrity," with "integrity" being defined simply as "the state of being whole and undivided" (*versus* morally upright). When a team experiences a breakdown in integrity, it is by definition divided and not whole, and therefore cannot possibly perform to the limit of its potential. Consequently, when such breakdowns occur, it is imperative that integrity be restored as soon as possible; that open wounds be closed. This is essential irrespective of the size of the break in integrity; the smallest of breaks can grow overtime and negatively affect individuals or teams. Consider that closing wounds and restoring integrity is the primary purpose of "Closure Conversations."

c. In the space below, write a list of "key ingredients" you believe are must-have elements of an effective Closure Conversation. What must be said to truly gain closure on an issue in a way that allows a group to put a problem it its past and move forward with complete integrity?

d. Pair-share your list of key ingredients. Add any additional elements you did not previously include in the space above. Then discuss as a group, and again add any additional elements above.

e. Practice having a Closure Conversation with your partner. Use the situation you described before and act to restore the integrity of the group or relationship by addressing the individual who "inflicted the wound." Once you are done practicing the conversation, ask your partner the following questions. Once you have received answers to all your questions, reverse roles and repeat.

    i. Did I effectively facilitate your understanding and acknowledgement of the problem and its impact?

    ii. Did I elicit the necessary apology(ies), and were they authentic?

    iii. Did I facilitate the creation of a plan to "make it right"?

iv. Did I elicit a commitment to the execution of that plan, and a recommitment to the relationship or group as a whole?

v. Is there anything I said or did that could have made you overly defensive?

f. Now that you possess an understanding of the importance and power of Closure Conversations, identify two people with whom you can commit to having such a conversation. Document your commitment in the space below:

By _____ (date), I will have a closure conversation with ✍ _____ ⌨

about: ✍ _____ ⌨

By _____ (date), I will have a closure conversation with ✍ _____ ⌨

about: ✍ _____ ⌨

g. Share your commitments with your partner and discuss setting mutual accountability appointments, which may extend beyond this current Module.

Step 6. Closure Conversations: Gaining and Sustaining Momentum

a. Sometimes a group can suffer a loss of integrity even without experiencing a specific, obvious wound. This usually occurs when the group perceives that the pursuit of its WHY has stalled. Identify a time when you were part of a group that began to believe it was "spinning its wheels" – that it was not operating efficiently or effectively. Describe that situation to your partner and pair-share on the following:

i. Was the group's progress toward its goal really stalled? In other words, was nothing worthwhile being done?

ii. Was progress being measured and communicated? If so, how? If not, why not?

iii. How might a perceived lack of progress affect a less engaged "fringe" member *versus* a member who was spending a lot of time and energy on the effort?

iv. What could be done to help prevent an actively engaged member from feeling like their contributions were not contributing to meaningful progress?

b. Based on your conversation, make a list of actions a leader can take to avoid breakdowns in integrity resulting from a perceived lack of progress.

c. Discuss these actions as a group and add any you did not previously identify in the space above. Then as a group, discuss the following:

i. Should a person's motivation for pursuing a goal be based upon an expectation for recognition and celebration? Why?

ii. Regardless of whether a person should be motivated by external recognition, how does the practice of recognition affect the motivation of the person receiving it? How does it affect others in the group who observe the recognition?

iii. Why might a leader be reluctant to provide recognition? Are these valid reasons? Why? What does it cost the leader to offer recognition? What does it cost the leader to withhold deserved recognition?

d. Reflect on how recognition and celebration show up in your group. In the space below, list three activities that work particularly well to increase the motivation of your members. Then list three that are not particularly effective.

Recognition/Celebration – Motivation:

1. ✍ _____ ⌨

2. ✍ _____ ⌨

3. ✍ _____ ⌨

Recognition/Celebration – Demotivation:

1. ✍ _____ ⌨

2. ✍ _____ ⌨

3. ✍ _____ ⌨

e. Share your list with your partner, then pair-share on the following:
    i. What are some ways to expand or spread items in the left column to further increase their motivational impact?
    ii. Are there ways to make the items in the right column more effective? If so, how? If not, could they be discontinued?

f. List two commitments you will make to help your group improve its acknowledgement of accomplishments and appreciation of individuals.

By _____ (date) I commit to: ✍ _____ ⌨

By _____ (date) I commit to: ✍ _____ ⌨

18.4. Discussion questions:

Per facilitator …
To what extent is the work of a pharmacist that of an individual contributor *versus* a team player?
How can pharmacists influence the behavior of others on the teams pharmacists join?

18.5. After-class assignments:

A. Reread Annex 16-1 on the four conversation types, especially performance (PC) and closure (CC). The next time you hear one of these words, «performance or closure», apply what you've learned to that conversation.
B. Fulfill the commitments you made to help your group improve its acknowledgement of accomplishments and appreciation of individuals.
C. Fulfill the commitments you made to hold performance conversations and closure conversations.

D. Fulfill the before-class activities for the next Module assigned by your facilitator.

18.6. Bibliography, references, & resources:

Annex 16-1. Summary of Ford's Four Conversations

Flashcards via Quizlet, https://quizlet.com/class/3716098/, Fords' Four Conversations » 4 terms; What to Cover » 8 terms; When to Use Which » 7 terms

Ford J, Ford L. *The Four Conversations: Daily Communication That Gets Results.* Oakland, CA: Berrett-Koehler Publishers, 2009. www.bkconnection.com

TeamSTEPPS®: Strategies and Tools to Enhance Performance and Patient Safety. Rockville, MD: Agency for Healthcare Research & Quality, March 2016. www.ahrq.gov/professionals/education/curriculum-tools/teamstepps/index.html, teamstepps.ahrq.gov/abouttoolsmaterials.htm

Module « **19** »   WHAT LEADERS DO – INFLUENCE OTHERS

☞ Learning Objectives:

Objective 1. To explore scenarios for themes of coaching others.

Objective 2. To explore their receptivity to being coached by others.

Objective 3. To allow pharmacists to test their problem-assessment and decision making skills in a series of realistic practice scenarios.

Each of us is a member of innumerable teams. One or more family teams. Work teams. College teams. Social and professional group teams. In many cases, teams involving a house of worship.

Each grouping of people in each of those examples is like a reshuffling of a deck of cards. So many combinations of individuals, individuals of more or less experience, more or less willingness to interact with others, more or less ability to accept information from others, more or less commitment to advance the group's goals.

This Module explores various stressful scenarios and lets you practice your analytical skills, your persuasion skills, your decision-making skills.

How do you become a better leader? Practice, practice, practice.

19.1. Readings or activities <u>before class</u>:

A. Read and be prepared to discuss: Janke KK, Sorensen TD, Traynor AP. Instruction for student pharmacists on leading change. *Am J Pharm Educ*. 2009 Apr 7;73(2):30.
www.ncbi.nlm.nih.gov/pmc/articles/PMC2690902/pdf/ajpe30.pdf.

B. John Kotter's book ***Leading Change*** (1996) is an important contribution to the field of change management and strategy implementation. The book outlines a practical 8-step process for change management:

  ‣ Establishing a Sense of Urgency
  ‣ Creating the Guiding Coalition
  ‣ Developing a Vision and Strategy
  ‣ Communicating the Change Vision
  ‣ Empowering Employees for Broad-Based Action
  ‣ Generating Short-Term Wins
  ‣ Consolidating Gains and Producing More Change
  ‣ Anchoring New Approaches in the Culture

C. Other relevant resources are the ***Mindset*** books by Carol Dweck. She contends that people can be placed on a continuum according to implicit views of where ability comes from. Some people believe their personal success is based on innate ability – these folks have a "fixed" theory of intelligence ("fixed mindset"). Other people believe their personal success is based on hard work, learning, training and doggedness – these folks have a "growth" or "incremental" approach to intelligence ("growth mindset"). Only some people are aware of their own frame of mind, but mindset can still be discerned based on behavior. It is especially evident in reaction to failure. Fixed-mindset people dread failure, because it is a

149

negative statement on their basic abilities. On the other hand, growth-mindset people do not fear failure as much, because they realize their performance can be improved and learning comes from failure. Dweck argues that a growth mindset allows people to live a less stressful and more successful life.

Dweck's insights are important because people with a growth mindset are more likely to continue working hard despite setbacks. Further, people's theories of intelligence can be affected by subtle environmental cues. Consider: children given praise like "good job, you're very smart" are more likely to develop a fixed mindset, whereas compliments like "good job, you worked very hard" are likely to lead to a growth mindset. Now, let's consider adults and adult learners.

19.2. Resources needed:

None other than this Module

19.3. In-class activities:

> *"Be a coach – help those who are alone or inexperienced.*
> *Find yourself a coach, allow yourself to be coached." John D. Grabenstein*

Step 1. Questions?
Step 2. Quotes.
Step 3. Exercise.

SCENARIOS: ON COACHING & BEING COACHED

a. Cluster into subgroups of two to three people each, so you can share possible solutions at appropriate points.

b. Follow your facilitator's directions in selecting a scenario. Work independently to identify a possible solution. Take 2 minutes to do so and to record in your Workbook.

c. Huddle with your group of 2 or 3 participants. Share each solution with the small group and record the other options in your Workbook. Take 2 minutes. Pick one of the solutions to share with the whole assembly and record.

d. Repeat the steps above with another scenario.

Scenario #1, "Struggles." You notice that a coworker struggles with tasks you find easy: Maybe it is deciding what to recommend to a physician. Or how to teach a patient how to use an inhaler. Or how to calculate the right dose or kinetics. Or maybe how to give useful advice in a short period of time. But the coworker never asks for help or advice. You tried once before, but the coworker changed the subject. What should you do?

Scenario #2, "Controls." The controlled substances inventory has been off by a disturbing amount each of the last three counts. You know you should try to determine the root cause of the discrepancy. This problem has not happened to you before and you are not sure what to do. If you seek advice from a peer, it might lead to a formal report, even though you have no idea why the count is off. If you seek help from your supervisor, you might be blamed for not supervising things well enough. What would be a reasonable approach to this sensitive situation?

Scenario #3, "Oops." You arrive at work and somebody asks you a question. That question triggers a realization: you realize that you made a mistake while filing a prescription yesterday. What should you do?

Scenario #4, "Peeping Tom (or Tammy)." Traffic was light today, so you arrived at work five minutes early. As you walk toward the pharmacy, you feel a little mischievous, so you stop and just observe what is going on inside the pharmacy. Do you like what you see? Does it look like a professional and efficient operation? If you do not like what you see, what should you do? If you like what you see, what should you do?

Scenario #5, "Bossy." In your hospital, your direct boss is a real "pill." (S)he only points out your mistakes, never acknowledges your accomplishments or progress. You never get any constructive advice or mentoring. What should you do?

Step 4. Wrap Up: In your life, so far, who have been your favorite coaches? The most effective at coaching you? What characteristics did they have that you want to exhibit for your coworkers, your children, others near you?

Summary. We are all in this together. If you could sum up all the experiences of the people in the room, it would span centuries. If we work together and share our accumulated knowledge, experience, and wisdom, we can accomplish a lot.

19.4. Discussion questions:

Per facilitator …
What does it take for a pharmacist to influence change?
What skills are important for a pharmacist who wants to coach?

19.5. After-class assignments:

A. Find a friend or colleague or coworker or ___ who needs help and coach him or her.
B. Fulfill the before-class activities for the next Module assigned by your facilitator.

19.6. Bibliography, references, & resources:

Antonakis J, Fenley M, Liechti S. Learning charisma: Transform yourself into the person others want to follow. *Harvard Bus Rev* 2012;90:127-30.

Dweck CS. *Mindset: How You Can Fulfill Your Potential.* New York: Constable & Robinson Limited, 2012.

Dweck CS. *Mindset: The New Psychology of Success.* New York: Random House, 2006.

Gladwell M. *The Tipping Point: How Little Things Can Make a Big Difference.* NY: Little, Brown & Co., 2000.

Jacobs MR. *101 Ways to Improve Your Pharmacy Worklife.* Washington, DC: American Pharmacists Association, 2001.

Janke KK, Sorensen TD, Traynor AP. Instruction for student pharmacists on leading change. *Am J Pharm Educ.* 2009 Apr 7;73(2):30. www.ncbi.nlm.nih.gov/pmc/articles/PMC2690902/pdf/ajpe30.pdf

Kotter JP. *Leading Change.* Boston: Harvard Business Press, 1996.

Sorensen TD, Traynor AP, Janke KK. A pharmacy course on leadership and leading change. *Am J Pharm Educ.* 2009 Apr 7;73(2):23. www.ncbi.nlm.nih.gov/pmc/articles/PMC2690896/pdf/ajpe23.pdf

Module « **20** »   INNOVATION, CREATIVITY, ENTREPRENEURSHIP

☞ Learning Objectives:

Objective 1. To identify key elements in explaining a new idea to others.

Objective 2. To identify the major segments of an effective business plan.

Objective 3. To build an understanding in the interdependency of team members that produce better results than individuals.

Objective 4. To explore the aspects of innovation that fulfill human needs.

If you plan to undertake a small project (let's wash the dog!), you can go ahead and implement it on your own. You gather tools (tub, water, soap, towels) and you may need to enlist a human helper. But the degree of planning needed is modest, and the consequences of forgetting something is small (after you dry out).

But if you face a big, multi-faceted project, you may need support from lots of people. You may need to ask others to invest their money or time in the project. If so, you will need to explain lots of details, demonstrating that you've considered the project from all angles.

This Module explores innovation, creativity, and entrepreneurship in practical form. The word "entrepreneur" comes from the French for one who undertakes or manages. Hence, we will dive into a project proposal and develop the elements of a business plan.

Perhaps you've heard someone remark, "What's your elevator speech?" An elevator speech is a quick summary of what you propose and why it should be adopted. It is succinct form of persuasion, like the Initiative Conversation addressed in Module 16.

The next level of complexity beyond an elevator speech may be a business case. Perhaps you've heard someone remark, "Well, what's the business case for doing XYZ?" That call for a business case is the request to hear the details explained.

Sometimes a verbal explanation will suffice. But for big projects, a multipage business plan (the business case in written form) is expected. In a business plan, specific sections hold specific kinds of details. The disciplined format helps focus the mind and assure that the key facets of the project are each described and explored.

As we proceed, you might want to keep in mind a humorous effort to persuade your dean of pharmacy of all the advantages to installing a swimming pool on the roof of the pharmacy school. That image should carry you through, in case some of the details below get a little tedious.

20.1. Readings or activities <u>before class:</u>

Re-read Annex 16-1 regarding Initiative Conversations and Understanding Conversations and be prepared to discuss for this Module.

Read and be prepared to discuss the elements of a business plan, as described by the U.S. Small Business Administration.

After reading, complete Annex 20-1: Entrepreneur/Business Plan Crossword Puzzle (or follow facilitator instructions).

20.2. Resources needed:

None other than this Module

20.3. In-class activities:

"Learning and innovation go hand in hand. The arrogance of success is to think that what you did yesterday will be sufficient for tomorrow." William Pollard

Step 1. Questions?
Step 2. Quote.
Step 3. Exercise.

ESSENTIAL ELEMENTS OF A GOOD BUSINESS PLAN

The website of the U.S. Small Business Administration (SBA) provides detailed guidance on crafting good business plans for starting or expanding a business. Business plans or business cases can also be written to explain or to seek funding for projects (small, medium or large) within an existing business or institutional environment. Such plans are helpful for organizing an entrepreneur's ideas. Pivotal elements of a good plan appear below.

Executive Summary: The executive summary can be the most important section of a business plan. In one page, this section summarizes for a reader where your company is, where you want to take it, and why your business idea will be successful. If you are seeking financing, the executive summary is also your first opportunity to grab a potential investor's interest. The executive summary should highlight the strengths of your overall plan and therefore may be the last section you write. However, it usually appears first in your document. Executive Summaries of this type typically include a mission statement (one or several sentences), company information, market analysis (the need or gap to be solved by this project), your products or services, funding needed, and future. Like a résumé, the Executive Summary is the first part of your business plan many people will see, so each word should count. Convince the reader that you can succeed.

Company Description: Information on what you (will) do, what differentiates your business from others, and the markets your business serves. This section is like an extended elevator speech and can help readers and potential investors quickly understand the goal of your business and its unique proposition.

Market Analysis: Before launching your business or starting work on your project, it is essential for you to research your business industry, market and competitors. The market-analysis section should illustrate your industry and market knowledge, as well as any research findings and conclusions. Narrow your target market to a manageable size.

Organization & Management: Businesses are structured differently. Describe the proposed organization and management structure.

Marketing & Sales: How do you plan to market your business? Marketing is the process of creating customers, the lifeblood of your business. Your marketing strategy should be part of an ongoing business-evaluation process and specific to your company. What is your sales strategy – how do you plan to sell your product? This often includes two primary elements: a sales force strategy and sales activities.

Service or Product Line: Include information about the specific benefits of your product or service – from your customers' perspective. You should also talk about your product or service's ability to meet consumer needs, any advantages your product has over that of the competition, and the current development stage your product is in (e.g., idea, prototype).

Funding Request: If you need funding, providing financial projections helps show you can allocate resources efficiently.

Appendix

or Appendices (optional): Appendices are optional, but are useful places to include detailed or authorizing information such as résumés, permits and leases, credit history, details about intellectual property, letters of reference, and additional information that a funder or approver may request.

Adapted from: U.S. Small Business Administration, https://www.sba.gov/tools/business-plan/1, May 2016, where many additional details appear.

▸

Step 4. Be aware: To promote interest in independent community pharmacy ownership and entrepreneurial leadership in general, the National Community Pharmacists Association (NCPA) and the NCPA Foundation have established the Good Neighbor Pharmacy NCPA Pruitt-Schutte Student Business Plan Competition. The competition aims to motivate student pharmacists to create the blueprint necessary for buying an existing independent community pharmacy or to develop a new pharmacy. The competition is named to honor two champions of independent pharmacy, Neil Pruitt, Sr., and H. Joseph Schutte.

See the NCPA website (www.ncpanet.org/students/business-plan-competition) for current rules, instructions, and dates. The rubric domains are: Cover Sheet, Table of Contents, Mission Statement and Vision Statement, Description of Business, Physical Description of the Business, Summary of Loan Request, Financial Documents, Marketing Plan, Supporting Documents, Originality and Creativity, Feasibility/Ability to Implement and Neatness and Professionalism. The specific criteria that must be met within each of these categories are described in the grading rubric.

INNOVATION AS A SOURCE OF CONTINUOUS NEED FULFILLMENT

Step 5. As an organization, remembering that you must effectively meet needs is a huge part of being successful. Another huge part is being adept at actually meeting needs. Much of the remainder lies in the space between: Being able to identify new needs that are not being met, or finding ways to better meet needs you are already working to fulfill. This type of work is often called "innovation."

Reflect on how innovation shows up in your group and ponder these questions:

▸ If innovation does not show up (i.e., you pretty much do the same things year after year), why is that? What are the pros and cons of doing the same things over and over? What are some ways you might begin to stimulate innovation into your group?

▸ If innovation does show up in your group, what does it look like?

▷ Is it strategically planned? In other words, is there a formal process for identifying new needs, generating new ideas, evaluating their risks, benefits, or costs, and aligning them with values, strengths, and passions?

▷ Is there a clear purpose for doing new things, or are new things being done "just to try something new," or because new leadership has taken over and it is expected to start with a clean slate? When a new program IS created to serve a clear need, what kind of an evaluation process is created to assess whether it is successful in meeting that need?

▷ Is it easier for organizations to start new programs, or discontinue existing programs? Why?

▷ Can "over-innovation" exist? What are the costs to an organization that innovates too much?

20.4. Discussion questions:

Per facilitator …

How many scenarios can you name (other than starting your own pharmacy) where a business plan might be helpful?

20.5. After-class assignments:

A. Develop a _-page business plan (business case). Each business plan must justify the hiring of two additional full-time employees (FTEs) in the scenario described. It can be a fictional, humorous effort to persuade the dean of pharmacy to install a swimming pool on the roof of the pharmacy school, hiring a life guard and a pool attendant. Or it can be a real or imagined effort to add two workers to the staff of the library, add a new pharmacy service, add two paid internships or fellowships, add two people to the staff of a fraternity's national office, or whatever scenario you can envision.

B. Fulfill the before-class activities for the next Module assigned by your facilitator.

20.6. Bibliography, references, & resources:

Brazeau G. Entrepreneurial spirit in pharmacy. *Am J Pharm Educ*. 2013 Jun 12;77(5):88. www.ncbi.nlm.nih.gov/pmc/articles/PMC3687121/pdf/ajpe77588.pdf

Flashcards via Quizlet, https://quizlet.com/class/3716098/, Innovation, Creativity, Entrepreneurship » 17 terms

Ford J, Ford L. *The Four Conversations: Daily Communication That Gets Results*. Oakland, CA: Berrett-Koehler Publishers, 2009. www.bkconnection.com

Holiday-Goodman M. Entrepreneurship, resource management, organizational culture, and other "business" factors influencing pharmacy practice change. *Res Social Adm Pharm*. 2012 Jul-Aug;8(4):269-71.

Annex 20-1. Entrepreneur/Business Plan Crossword Puzzle

Separate annex documents available to facilitators upon request (LeadGrowShape@plei.org).

Across

2. Choice among several options of the plan or action to achieve the result
4. A person who organizes an enterprise with considerable initiative and risk
5. A field of trade or business
7. Introduction of new things or methods
8. Explanation of details
9. Process of creating customers

Down

1. Describes the group as it would appear in a future successful state
2. Elevator speech
3. A written business case
6. Executive summary

See also Annex 17-1. Mission-Values-Vision Crossword Puzzle

Module « 21 »   CAN YOU SEE LEADERSHIP?

☞ Learning Objectives:

Objective 1. To compare and contrast participants' self-image to the image perceived by others.
Objective 2. To describe the importance of, and limitations with "leading by example."
Objective 3. To compare and contrast leadership behaviors, in light of leadership models described earlier.
Objective 4. To evaluate leadership behaviors in actual situations visible to the participant (after class).

Leadership is in the visible spectrum, if you know what to look for. You've seen flags used to project a national presence or organizational presence. The same applies to individuals, so you really deserve to design your own flag. We'll give you your chance.

Then we'll send you out onto campus and into the community, looking at leaders. Critiquing them. Listing their attributes and "opportunities for improvement." Brutal honesty, because honesty is the best policy.

Leadership is all around us. Maybe it would be more accurate to say: adequate and inadequate leadership is all around us. If you look long enough, you will find good and less-good examples. Let's look and learn lessons from both types.

21.1. Readings or activities <u>before class</u>:

Read and be prepared to discuss the content of this Module.
If readily available, read: Rickert DR, Smith RE, Worthen DB. The 'seven habits': Building pharmacist leaders. *Am Pharm*. 1992;32(Aug):48-52.

Covey's 7 Habits of Highly Effective People
Habit 1: Be proactive.
Habit 2: Begin with the end in mind.
Habit 3: First things first.
Habit 4: Think win-win.
Habit 5: Seek first to understand.
Habit 6: Synergize.
Habit 7: Sharpen the saw.

21.2. Resources needed:

Directory of student organizations on campus (explore school or university website)

21.3. In-class activities:

"Be the change you want to see in the world." Mohandas K. Gandhi

"What you are speaks so loudly, I can't hear what you are saying." Ralph Waldo Emerson

Step 1. Questions?
Step 2. Quotes.
Step 3. Exercise.

MODEL THE WAY

Step 4. **Your Personal Flag**

a. Create Your Own Personal Flag. Take 5 minutes to draw a picture or select a clip-art image, to create a graphical representation of "who you are" as a person. Do not underestimate the power of images to convey meaning. National flags evoke powerful emotions. You can use drawings, pictures from magazines, or anything else your creative mind can find.

b. Exchange flags with your partner BUT DO NOT SAY ANYTHING ABOUT THEM YET. Examine their work. Write a brief "profile" of your partner, based upon what you see in their flag and what your experience with them has been thus far. Based upon what you see, what do you believe they value and for what do they have passion? What do you believe is of importance in terms of how their time and treasure is spent? What do you imagine it would be like to live or work with your partner based upon what you see in the flag?

Meaning(s) within your partner's flag:

BONUS: If you and your partner are willing, check out each other's Facebook pages to gain an even richer set of information about each other.

Step 5. **Gallery Walk**. Now, imagine you are in a gallery. The flags are "portraits" representative of individuals of the group and are valued pieces of art. What can you learn about the individuals around you by examining their portraits? Focus your attention and find out.

Over the next 5 to 10 minutes, jot down thoughts that come to mind about a specific flag and questions you would ask if given the chance. Record what you learn about the individuals in your group.

What did you see? What did you learn about the individuals' interests, knowledge, skills or attitudes from their portrait? How might this information serve you as a leader? What are the benefits of gathering information about others through observation? What are the limitations?

Step 6. **Can You See Your Reflection?**

a. Interview your partner to gain an appreciation for "how you occur" to them. (Do not have them share the actual profile they wrote up on you... yet). Use this opportunity to practice interviewing your partner as a "curious LEARNER" (*versus* a "judgmental KNOWER").

Note: there are no right or wrong answers here. All you are trying to see is how the information you have presented has been perceived through their personal "lenses."

Here are some questions you may ask. Feel free to add any others as you see fit.

    i. What kind of first impression did I give off?

    ii. What kinds of things did I say or do to give that impression? (After their initial response, ask them to talk about the little things if they did not already do so... like facial expressions, speaking too much or too little, tone of voice, eye-rolling, frequent or loud sighing, being distracted by your cell phone, even bad breath or body odor!)

    iii. What would you guess are my top values and passions? On what kinds of objects and activities do you think I invest my time and money?

    iv. What would you guess are my top strengths?

    v. What would you guess are my biggest weaknesses?

    vi. What would you guess are my biggest insecurities or fears?

    vii. If you had to describe me to a potential employer in 30 seconds or less, what would you say?

    viii. If you had to describe me to a prospective spouse in 30 seconds or less, what would you say?

b. Take a few minutes to present or interpret your flag to your partner. When you are done, have them share the "profile" they wrote about you. Then reverse roles and repeat.

c. Reflect upon the exercise and discuss the following with your partner:

    i. Compare and contrast internal *versus* external "realities." Did any of the ways you occurred to your partner "miss the mark"? Can you understand how your partner may have been led to that way?

    ii. Which of your partner's interpretations made you feel good? Why?

    iii. Which of your partner's interpretations made you the most uncomfortable? Why?

    iv. Do you believe any other group members, classmates, co-workers, *et cetera* would be likely to make the same "uncomfortable interpretations" about you?

    v. Should you even care what others think about you? Why?

    vii. Think about the phrase: "Perception is reality." How does this apply (or not) in the world of personal interpretations? If it does apply, what are the implications?

d. What have you learned about yourself as an "observer"? How easy was it for you to write a story based on what you "saw"? How easy or difficult was it to ask your partner questions that permitted you to see him/her from their point of view, rather than your perception of them? If they shared something with you and it caused you to wonder more, how willing were you to stop and probe further *versus* moving on to the next question? Reflect on this important point and determine what effect your answers have on your current relationships within the group and elsewhere (i.e., work, classroom, home, *et cetera*).

WHAT I HAVE LEARNED AS AN OBSERVER

Step 7: In the space below, write the names of three other individuals (friends, family, coworkers, *et cetera*) that you would like to interview to see how you occur to them. Note that for people who know you fairly well, the flag portion of the exercise is not necessary, and additional questions may apply.

1. ✍ _____

2. ✍ _____

3. ✍ _____

Step 8. The Imperative and Risks of "Leading by Example"

a. Work with your partner to identify the top three reasons why people are so much more willing to follow individuals who "walk the talk."

1. ✍ _____

2. ✎_____ ⌨

3. ✎_____ ⌨

b. Identify a once respected leader (preferably one from your own life) who experienced a sudden "fall from grace." Share the story of that person's downfall with your partner and discuss the following:

   i. Did their downfall result from a specific inability to fulfill a formal requirement of their job or role? If not, why were their actions even relevant? Was there an implicit agreement that they violated? What serves as the basis for such agreements?

   ii. What role did trust play in that person's downfall? What effect does a lack of trust have on followers? What is the effect on the organization?

   iii. Was the fallen leader ever able to redeem themselves in the eyes of their followers? If so, how?

c. Obviously, "leading by example" is a foundational principle of leadership. However, is it possible to take it too far? Consider the following quotes:

"Setting an example is not the main means of influencing others, it is the only means." Albert Einstein

"Example is not the main thing in influencing others. It is the only thing." Albert Schweitzer

Imagine someone whose only tool in their leadership toolbox is "leading by example." What do you think their experience as a leader is likely to be? Share your thoughts with your partner.

Notes: ✎_____ ⌨

21.4. Discussion questions:

Per facilitator …
Name some scenarios where a pharmacist must represent pharmacy to non-pharmacists.

21.5. After-class assignments:

A. Observe campus activities for how individuals interact with each other: class officers, APhA-ASP, CAPSI, fraternities and sororities, sports teams and coaches, student government, campus newspaper editors and readers, multi-person research project.

   1 – Observe positional leaders

   2 – Observe nonpositional leaders

   3 – Name someone on campus with least amount of positional authority, yet with great influence.

   Be prepared to discuss your findings (or submit a short __-page paper about your observations – ask your facilitator) at the time specified by your facilitator.

Alternately, invite a panel of presidents of student associations and use your questions [consider interview suggestions offered in Module 22].

B. Fulfill the before-class activities for the next Module assigned by your facilitator.

21.6. Bibliography, references, & resources:

Covey SR. *The 7 Habits of Highly Effective People*. New York: Simon Schuster, 1989.

Kofman F. *Conscious Business: How to Build Value Through Values.* Boulder, CO: Sounds True, 2006.

Rickert DR, Smith RE, Worthen DB. The 'seven habits': Building pharmacist leaders. *Am Pharm.* 1992;32(Aug):48-52.

Module « 22 »   INTERVIEWS & GUEST SPEAKERS

☞ Learning Objectives:

Objective 1. To identify what knowledge transfer is most needed when a guest speaker visits with a group, or when a participant goes out to conduct an interview.

Objective 2. To identify learnings from leadership positions previously held.

Objective 3. To identify what aspects of a desirable position are most attractive to a participant.

Other people know more than I do – that's a basic premise to the lot of a college student. True, but we've already mentioned a few times in this Workbook that you (and everyone) should take as much control of your environment as possible.

So, the Prof is going to invite some Esteemed One in to talk to the class. Could be boorrinngg.... Seize control! What do you want to know from this alleged expert? Put the guy/gal on the spot and ask hard questions, not softballs! It's your time in that room, make it worth your while!

This Module considers how to get the most learning from interviews and guest speakers. It explores what to listen for with role models and exemplars. And how to ask questions to help find the elements of their expertise most relevant to you. Leverage curiosity! Take control!

22.1. Readings or activities <u>before class</u>:

Read the list of proposed questions below [Step 3(b)], and identify other questions that should be asked to specific kinds of guests.

22.2. Resources needed:

None other than this Module

22.3. In-class activities:

"If your actions inspire others to dream more, learn more, do more and become more, you are a leader."
John Quincy Adams

Step 1. Questions?
Step 2. Quote.
Step 3. Plan the Interview.
   a. What do you most want to learn from the person to be interviewed?

b. Modify the following list of questions to match the information you most want to gather from this person. Remember, time is finite, so do not waste too much time on pleasantries, at the expense of not having time later to get into "the good stuff."

Questions [for you to adapt, while considering the individual to be interviewed]:

1. What is your leadership position? What are your responsibilities?
2. How and why were you selected? How did you prepare?
3. Why did you become a leader?
4. How did you become a leader?
5. How would you describe your leadership style?
6. Why did you choose this specific pharmacy organization to serve as a leader?
7. What have been your biggest leadership challenges and celebrations?
8. What do you find most rewarding?
9. What regrets do you experience by being a leader? Are there times when you would rather be a follower?
10. Can you name any occasions when you used failure to improve the next time around?
11. In what way(s) has your leadership activity had an impact on pharmacy or healthcare?
12. Do you feel your gender, culture, or ethnicity affected your view of leadership or how to lead?
13. Have you observed differences in the way men and women lead? If yes, what differences have you noted? If no, why do you think this is?
14. What advice would you give someone who is beginning a career regarding leadership?
15. Who is your leadership role-model or mentor?
16. If you had to train someone to replace you in your current job, what key abilities would you focus on?

Modifications, deletions, additions: ✎ _____ ⌨

Step 4. Conduct the interview. Keep notes:

✎ _____ ⌨

Step 5. Debrief as a group after the interview.

Step 6. Individually compile your learnings from the interview into a coherent essay, as directed by the facilitator.

A. Write your personal responses to the following questions in essay format:

i. How did this interview influence your perception of leadership activities? Explain.

ii. What did you learn from this interview that made the most impact on you and why?

iii. How does what you learned in the interview validate, refute, or reinforce what you have learned about leadership in this class?

22.4. Discussion questions:

Per facilitator

22.5. After-class assignments:

A. *Facilitator discretion*: Report of an interview.

B. *Facilitator discretion*: Retrospective Reflection on a Position You Have Held: Include the following information in the reflection paper:

    i. The organization(s), your leadership role, how long you were in that role, and what specific activities you completed as a leader.

    ii. Discuss why you pursued these leadership opportunities.

    iii. Identify and reflect upon your positive (and negative) experiences of these leadership experiences (professionally and personally) and any effect they had on others.

    iv. Describe how these experiences influenced your plans for pursuing leadership opportunities.

C. *Facilitator discretion*: Prospective Projection to a Position You Would Like to Hold: Identify one leadership position in a pharmacy organization you may consider pursuing either while a student or after graduation. Do not list a position that you already hold or have held or a position you know you will assume in the next officer transition for your organization. List a specific position that is available in a specific pharmacy organization. (For instance, do not say that you would like to be a committee chair. State that you would like to chair the Service Committee or Social Committee.)

    i. Explain why you would like to be elected or appointed to that specific position.

    ii. Explain why you chose that specific organization.

D. Fulfill the before-class activities for the next Module assigned by your facilitator.

22.6. Bibliography, references, & resources:

Mort JR, Strain JD, Helgeland DL, Seefeldt TM. Perceived impact of a longitudinal leadership program for all pharmacy students. *Innov Pharm.* 2014;5(3): Article 167. pubs.lib.umn.edu/innovations/vol5/iss3/7

Smith DN, Roebuck DB. Interviews: Linking leadership theory to practice. *J Lead Educ.* 2010;9(2):135-43. www.journalofleadershiped.org/attachments/article/149/Smith_and_Roebuck.pdf

Module « **23** »   INTERPROFESSIONAL RELATIONS: WHERE TO START

☞ Learning Objectives:

Objective 1. To describe the role of communication in the productivity of teams.
Objective 2. To describe the role of leadership in the productivity of teams.
Objective 3. To describe various roles individual team members may fulfill, both productive and counterproductive.

Healthcare teams. We've been on good ones, effective ones, teams worthy of celebration. And we've been on lethargic ones, officious ones, in-name-only ones. What does it take to turn the less-good ones into the praiseworthy ones? And why is it important for the delivery of effective patient care?

This Module scratches the surface on this topic (admittedly, very shallow). But it is inescapable that a healthcare team brings together multiple species of healthcare workers: pharmacists, nurses, physicians, sometimes psychologists or dentists or physical therapists or others who come together to enable a patient's recovery or well-being.

If we are exerting as much energy as we are, simply on getting a pharmacy team humming, how much more complicated must it be to coordinate the differing ego and other needs of these other human species? Well, each of these other professions is composed of humans, not some other species. And we're united in a common goal to prevent or relieve human suffering. So, can it be all that hard? Maybe the lessons we're learning about our fellow pharmacists are directly applicable to those "others" as well....

In this Module, we consider stereotypes. We consider team building. We consider hierarchies and influence. Want to join us?

23.1. Readings or activities before class:

A. Name some stereotypes you have about physicians.

✍ _____ ▦

B. Name some stereotypes you have about nurses.

✍ _____ ▦

C. Name some stereotypes you have about dentists.

✍ _____ ▦

What forms the basis for your stereotypes? To what have you been exposed that shapes what you think about these healthcare professionals? Thinking about these healthcare professionals with greater depth,

165

how do you know that what you think is true?

✎ _____ ⌨

D. Name some stereotypes you have about pharmacists.

✎ _____ ⌨

E. What do you know for a fact that physicians or nurses know about pharmacists?

✎ _____ ⌨

F. Watch **Video 1** and take notes about helpful behaviors and disruptive behaviors. Keep one list of each to discuss in class. www.ahrq.gov/professionals/education/curriculum-tools/teamstepps/officebasedcare/bad_combination/index.html

✎ _____ ⌨

23.2. Resources needed:

Internet access to play videos from TeamSTEPPS® website. Note: You may download the TeamSTEPPS® video files in MP4 format for local use without an Internet connection. Videos are compressed in Zip format for easier downloading.

23.3. In-class activities:

"You treat a disease, you win, you lose. You treat a person, I guarantee you, you'll win, no matter what the outcome." Patch Adams

Step 1. Questions?
Step 2. Quote.
Step 3. Exercise.

TEAMSTEPPS®

TeamSTEPPS® is an evidence-based teamwork system aimed at optimizing patient care by improving communication and teamwork skills among healthcare professionals, including frontline staff. It includes a comprehensive set of ready-to-use materials and a training curriculum to successfully integrate teamwork principles into a variety of settings. Several versions of TeamSTEPPS® are available, along with individual modules related to specific audiences, settings, or situations. Each is posted online.

Adapted from: TeamSTEPPS®: Strategies and Tools to Enhance Performance and Patient Safety (STEPPS), developed by the Agency for Healthcare Research & Quality (AHRQ), with support from the U.S. Department of Defense.

a. Watch **Video 1** and identify helpful behaviors and disruptive behaviors.

b. Pair-share the helpful behaviors you identified in Video 1.

c. Pair-share the disruptive or unfortunate behaviors you identified in Video 1.

d. Discuss: How often do patients realize how chaotic an office or clinic may be?

TeamSTEPPS® for Office-Based Care Training Videos

e. As a group, view **Video 2**: Good Teamwork – Communication Video:

www.ahrq.gov/professionals/education/curriculum-
tools/teamstepps/officebasedcare/1_communication_good/index.html.
     Pair-share: What changes or improvements did you notice in this video?

✎_____ ⎕

     d. As a group, view **Video 3**: Good Teamwork – Leadership Video:
www.ahrq.gov/professionals/education/curriculum-
tools/teamstepps/officebasedcare/2_leadership_good/index.html
     Pair-share: What changes or improvements did you notice in this video?

✎_____ ⎕

     e. Pharmacists and pharmacy technicians were not portrayed in these videos. Would you expect them to contribute in any different way, if they had been portrayed?

✎_____ ⎕

Step 4. Key Points from TeamSTEPPS®. Effective teamwork depends on each team member being able to:
     a. Anticipate the needs of others
     b. Adjust to each other's actions and to the changing environment. Communicate clearly to do so.
     c. Have a shared understanding of how a procedure should happen, to identify when errors (may) occur and how to correct for (or prevent) these errors.

Discuss. ✎_____ ⎕
     d. Obstacles to productive teamwork: Lack of coordination, workload, miscommunication.

Discuss. ✎_____ ⎕

Step 5.

TEAM ROLES:

Consider the following passage, then answer the following questions.

     Within any team, members assume different roles. Several of these roles are known to help effective teams function smoothly. These beneficial roles may be assumed by separate members or shared by various members at different points in time. Any given individual may fulfill more than one role.

     Every team has both **task** and **maintenance** needs. Some of the essential team roles are task-related, in that they help the team to accomplish things. Some are maintenance-related, in that they facilitate the participation of the members.

     Task roles include these:
          Initiator: Proposes tasks, goals, or actions. Defines team problems. Suggests procedures.
          Information seeker: Asks for factual clarification. Requests facts pertinent to the discussion.
          Opinion seeker: Asks for clarification of values pertinent to a topic. Questions values involved in options.
          Informer: Offers facts. Expresses feelings. Gives opinions.

Clarifier: Interprets ideas or suggestions. Defines terms. Clarifies issues. Clears up confusion.

Summarizer: Pulls together related ideas. Restates suggestions. Offers decisions or conclusions for the team to consider.

Reality tester: Offers critical analyses of ideas. Tests ideas against data, to see if ideas would work.

Orienter: Defines team position vis-à-vis its goals. Points out departures from agreed-on goals. Raises questions about direction pursued.

Follower: Goes along with the crowd. Passively accepts ideas of others. Serves as an audience in discussion and decision making.

Maintenance roles include these:

Harmonizer: Tries to reconcile disagreements. Reduces tension. Gets people to explore differences.

Gatekeeper: Helps keep communication channels open. Facilitates participation of others. Suggests procedures that permit sharing.

Consensus taker: Asks to see whether the team is nearing a decision. Sends up trial balloons to test possible solutions.

Encourager: Is friendly, warm, and responsive to others. Accepts others' contributions via facial expressions or remarks.

Compromiser: Offers compromises that yield status when his or her own ideas are involved in conflicts. Changes position in the interest of team cohesiveness or growth.

Standard setter: Expresses standards to aim for. Applies standards in evaluating quality of team processes.

It can be useful for a team to consider which roles are fulfilled by which members. If certain roles appear to be missing, members can plan to incorporate the associated behaviors into their team activities. Determining roles allows the members to form a clear perception of their value to the team. They can consciously build on the behaviors that they naturally exhibit and that are comfortable to them, thereby helping the team to realize its full potential.

a. Which of these roles did you see portrayed in the videos?

b. Which of these roles have you found yourself playing in various teams you belong to?

c. Consider when you may have played one role in one circumstance, but a vastly different role in a different circumstance. Pair-share with a colleague. Discuss with the whole group.

d. Why would it be important to have a mix of task and maintenance roles?

e. How do your values, interest, strengths and needs influence the role(s) you play?

23.4. Discussion questions:

Per facilitator
Facilitator discretion: Use of Annex 23-2. Team-Role Crossword Puzzle
Facilitator discretion: Use of Annex 23-3. Team-Role Unscramble

23.5. After-class assignments:

A. Next time you are in a healthcare setting (whether working or as a patient or visitor), evaluate the staff around you in terms of their communication competence and their teamwork (or lack thereof). If you were the supervisor, what would you say to the staff?
B. Fulfill the before-class activities for the next Module assigned by your facilitator.

23.6. Bibliography, references, & resources:

TeamSTEPPS®: Strategies and Tools to Enhance Performance and Patient Safety. Rockville, MD: Agency for Healthcare Research & Quality, March 2016. www.ahrq.gov/professionals/education/curriculum-tools/teamstepps/index.html, teamstepps.ahrq.gov/abouttoolsmaterials.htm

TeamSTEPPS® 2.0 Video Training Tools. March 2014. Agency for Healthcare Research and Quality, Rockville, MD. www.ahrq.gov/professionals/education/curriculum-tools/teamstepps/instructor/videos/index.html

TeamSTEPPS® for Office-Based Care Classroom Course. Rockville, MD: Agency for Healthcare Research & Quality, December 2015. www.ahrq.gov/professionals/education/curriculum-tools/teamstepps/officebasedcare/classroom.html; www.ahrq.gov/professionals/education/curriculum-tools/teamstepps/officebasedcare/videos.html

Hospital brochure: www.ahrq.gov/sites/default/files/wysiwyg/professionals/education/curriculum-tools/teamstepps/instructor/essentials/pocketguide.pdf

Long-Term Care (LTC) brochure: www.ahrq.gov/professionals/education/curriculum-tools/teamstepps/longtermcare/essentials/index.html

Chatalalsingh C, Reeves S. Leading team learning: what makes interprofessional teams learn to work well? *J Interprof Care*. 2014 Nov;28(6):513-8.

Drummond N, Abbott K, Williamson T, Somji B. Interprofessional primary care in academic family medicine clinics: Implications for education and training. *Can Fam Physician*. 2012 Aug;58(8):e450-8.

Farrell B, Ward N, Dore N, Russell G, Geneau R, Evans S. Working in interprofessional primary health care teams: What do pharmacists do? *Res Social Adm Pharm*. 2013 May-Jun;9(3):288-301.

Flashcards via Quizlet, https://quizlet.com/class/3716098/, Interprofessional (TeamSTEPPS): I Pass the Baton » 10 terms; Key Principles » 5 terms; Mutual Support » 5 terms; SBAR » 4 terms; Team Events » 3 terms; Team Roles » 15 terms

Annex 23-1. Team-Role Summary (Strategies and Tools to Enhance Performance and Patient Safety)

Separate annex documents available to facilitators upon request (LeadGrowShape@plei.org).

Key Principles:

Team Structure: Identification of the components of a multi-team system that must work together effectively to ensure patient safety.

Communication: Structured process by which information is clearly and accurately exchanged among team members. See SBAR, Check-Back, and Handoff for recommended techniques.

Leadership: Ability to maximize the activities of team members by ensuring that team actions are understood, changes in information are shared, and team members have the necessary resources.

Situation Monitoring: Process of actively scanning and assessing situational elements to gain information or understanding, or to maintain awareness to support team functioning.

Mutual Support: Ability to anticipate and support team members' needs through accurate knowledge about their responsibilities and workload.

SBAR: A technique for communicating critical information that requires immediate attention and action concerning a patient's condition.

Situation – What is going on with the patient? "I am calling about Mrs. Joseph in room 251. Chief complaint is shortness of breath of new onset."

Background – What is the clinical background or context? "Patient is a 62-year-old female postop day one from abdominal surgery. No prior history of cardiac or lung disease."

Assessment – What do I think the problem is? "Breath sounds are decreased on the right side with acknowledgment of pain. Would like to rule out pneumothorax."

Recommendation & Request – What would I do to correct it? "I feel strongly the patient should be assessed now. Can you come to room 251 now?"

Check-Back: Use closed-loop communication to help ensure that information conveyed by the sender is understood by the receiver. Follow these steps:

1. Sender initiates the message

2. Receiver accepts the message and provides feedback

3. Sender double-checks to ensure that the message was received. Example:

Prescriber: "Give 25 mg diphenhydramine IV push"

Nurse: "25 mg diphenhydramine IV push"

Prescriber: "That's correct"

Communication Handoff: The transfer of information (along with authority and responsibility) during transitions in care. It includes an opportunity to ask questions, clarify, and confirm. Examples of transitions in care include shift changes; transfer of responsibility between shifts; and during patient transfers.

"I PASS THE BATON"

I - Introduction - Introduce yourself and your role/job (include patient)

P - Patient - Name, identifiers, age, sex, location

A - Assessment - Present chief complaint, vital signs, symptoms, and diagnoses

S - Situation - Current status/circumstances, including code status, level of (un)certainty, recent changes, and response to treatment

S - Safety Concerns - Critical lab values/reports, socioeconomic factors, allergies, and alerts (falls, isolation, *et cetera*)

THE

B - Background - Comorbidities, previous episodes, current medications, and family history

A - Actions - Actions that were taken or are required. Provide rationale.

T - Timing - Level of urgency and explicit timing and prioritization of actions

O - Ownership - Identify who is responsible (person/team), including patient/family members

N - Next - What will happen next? Anticipated changes? What is the plan? Are there contingency plans?

Effective Team Leaders. Responsibilities of effective team leaders:

- Organize the team
- Identify and articulate clear goals (i.e., the plan)
- Assign tasks and responsibilities
- Monitor and modify the plan; communicate changes
- Review the team's performance; provide feedback when needed
- Manage and allocate resources
- Facilitate information sharing
- Encourage team members to assist one another
- Facilitate conflict resolution in a learning environment
- Model effective teamwork

Leadership Team Events Sharing the Plan

- ▸ Brief - Short session to share the plan, discuss team formation, assign roles and responsibilities, establish expectations and climate, anticipate outcomes and likely contingencies
- ▸ Huddle - Ad hoc meeting to re-establish situational awareness, reinforce plans already in place, and assess the need to adjust the plan
- ▸ Debrief - Informal information exchange session designed to improve team performance and effectiveness through lessons learned and reinforcement of positive behaviors

Brief Checklist: Address the following questions:

- ▷ Who is on the team?
- ▷ Do all members understand and agree upon goals?
- ▷ Are roles and responsibilities understood?
- ▷ What is our plan of care?
- ▷ What is staff and provider's availability throughout the shift?
- ▷ How is workload shared among team members?
- ▷ What resources are available?

Debrief Checklist: Address the following questions:

- Was communication clear?
- Were roles and responsibilities understood?
- Was situation awareness maintained?
- Was workload distribution equitable?
- Was task assistance requested or offered?
- Were errors made or avoided?
- Were resources available?
- What went well?
- What should improve?

Situation monitoring involves continually scanning and assessing a situation, to gain and maintain an understanding of what's going on around you. Situation awareness is the state of "knowing what's going on around you." A shared mental model results from each team member maintaining situation awareness and ensures that all team members are "on the same page."

Cross-Monitoring: A harm/error-reduction strategy that involves:
▷ Monitoring actions of other team members
▷ Providing a safety net within the team
▷ Ensuring that mistakes or oversights are caught quickly and easily
▷ "Watching each other's back"

Task Assistance: Helping others with tasks builds a strong team. Key strategies include:
- Team members protect each other from work overload situations
- Effective teams place all offers and requests for assistance in the context of patient safety
- Team members foster a climate where it is expected that assistance will be actively sought and offered

Mutual Support: Feedback Information provided to team members to improve team performance. Feedback should be:
▷ Timely – Given soon after the target behavior has occurred
▷ Respectful – Focuses on behaviors, not personal attributes
▷ Specific – Relates to a specific task or behavior that requires correction or improvement
▷ Directed toward improvement – Provides directions for future improvement
▷ Considerate – Considers a team member's feelings; delivers negative information with fairness and respect

Team Performance Observation Tool
    Team Structure
        Assembles team
        Assigns or identifies team members' roles and responsibilities
        Holds team members accountable
        Includes patients and families as part of the team
    Communication
        Provides brief, clear, specific, and timely information
        Seeks information from all available sources
        Uses check-backs to verify information that is communicated

Uses SBAR, call-outs, check-backs, and handoff techniques to communicate with team members

Leadership

Identifies team goals and vision

Utilizes resources efficiently to maximize team performance

Balances workload within the team

Delegates tasks or assignments, as appropriate

Conducts briefs, huddles, and debriefs

Role models teamwork behaviors

Situation Monitoring

Monitors the state of the patient

Monitors fellow team members to ensure safety and prevent errors

Monitors the environment for safety and availability of resources (e.g., equipment)

Monitors progress toward the goal and identifies changes that could alter the care plan

Fosters communication to ensure a shared mental model

Mutual Support

Provides task-related support and assistance

Provides timely and constructive feedback to team members

Effectively advocates for the patient using the Assertive Statement, Two-Challenge Rule, or CUS (Concerned-Uncomfortable-Safety) Statements

Uses the Two-Challenge Rule or DESC (Describe-Express-Suggest-Consequences) script to resolve conflict

Resource: Pocket Guide TeamSTEPPS® 2.0: Team Strategies & Tools to Enhance Performance and Patient Safety. Rockville, MD: Agency for Healthcare Research & Quality, December 2013. www.ahrq.gov/professionals/education/curriculum-tools/teamstepps/instructor/essentials/pocketguide.html

Annex 23-2. Team-Role Crossword Puzzle

Separate annex documents available to facilitators upon request (LeadGrowShape@plei.org).

Across

1. Asks for clarification of values pertinent to a topic.
3. Helps keep communication channels open. Facilitates participation.
7. Offers facts, expresses feelings, gives opinions.
8. Proposes tasks, goals, or actions. Defines problems.
10. Attempts to reconcile disagreements. Reduces tension.
11. Offers critical analyses of ideas. Tests ideas against data.
12. Modifies in the interest of team cohesiveness or growth.

Down

2. Pulls together related ideas. Restates suggestions.
4. Interprets ideas or suggestions. Defines terms.
5. Goes along with the team. Passively accepts ideas of others.
6. Friendly, warm, and responsive to others.
9. Defines position of team with respect to its goals. Points out departures from goals.

Annex 23-3. Team-Role Unscramble

Separate annex documents available to facilitators upon request (LeadGrowShape@plei.org).

Key Principles	Enter nomenclature
Ability to maximize activity of team members	▸
Actively scanning and assessing situation to gain understanding	▸
Anticipating team members' needs	▸
Assures team actions are understood, changes in information are understood	▸
Components of multi-team structure that must work together	▸
Information is clearly and accurately exchanged	▸

SBAR	Enter nomenclature
What do I think the problem is?	▸
What is going on with the patient?	▸
What is the clinical context? E.g., prior history	▸
What would I do to correct it?	▸

I Pass THE Baton	Enter nomenclature
Actions taken or required (rationale?)	▸
Chief complaint, vital signs, symptoms, diagnoses	▸
Comorbidities, previous episodes, current meds, family history	▸
Critical lab values, socioeconomic factors, allergies, alerts	▸
Current status, level of (un)certainty, recent changes, response to treatment	▸
Introduce yourself and your role	▸
Level of urgency, explicit timing, prioritization of actions	▸
Name, identifiers, age, sex, location	▸
What happens next? Anticipated changes? Plan?	▸
Who is responsible?	▸

Leadership Team Events	Enter nomenclature
Share the plan, discuss team formation, assign roles	▸
Ad hoc meeting for situational awareness, reinforce plans, assess need to adjust plan	▸
Information exchange to improve team performance	▸

Mutual Support	Enter nomenclature
Given soon after target behavior occurred	▸
Focuses on behaviors, not personal attributes	▸
Related to isolated behaviors that require improvement	▸
Provides approaches for making things better	▸
Allows for team member's feelings (fairness, respect)	▸

Module « 24 »   FOLLOWERSHIP

☞ Learning Objectives:

Objective 1. To explore how understanding one's self helps contribute to the success of other leaders.
Objective 2. To describe how leaders frequently exhibit follower behaviors.
Objective 3. To describe various followership patterns.

Leaders, by definition, need followers. Followers need leaders.

But we are using a very specific definition of follower in this Module – the person who is devoted to the success of the group, the team.

In most cases, leaders have supervisors, managers, reporting chains. This means that leaders often wear two hats: leader of some segment of their environment and, simultaneously, a follower within a larger structure with the bigger (higher) boss.

Get used to it. Every leader will also be a follower, so it's important to understand both roles. This understanding is useful in multiple ways.

24.1. Readings or activities <u>before class</u>:

Re-reading the Delegation section of the pre-class reading in Module 4 may be helpful.
Re-reading Annex 16-1 regarding Performance Conversations and Closure Conversations will be helpful while discussing this Module.
Read the following text and be prepared to discuss.
After reading, complete Annex 24-1: Followership Crossword Puzzle (or follow facilitator instructions).

DELEGATION: THE ART OF SERVICE

Followership refers to a role held by certain individuals in a group. Specifically, it is the capacity of an individual to actively follow a leader. Followership is the reciprocal behavior to leadership. The study of followership contributes to better understanding of leadership. The success and failure of teams depends both on how well a leader can lead and also on how well followers can follow. Good followership is active, not passive. Effective followers are enthusiastic, intelligent, ambitious, and self-reliant.

The field of followership is attributed to scholar Robert Kelley. Kelley described four main qualities of effective followers:

▸ <u>Self-Management</u>: This refers to the ability to think critically, to be in control of one's actions, and work independently. It is important that followers manage themselves well, to be ready when leaders delegate tasks to capable individuals.

▸ <u>Commitment</u>: This refers to an individual being committed to the goal, vision, or cause of a group, team, or organization. This is an important quality of followers as it helps keep one's (and other member's) morale and energy levels high.

▸ <u>Competence</u>: It is essential that individuals possess the skills and aptitudes necessary to complete the goal or task of the group, team, or organization. Individuals high on this quality often hold skills higher than their average co-worker (or team member). Further, these individuals continue their pursuit of knowledge by upgrading their skills through classes and seminars.

- Courage: Effective followers hold true to their beliefs and maintain and uphold ethical standards, even in the face of dishonest or corrupt superiors (leaders). These individuals are loyal, honest, and importantly, candid with their superiors.

Followership Patterns: Kelley identified two underlying behavioral dimensions that help identify the difference between followers and non-followers. The first dimension is whether the individual is an independent, critical thinker. The second dimension is whether the individual is active or passive. From these dimensions, Kelley has identified five followership patterns, or types of followers:

- The Sheep: These individuals are passive and require external motivation from the leader. These individuals lack commitment and require constant supervision from the leader.

- The Yes-People: These individuals are committed to the leader and the goal (or task) of the organization (or group/team). These conformist individuals do not question the decisions or actions of the leader. Further, yes-people will defend adamantly their leader when faced with opposition from others.

- The Pragmatics: These individuals are not trail-blazers; they will not stand behind controversial or unique ideas until much of the group has expressed their support. These individuals often remain in the background of the group.

- The Alienated: Alienated people are negative. They often attempt to stall or bring the group down by constantly questioning decisions and actions of the leader. These individuals often view themselves as the rightful leaders of the organization and criticize the leader and fellow group members.

- The Star Followers: These exemplary individuals are positive, active, and independent thinkers. Star followers will not blindly accept the decisions or actions of a leader until they have evaluated them completely. Furthermore, these types of followers can succeed without the presence of a leader.

24.2. Resources needed:

None other than this Module

24.3. In-class activities:

"Employees do a great deal more following than leading, even as leaders. For the most part, followership behaviors drive tactical successes. Leadership talents and skills propel strategic accomplishments." Rodger Adair

Step 1. Questions?
Step 2. Quote.
Step 3. Exercise.

HOW DO YOU FOLLOW?

a. Consider Kelley's four main qualities of effective followers. For each of the qualities, write down times when you do and do not exhibit the quality:

Self-Management: 🖎 _____ ⌨

Commitment: 🖎 _____ ⌨

Competence: ✍ _____ ⌨

Courage: ✍ _____ ⌨

b. When you do not exhibit these qualities, why not? Could you be a less effective follower in that case? Thinking about it now, has this approach worked for you?

✍ _____ ⌨

c. Compare notes in pair-share mode. Listen well to the reasons that others offer when they do not exhibit qualities of an effective follower.

Step 4. Consider Kelley's list of five followership patterns. Also consider the behavioral dimensions of critical thinking and activity/passivity.

a. For each of the followership patterns, write down an example of when this pattern is appropriate and another example of when this pattern is not appropriate:

The Sheep: ✍ _____ ⌨

The Yes-People: ✍ _____ ⌨

The Pragmatics: ✍ _____ ⌨

The Alienated: ✍ _____ ⌨

The Star Followers: ✍ _____ ⌨

b. Pair-share to compare notes. What do you think of these reasons for appropriate behavior? What about the "inappropriate" ones? How might you help people change patterns that are not appropriate?

Step 5. Pair up with another participant.

a. Think about a scenario where you have a task to delegate and conduct a Performance Conversation (Annex 16-1) in which you delegate this task to your partner. Be sure to follow the steps in the Annex to arrive at what you agree upon (e.g., task XYZ will be performed by a specific date/time and follow up will occur along the way at specific date/time). Be sure you determine that the person is equipped to assume the task. What did you learn, either as "leader delegating task" or as "worker assigned task"? Offer feedback to each other.

✍ _____ ⌨

b. Repeat the exercise, so that the other participant thinks of a scenario, identifies a task, and conducts the PC. What did you learn when you assumed the opposite role?

_____

c. How does a PC facilitate task delegation? What was difficult in having this kind of conversation with someone to whom you have assigned a task?

_____

24.4. Discussion questions:

Per facilitator …
In what ways are pharmacists better followers than leaders?
In what ways are pharmacists more inclined to lead than to follow?

24.5. After-class assignments:

A. While in a public setting, find examples of an exemplary follower. What are the characteristics that make this one your choice? Do in groups, if you wish.
B. Fulfill the before-class activities for the next Module assigned by your facilitator.

24.6. Bibliography, references, & resources:

Baker SD. Followership: The theoretical foundation of a contemporary construct. *J Leadership & Org Studies.* 2007;14:50-60.
Flashcards via Quizlet, https://quizlet.com/class/3716098/, Followership-Delegation Lexicon » 10 terms
Ford J, Ford L. *The Four Conversations: Daily Communication That Gets Results.* Oakland, CA: Berrett-Koehler Publishers, 2009. www.bkconnection.com
Kelley RE. In praise of followers. *Harvard Business Review* 1988;66:142-148.

Annex 24-1. Followership Crossword Puzzle

Separate annex documents available to facilitators upon request (LeadGrowShape@plei.org).

Across

1. Holding true to beliefs and standards, even in face of contrary forces
2. Ability to think critically, control one's actions, work independently
6. Negative people who stall or repeatedly question decisions
7. Skills and aptitudes needed to complete the goal or task of the group
8. People who wait for a majority to express support
9. Require external motivation from leader

Down

1. Pledged to goal, vision, or cause of a group
3. Capacity to actively follow a leader
4. Positive, active, independent thinkers
5. Conformists who do not question actions of the leader

Module « 25 »   SAUSAGE, LEADING TO POLICY

☞ Learning Objectives:

Objective 1. To identify who represents each participant in state, provincial, and federal legislatures.
Objective 2. To describe the committee structure with jurisdiction for health matters in various legislatures.
Objective 3. To identify the state or provincial pharmacist association's legislative priorities.

This Module explores how governments govern, how bills become law. There is another control category, known as regulation, that we don't address directly, but you'll get the drift.

Laws don't descend from the skies (with the notable exception of the Ten Commandments). Human beings arrange them, write them, amend them, influence them. Maybe you've heard about how legislation is like sausage... Well, let's take a peek.

The best approach will be to hear from experienced people, so we suggest interviews with the legislative directors of pharmacist associations. But we will also introduce you to resources available to all citizens.

You have registered to vote, haven't you?

And you know how to order absentee or special ballots if you're away from home, right?

25.1. Readings or activities before class:

Based on your home town [where you vote], complete the top parts of Annex 25-1, describing the representatives (members) and senators who represent you in the various legislatures.
Re-read Annex 16-1 regarding Initiative Conversations and Understanding Conversations and be prepared to discuss for this Module.

25.2. Resources needed:

Before class, invite a member of your state or provincial pharmacist association to join the class in-person, on the telephone, or via the web. The legislative director would be ideal, but others in the association will also be knowledgeable.
Annex 25-1. Legislative Environment Summary

25.3. In-class activities:

"Laws, like sausages, cease to inspire respect in proportion as we know how they are made."
John Godfrey Saxe, University of Michigan, 27 March 1869

"It's a long, long wait
While I'm sitting in committee
But I know I'll be a law someday

183

At least I hope and pray that I will
But today I am still just a bill."
"I'm Just a Bill," Schoolhouse Rock
Music & Lyrics: Dave Frishberg, 1975; https://www.youtube.com/watch?v=FFroMQlKiag

Step 1. Questions?
Step 2. Quotes.
Step 3. Exercise.

WHERE DO POLICIES & REGULATIONS COME FROM?

a. Review the home-town information participants collected before class in section A of Annex 25-1. Spend a little time considering legislative structures for states and provinces other than the one where your school is located.

b. Complete the tables regarding legislative committees and subcommittees with jurisdiction for health matters, both local and federal.

c. Consult face-to-face, telephonically, or virtually with the legislative director for your state or provincial pharmacist association and ask questions about goals and legislative agenda.

d. Based on the legislative priorities of your pharmacist association, develop a group project to craft a message to legislators, such as supporting provider status or another pending topic relevant to your area.

e. Gather data from websites, *et cetera*, about legislative directors for other pharmacist associations.

25.4. Discussion questions:

Per facilitator …
What kinds of requests can (or should) pharmacists make of legislators? Government agencies?

25.5. After-class assignments:

A. Complete legislative-message project described in Part D of Annex 25-1.
B. Fulfill the before-class activities for the next Module assigned by your facilitator.

25.6. Bibliography, references, & resources:

Flashcards via Quizlet, https://quizlet.com/class/3716098/, Pharmacy Associations, Canada » 7 terms; USA
    » 8 terms
Ford J, Ford L. *The Four Conversations: Daily Communication That Gets Results*. Oakland, CA: Berrett-Koehler
    Publishers, 2009. www.bkconnection.com
US Junior Chamber [of Commerce, Jaycees]. Get Out the Vote,
    www.jci.cc/controlpanel/documents/Get%20Out%20the%20Vote%202010.pdf

Annex 25-1. Legislative Environment Summary

Separate annex documents available to facilitators upon request (LeadGrowShape@plei.org).

A. Based on your home town [where you vote], research and enter the names of the legislators who represent you in state or provincial legislatures, the U.S. Congress, or the Parliament of Canada. [Yes, Nebraska, we know you have a unicameral state legislature, so you have less work to do.]

Home town [where you vote]	▸	
State / Province	▸	
	State or Provincial House of _____ or Assembly	State or Provincial Senate
Name of district (e.g., 5ᵗʰ)	▸	▸
Name of legislator ("member")	▸	▸
	U.S. House of Representatives House of Commons of Canada	U.S. Senate Senate of Canada
Name of district (e.g., 5ᵗʰ)	▸	
Name of legislator ("member")	▸	1.
		2.

Hint: The U.S. federal information is available at congress.gov.

🍁 For Canadian federal information, go to www.parl.gc.ca/senatorsmembers.aspx

Are you registered to vote? YES NO

If you aren't registered yet, you can find out how at:

USA: vote.usa.gov   🍁 Canada: www.elections.ca

USA: For absentee ballots, vote.org. 🍁 Canada: For special ballots, www.elections.ca/ voting-by-mail

When are the next elections in your state or province? _____

B1. Use the grid below to record the names of <u>house and senate</u> committees with jurisdiction for health matters. Include the names of their chairs (and ranking members of the minority party).

	State or Provincial House of _____ or Assembly	State or Provincial Senate
Committee with jurisdiction for health matters	▶	▶
Chair	▶	▶
Ranking member	▶	▶
Subcommittee for health, *if applicable*	▶	▶
Chair	▶	▶
Ranking member	▶	▶

B2. Use the grid below to record the names of the chairs of the <u>federal house and senate</u> committees with jurisdiction for health matters. Include the names of ranking members of the minority party.

	U.S. House of Representatives House of Commons of Canada	U.S. Senate Senate of Canada
Committee with jurisdiction for health matters	U.S.: Energy & Commerce Committee Can: Standing Committee on Health	U.S. Health, Education, Labor & Pensions (HELP) Committee Can: Committee on Social Affairs, Science & Technology
Chair	▶	▶
Ranking member	▶	▶
Subcommittee for health	U.S.: Subcommittee on Health Can:	U.S.: Subcommittee on Primary Health & Retirement Security Can:
Chair	▶	▶
Ranking member	▶	▶

Hint: the U.S. federal information is available at congress.gov.

🍁 The Canadian federal information is available at www.parl.gc.ca/senatorsmembers.aspx?Language=E.

C. Consult face-to-face, telephonically, or virtually with the legislative director for your state or provincial pharmacist association. Sample questions to ask:

What are the organization's priority goals?

✎ _____ ▦

What is the organization's legislative agenda (priorities)?

✎ _____ ▦

What proposed legislation or hearings are pending?

✎ _____ ▦

Discuss upcoming elections and positions of representatives.

✎ _____ ▦

Discuss allies and opponents.

✎ _____ ▦

Which months is your legislature typically in session?

✎ _____ ▦

What proportion of legislation introduced passes into law in your state or province?

✎ _____ ▦

D. Based on the legislative priorities of your local pharmacist association, develop a group project to craft a message to legislators, such as supporting provider status or another pending topic relevant to your area.

Ideas: ✎ _____ ▦

E. Gather information from websites or other sources about the legislative directors for other pharmacist associations. National Groups...

APhA or CPhA: ✎ _____ ▦

AACP or AFPC: ✎ _____ ▦

ASCP or CSCP: ✎ _____ ▦

ASHP or CSHP: ✎ _____ ▦

NCPA or NPAC: ✍ _____ ⌨

NACDS or CACDS: ✍ _____ ⌨

_____ : ✍ _____ ⌨

State or Provincial Groups...

_____ : ✍ _____ ⌨

_____ : ✍ _____ ⌨

_____ : ✍ _____ ⌨

AACP – American Association of Colleges of Pharmacy

ACPE – Accreditation Council for Pharmaceutical Education

AFPC – Association of Faculties of Pharmacy of Canada [Association des Facultés de Pharmacie du Canada]

APhA – American Pharmacists Association

ASCP – American Society of Consultant Pharmacists

ASHP – American Society of Health-System Pharmacists

ASP – Academy of Students of Pharmacy (APhA-ASP)

CACDS – Canadian Association of Chain Drug Stores [Association Canadienne des Pharmacies de la Chaîne]

CAPSI – Canadian Association of Pharmacy Students & Interns [Association Canadienne des Étudiants et Internes en Pharmacie (ACEIP)]

CCAPP – Canadian Council for Accreditation of Pharmacy Programs [Conseil Canadien d'Agrément des Programmes de Pharmacie]

CPhA -- Canadian Pharmacists Association (CPhA) [Association des Pharmaciens du Canada]

CSCP – Canadian Society of Consultant Pharmacists [Société Canadienne des Pharmaciens Consultant]

CSHP – Canadian Society of Hospital Pharmacists [Société Canadienne des Pharmaciens d'Hôpitaux]

NACDS – [US] National Association of Chain Drug Stores

NCPA – [US] National Community Pharmacists Association

NPAC – Neighbourhood Pharmacy Association of Canada [Association Canadienne des Pharmacies de Quartier Est]

Module « 26 »   SKILLS FOR GETTING YOUR MESSAGE ACROSS

☞ Learning Objectives:

Objective 1. To describe best practices in communication methods.

Objective 2. To describe how to get a message across in 30 seconds or less.

Objective 3. To define and understand the word "impeccable" (flawless, perfect, unsullied) as it relates to the actions and words of the leader.

Objective 4. To describe the power a leader's words have and the responsibility to use it positively.

Objective 5. To discuss the way in which emotions, feelings, thoughts, judgments, attitudes, opinions or gossip are transmitted between people.

This Module compares and contrasts transmitting and receiving: getting the message across. This Module explores the importance of communication for group achievement, and the role of the leader in setting the tone for group interaction. The communication example set by the leader is the basis for group members. This section is designed to explore the responsibility that a leader has for creating an environment conducive for optimal interaction.

This Module considers barriers to effective interpersonal communication and illustrates risks for group development. Moreover, it considers the importance of developing relationships to be an effective leader.

Do you find yourself using lots of words, but not getting your message across? This Module will help you work on organizing your messages, using brevity, clarity, and punch.

Do you realize all the messages being transmitted to you? Do you listen with all your senses? We will talk about why Sherlock Holmes would have made a good pharmacist. The secrets are good listening and observation skills.

Communication may be the single most important area for development and continual refinement for effective leadership. Groups of people who talk regularly, share information with each other, listen to one another, work through problems and spend time together find themselves connected to one another. This cohesion fosters understanding, commitment and often a desire to serve one another. Possibility can flourish into reality in this type of positive environment.

26.1. Readings or activities <u>before class</u>:

Read and be prepared to discuss the text below.

After reading, complete Annex 26-2: Communication Crossword Puzzle (or follow facilitator instructions).

Communication is vital to the pharmacist. Without effective communication, how can we adequately counsel patients, provide drug information, or work with physicians or nurses or our fellow pharmacists?

PLANNING FOR COMMUNICATION

Communication is defined as any situation where a communicator constructs a message, chooses, and then employs a communication medium (e.g., voice, memo) to transmit the message to a receiver. But the process does not end until the receiver interprets the message as he receives it and sends feedback to the communicator.

Preparation for communication is essential. The communicator should define his or her specific, achievable, desired outcome(s). The communicator should define the target audience, develop plans of action (i.e., strategies), select a medium, and identify any evidence or resources needed before communication begins. Effective, successful communication requires proper timing, setting, style, and approach as well.

GETTING YOUR POINT ACROSS

Milo Frank makes a great point that any effective message can be delivered in 30 seconds or less. In fact, if it cannot be delivered in that amount of time, you might not be able to get it across at all. Think: "elevator speech." An elevator speech is a quick summary of what you propose and why it should be adopted. It is a succinct form of persuasion, like the Initiative Conversation addressed in Module 16.

Any message in 30 seconds or less: TV and radio commercials do it all the time. Even the most complex problems can be summarized in this way. Milo Frank's principles:

1 – Have a single, clear-cut objective

2 – Go to the right person, the one who can grant your wish

3 – Use the right approach, the single best thought or sentence leading to your objective. It takes into consideration the needs of your listener

4 – Use a hook, a statement or object to get attention

5 – Know your subject

6 – Ask for your wish, either specifically or subtly

These concepts are valid for interviews, telephone calls, beginnings and ends of speeches, letters, and all other forms of communication. In asking your boss for a raise, for example, assemble a 30-second package; your approach might be "I've proven the value of my work to the company." Alternately: "What specifically may I do to position myself for a promotion, given my focus, drive, and accomplishment of key assignments such as XYZ?"

ORAL COMMUNICATION

Speaking effectively is important whether you are counseling patients, working with prescribers, dealing with business associates, or talking with your family. Every oral interchange has an opening, a middle, and a closing.

Opening: Make sure you have the other person's attention before proceeding any further. Communicate your own readiness to begin through eye contact and posture. Give the reason for the communication and move the conversation toward your desired outcome.

Middle: Monitor yourself to be sure your statements and questions reflect the desired outcome. Use summary statements or one of the several types of questioning techniques (see below) to keep the conversation on track. If you find yourself out on a tangent, use an appropriate statement or question to get back on course. Look for verbal and nonverbal feedback to determine if the other person received your message(s) and is interpreting it the way you intend.

Close: Use feedback techniques such as summary statements (e.g., "the most likely side effects you'll have are...") to make sure the issues discussed are mutually understood. Make any necessary contracts. Repeat specifically any agreements for action you both have made. Specify time requirements, milestones, and deadlines. Get a receipt in the form of verbal or nonverbal assurance that you achieved your desired outcomes.

QUESTIONING TECHNIQUES

Open-ended questions allow maximum freedom of response. "How does your medicine make you feel?" "What kind of reaction did you have?" "What type of infection are you treating?" "Tell me more..." Use this kind of question to open discussions, to explore sensitive areas, to elicit ideas, and to avoid biasing the answers.

Directive questions limit possible answers. "Does this drug cause you drowsiness or excitability?" "Are you using this drug for prophylaxis or treatment?" Use this type to guide conversation in a direction, to get a decision from several alternatives, or for a short specific answer.

Leading questions suggest the desired response within the question. "Surely you unwrapped the suppository before inserting it?" "Do you really want to dose the gentamicin four times a day?" Use leading questions to get approval of your opinion, to test how closely the two of you agree, or to introduce a new idea or approach. Be careful; leading questions bias the answers. They affect the accuracy and validity of the response.

Hypothetical questions pose a possibility or suggestion. "How about continuing the cream for one more week?" "What if we increased the dose?" Use these if you want to open discussion of alternatives, to introduce new ideas, to challenge an idea, or to lead the respondent toward a conclusion or agreement.

Specifier questions ask for specific information. "When did the rash begin?" "What is the diagnosis?" "Where is that emotion coming from?" Use this type to gather more definitive or additional information or to get the respondent to describe a feeling in greater detail.

Justifying questions ask for explanation of reasons, attitudes, or feelings. "What made you stop taking the drug?" "Why are you using this drug for this infection?" Use justifying questions to challenge the validity or authority of a decision, to find out the rationale, or to help the other person reason through the problem. Use this type with care; they may evoke an emotional or defensive response. Consider using other questioning techniques first.

NONVERBAL COMMUNICATION

Sherlock Holmes understood nonverbal communication exquisitely well. Sherlock Holmes would have made an excellent pharmacist. In "The Adventure of the Norwood Builder," Holmes easily diagnoses a client as an asthmatic from his labored breathing. Holmes' extraordinary powers of observation solve a dermatologic mystery in "The Adventure of the Lion's Mane." Many other tales in this Arthur Conan Doyle series provide an allegorical version of medical observation, interpretation, and diagnosis.

Pharmacists can make good use of nonverbal cues from patients. Hesitation, a questioning look, an embarrassed cough, and other clues can speak volumes about patients' concerns. Detailed articles about pharmacist-patient communication are now common and should be considered for a more in-depth analysis. But using nonverbal communication solely, without any other techniques, can be detrimental. This is particularly true if one makes incorrect assumptions (e.g., assume a nodding head equates to agreement or understanding).

PRESENTATIONS

When you give an oral presentation, keep several tips in mind. Keep an erect posture and good eye contact with your listeners. Use natural gestures, but not distracting ones. Use pauses for rhythm, emphasis, and punctuation. Use index cards to cue key words. Note how an index card can fit in the palm of your hand. If you will speak without a podium, write your notes in sequence down the long axis of the card; this trick will tend to hide the cards from the view of the audience.

Neither read nor memorize your address; understand your topic thoroughly and speak about it naturally. If your current style is reading or memorization, work toward the natural delivery goal progressively, not all at once. With each speech you give, make your outlines broader and more general. Over time, you will trust yourself to get each of your important points across, while presenting an individualized talk to the audience on hand. Audiences appreciate being talked to personally.

Audio-Visual Aids

Audio or visual aids should enhance your presentation, never distract from it. Use graphs, charts, or tables as summary tools whenever detailed information is presented. Never block the audience's view or hearing of your aids.

Always, always check out the room where you will speak, well before the address begins. Rehearse using your audiovisual aids in the same room as they will be presented. Keep the contents of posters, charts, slides, and transparencies legible and uncluttered. Sit where the audience will sit so you can see their view of your material. Do not apologize for illegible material; make it legible in the first place. If you want the audience to keep its attention on you, do not distribute handouts until the end of the presentation.

Written Communication

Effective writing is clear, concise, correct, complete, and appropriate. Effective writing saves time and money and contributes to personal and departmental image.

Intent

To write well, you must first define your purpose. What do you want the reader to know? to do? to think? to feel? State your purpose clearly, early, and in a positive way. Select a writing style and tone that enhances the image you want to portray. Readers will likely respond well to correspondence written in the same style as their messages to you.

Do not write impulsively. And avoid saying unpleasant things in writing. Deciding to write is as important as deciding what to say. Telephone calls or personal visits may be more appropriate than a written message, although a written follow-up may still be appropriate.

Good writing involves three major stages: preparation, writing, and revising. Always revise your first drafts. Letting a day or two pass between drafting and revising, if possible, will tend to let you see the message as your reader will see it.

Language

Avoid jargon and buzz words. Avoid replacing words with abbreviations, as is common in text messaging. Use specific words to avoid ambiguity. Write in the active voice (e.g., "John wrote the letter," rather than "The letter was written by John"). Speak as you write. People "hear" writing, and the natural flow of speech is pleasant to read.

Organization

Writing is a form of brainstorming. Writing down ideas helps you shape your argument and check your logic. If you are writing with bad news, consider how the reader will react. Use the deductive approach, telling the bad news right away, then explaining the reasons. Or use an inductive approach, building your argument before stating the purpose of the message. Do use introductory statements of good will, and then reinforce the good will in the concluding paragraph.

Organize written ideas by order of importance (for busy readers), chronological order (to tell stories), cause-and-effect sequence (when writing about problems), or by compare-and-contrast sequence (for descriptions and evaluations).

Effective-Writing Checklist

Is it clear? Is the purpose stated clearly? Does the reader know what response is desired or expected? Are ideas organized to persuade the reader to accomplish your purpose? Have you used language the reader could misunderstand?

Is it concise? Have you deleted all unnecessary information? Have you eliminated all redundant words and phrases? Do not say "in conjunction with" if "and" will suffice.

Is it correct? Have you confirmed the accuracy of all information? Have you double-checked grammar, spelling, and usage?

Is it complete? Does it contain all information needed to persuade the reader and enable the desired action? Doing research for the reader will help speed up the response.

Know Your Readers

Who is your reader? Who else is competing for your reader's time? Who is the reader likely to share your correspondence with? What is the reader's attitude toward you, your group, your subject? How much does the reader already know about the subject? How much evidence will it take to persuade the reader? What style and tone will the reader best respond to? Use the answers to customize your correspondence.

Grammar & Punctuation

Do not underestimate the value of grammar and proper punctuation. Disregarding the rules stands out like a sore thumb. Take time to proofread your work or ask for help from others. Lack of attention to detail reflect poorly on the writer. It may even cause the reader to question the validity of the content or the credibility of the writer.

DISCUSSION

This Module has scratched the surface on communication. We have not even begun to address barriers to communication or their resolution. We mean for this to be a thought-provoking Module, not an all-inclusive one. If we have raised questions in your mind about how to communicate more effectively, we have succeeded.

Check it out: libraries have specialized books and tapes on the subject; so do bookstores. Mastering communication can be a key to a more successful, more satisfying life.

Here is a rule of thumb for better communication: practice. Repeated efforts, trial and error, and learning from "mistakes" help us each become ever better.

To a great extent, excellent pharmacists are excellent communicators. Plan today how you can become a better communicator.

26.2. Resources needed:

Annex 26-1. Elocution Exercise

26.3. In-class activities:

"If I had to name a single all-purpose instrument of leadership, it would be communication." John W. Gardner

Step 1. Questions?
Step 2. Quote.
Step 3. Exercise.
What does the word impeccable mean?

THE GIRL WITH THE BEAUTIFUL VOICE

There was a woman who was intelligent and had a very good heart. She had a daughter whom she adored and loved very much. One night she came home from a very bad day at work, tired, full of emotional tension and with a terrible headache. She wanted peace and quiet, but her daughter was singing and jumping happily.

The daughter was unaware of how her mother was feeling. She was in her own world, in her own dream. She felt so wonderful and she was jumping and singing louder and louder, expressing her joy and her love. She was singing so loud that it made her mother's headache even worse. And at a certain moment, the mother lost control.

Angrily, she looked at her little girl. "Shut up, you have an ugly voice, can you just shut up!"

The daughter believed what her mother said and in that moment she made an agreement with herself. After that she no longer sang, because she believed her voice was ugly and would bother anyone who heard it. She became shy at school and if she was asked to sing, she refused. Even speaking to others became difficult for her. Everything changed in the little girl because of this new agreement. She believed she must repress her emotions to be accepted and loved.

This little girl grew up and even though she had a beautiful voice she never sang again. She developed a whole complex from one incident. The complex was created from the piercing comment made by the one person who loved her most—her mother. The little girl's mother never knew the damage she did with her word."

Adapted from: Ruíz DM. *The Four Agreements*.

Notes:

a. Questions for discussion:

    i. What do you think of the passage?

    ii. Was the mother impeccable?

    iii. What do you think about the way the little girl reacted?

    iv. What do you think about the "message" delivered by the mother and the long-term impact upon the daughter?

b. Summary

▷ The leader has great power.

▷ Simple words influence others – positively or negatively.

▷ Individuals are looking to the leader(s) to set the tone and direction for the group; they look to place trust in their leader(s).

▷ A tremendous amount of responsibility, not to mention obligation, to do all that can be done rests with the leader.

▷ In this effort, the leader must acknowledge the power that accompanies words and to manage this responsibility dutifully.

Step 4. Another way to think about ourselves is to liken our brains to a computer that is susceptible to a virus.

a. Think about it. How are emotions, feelings, thoughts, judgments, attitudes, opinions, or gossip transmitted between people? By words – written, spoken, unwritten, unspoken. Words are the agents by which emotions, feelings, judgments, and those others are transmitted.

b. Consider whether the following analogy – that of a computer and its susceptibility to viruses – can apply to that of our human minds. Consider the effect words can have.

THE POWER OF THE WORD

"A computer can be likened to the mind.

It calculates, stores, and processes data.

A computer accepts input readily and without discretion.

A virus can be introduced and, unless the computer has updated anti-virus software, the virus can run amuck and does.

The virus running amuck can cause dysfunction, which may vary in its degree.

The virus may then be transmitted via e-mail or thumb drive to other computers, starting a viral epidemic.

The energy and resources involved in managing an epidemic can be tremendous."

Source: Ruíz DM. *The Four Agreements*.

c. What are some ways a computer is like a human brain? What happens when the human brain is resilient against negative words (analogous to a computer with virus protection)? How is this different from the situation where a human brain is **fertile ground** for negative words to take root (like the young girl who never sang)?

194

✍ _____ ⌨

d. Thinking about it this way, why is it important for a leader to be cognizant of the words he or she chooses? What are the risks to the individual (and group), when a leader is inattentive?

Step 5. Writing Task #1: Respond to these questions:

Has there been a situation when your mind was fertile that accepted a critical or unintended idea?

a. Which seeds grow in your mind? In other words, how fertile is your mind when thoughts are planted? What do you do with them?

✍ _____ ⌨

b. Is your mind able to discriminate between the impeccable words of others or not? What is your obligation to cultivate your mind to recognize and embrace impeccable words?

✍ _____ ⌨

c. Which seeds would grow in the minds of those you lead? Are they able to discriminate between your impeccable words and those that may not be?

✍ _____ ⌨

d. Thus lies the responsibility you accept as the leader to use impeccable words. You cannot possibly know the degree of fertility that exists in the minds of those you lead.

Notes: ✍ _____ ⌨

e. Seriously consider your entries above and ways to help your peers and teammates develop defenses against negative (non-impeccable) words. This involves helping them to develop resources for finding motivation from within themselves to guard against negativity, gossip, assumptions, *et cetera*. Find other things you can do to communicate clear and consistent messages, often.

Keep members informed of the activities of the "leadership." Offer an open-door policy and encourage people to talk to you openly and honestly (realizing that what you hear may not be what you want to hear). Foster positive interaction between leaders and members and between members.

Focus on offering events that can develop relationships. Investment in others permits relationships to evolve and flourish. This also guards against "infertile" ground and forms the basis for productive, healthy group activity. Without strong relationships, leading the group to work to its potential will be difficult, if not impossible.

f. Consider the following exercise for grooming future officers—to consider the positive and negative aspects of words. Help them to realize the duty they must be impeccable with their words and actions.

Activity: How are emotions, feelings, thoughts, judgments, attitudes, opinions, or gossip transmitted between people?

Step 6. Writing Task #2: Respond to these questions:

a. Describe as many different functions that words can have on other people. For example, words can create beautiful poetry. Words can instill fear in others through intimidation. *Et cetera.*

✎ _____ ⌨

b. Who is willing to share some of the effects that words can do?

Positive Effects	Negative Effects
▸	▸
▸	▸
▸	▸
▸	▸
▸	▸
▸	▸

26.4. Discussion questions:

Name several ways that pharmacists can use their communication skills to improve the lives of their patients. Name several ways that pharmacists should take guard in their communication to avoid harming a patient.

26.5. After-class assignments:

A. Practice the communication techniques you learned in this Module in your daily life.
B. Fulfill the before-class activities for the next Module assigned by your facilitator.

26.6. Bibliography, references, & resources:

Caplan RM. "The Lion's Mane:" Concerning the diagnostic acumen of Sherlock Holmes. *Am J Dermatopathology* 1983;5:577-579.

Flashcards via Quizlet, https://quizlet.com/class/3716098/, Communication-Skills Lexicon » 8 terms

Frank MO. *How to Get Your Point Across in 30 Seconds—Or Less.* New York: Simon & Schuster, 1986.

Oliver CH. Communication awareness: Rx for embarrassing situations. *Am Pharm.* 1982;22: 533-535.

Polanski RE, Polanski VG. Environment for communication. *Am Pharm.* 1982;22:545-546.

Ruíz DM. *The Four Agreements: A Practical Guide to Personal Freedom.* NYC: Amber-Allen Publishing, 1997.

Weissman G: The game is afoot, or Holmes and Watson at Bellevue. *Discover* March 1986, 1416.

Witte KW, Bober KF. Developing a patient-education program in the community pharmacy. *Am Pharm.* 1982;22:540-544.

Zellmer WA. Let's talk. *Am J Hosp Pharm.* 1987;44:1323.

Annex 26-1. Elocution Exercise

Separate annex documents available to facilitators upon request (LeadGrowShape@plei.org).

Elocution, defined: The skill of clear and expressive speech, especially of distinct pronunciation and articulation. Radio announcers often have evocative and melodious forms of phrasing and pacing that help listeners absorb meaning, sense emotion, and visualize circumstances.

Session Goal: To help participants explore how variations in tone, speed, and emphasis convey meaning to listeners.

Purpose: Leaders are often called on to deliver greetings or specific remarks, participate on panels, lead ceremonies. Leaders typically craft their own messages suitable to the occasion. In other circumstances, leaders may be given other people's words to speak, such as with traditional or ritualized text at induction ceremonies or award presentations. At memorial services, people may be asked to read with meaning passages from the Torah, Bible, or Qur'an or writings of the philosophers.

If given a script, you can choose to simply say the words in a monotone voice. Or you can study the passage and bring it alive with your voice, your inflection, the nuances you give the words.

A full discussion of rhetorical appeal is beyond the scope of this exercise. But these activities may help participants begin to appreciate the topic and identify an interest in learning more.

Meaning:

- ‣ In these settings, the audience is often looking to the speaker at the podium for inspiration, tradition, and morale building.
- ‣ The speaker needs to understand the context, the audience, and have a goal. What is the purpose of and the meaning behind the words? It could be to:
  - ▷ Give information...
  - ▷ Explain...
  - ▷ Inspire...
  - ▷ Threaten...
  - ▷ Persuade...
  - ▷ Share emotion...
  - ▷ Ask (or beg) ...
  - ▷ Question (or doubt) ...

General Principles:

1. Emphasize the new idea or contrast; subdue the old idea.

   Lewis Carroll: "My rule for knowing which word to lean on is the word that tells you something new, something that is different from what you expected."

   The emphasis may contrast similar or different parts of speech (e.g., nouns, verbs, adjectives, etc.)

2. First-time-ness: Sound as if you are saying the words for the first time.

3. Take advantage of the punctuation, road signs on the vocal highway.

   Be alert, though. The primary goal of punctuation is to convey logic. There will be times when the intended meaning of the speaker will override a logical interpretation of punctuation.

4. Pace yourself: Slowing the rate of speech arrests the attention of listeners. Try slow and fast deliveries of the indented sentence. Try it again, variously putting emphasis on the first word, then the fourth

word, then the fifth word. Alternately, insert very short pauses between words.

» "He has truthfulness and integrity."

5. Speaking more softly attracts attention, for similar reasons.

6. Abrupt changes in speed or volume attracts attention.

7. Any time you are in an audience, observe the subtleties of sound, sense, and structure used by the speakers. Goal: Spontaneity, enjoyment.

Prescription: Rehearse aloud and experiment in rehearsal.

▸

So, let's continue with part 1 of a **practical exercise** in elocution. Your facilitator will give several of you passages to read with meaning.

▸

Now, part 2, using selected passages from William Shakespeare's *Romeo and Juliet*. Use some or all of these passages to experiment with pacing, emphasis, volume, and other vocal attributes. Pay attention to whether the intended emotion is love, humor, anger, reflection, or other emotions. Your facilitator will guide you.

9. Romeo: "Under love's heavy burden do I sink.
[Act 1, Scene 4]

10. Juliet: "My lips, two blushing pilgrims, ready stand
To smooth that rough touch with a tender kiss."
[Act 1, Scene 5]

11. Romeo: "Is love a tender thing? it is too rough,
Too rude, too boisterous, and it pricks like thorn."
[Act 1, Scene 4]

12. Tybalt [nephew to Lady Capulet]:
"...talk of peace! I hate the word,
As I hate hell, all Montagues, and thee..."
[Act 1, Scene 1]

13. Romeo [as Juliet appears above at a window]
"But, soft! what light through yonder window breaks?
It is the east, and Juliet is the sun.
Arise, fair sun, and kill the envious moon..."
[Act 2, Scene 2]

14. Juliet: "Romeo, Romeo, wherefore art thou Romeo?"
Deny thy father and refuse thy name."
[Act 2, Scene 2]

15. Romeo: "The brightness of her cheek would shame those stars,
As daylight doth a lamp; ..."
[Act 2, Scene 2]

16. Juliet [to Nurse]: "How art thou out of breath when thou hast breath
To say to me that thou art out of breath?"
[Act 2, Scene 5]

17. Romeo: "See how she leans her cheek upon her hand.
O, that I were a glove upon that hand
That I might touch that cheek!"
[Act 2, Scene 2]

18. Juliet: "My bounty is as boundless as the sea,
My love as deep; the more I give to thee,
The more I have, for both are infinite."
[Act 2, Scene 2]

19. Romeo: "It is my lady, O, it is my love!
O, that she knew she were!"
[Act 2, Scene 2]

20. Juliet: "Parting is such sweet sorrow,
That I shall say good night till it be morrow."
[Act 2, Scene 2]

21. Friar Laurence:
"Wisely and slow; they stumble that run fast."
[Act 2, Scene 3]

22. Juliet: "What's in a name? that which we call a rose
By any other name would smell as sweet."
[Act 2, Scene 2]

23. Romeo: "I must be gone and live, or stay and die."
[Act 3, Scene 5]

24. Second Servant:
"...'tis an ill cook that cannot lick his own fingers..."
[Act 4, Scene 4]

25. Romeo: "O true apothecary!
Thy drugs are quick. Thus with a kiss I die."
[Act 5, Scene 3]

Bibliography, references, & resources:

Aggertt OJ, Bowen ER. *Communicative Reading*. New York: Macmillan Co., 1956.
Bertram JD. *The Oral Experience of Literature: Sense, Structure, Sound*. San Francisco: Chandler Publishing
    Co., 1967.

Lamar NN. *How to Speak the Written Word: A Guide to Effective Public Reading*, rev. ed. Old Tappan, NJ: Fleming H. Revell Co., 1967.

Shakespeare W. *Romeo and Juliet*, 1597. Accessed at http://learningstorm.org/wp-content/uploads/2016/02/RMEOJLET-1.pdf

Annex 26-2. Communication Crossword Puzzle

Separate annex documents available to facilitators upon request (LeadGrowShape@plei.org).

Across
4. Type of questions that pose a suggestion
6. The only way to get your wish
7. Type of questions that ask for explanation of reasons

Down
1. Definition of your purpose
2. Type of questions that limit possible answers
3. Type of questions that ask for specific information
4. Statement or object to get attention
5. Type of questions that suggest the desired response

Module « **27** »   HOW DEEPLY DO YOU COMMUNICATE?

☞ Learning Objectives:

Objective 1. To learn the five levels of communication as described by John Powell.
Objective 2. To consider the depth of sharing in which participants engage with various individuals.
Objective 3. To broaden the awareness of involvement that participants have with others.

We talk to other people pretty much every day. But have you ever stopped to measure the depth of those conversations. You probably are shallow or reserved with some people and more expansive with others.

This Module explores communication in a way that promotes awareness of how people engage with others. The ability to cultivate relationships is pivotal to an effective leader. Because communication can be such an ethereal concept, participants will work to unravel its mysteries.

27.1. Readings or activities <u>before class</u>:

Read and be prepared to discuss the following text regarding Powell's Five Levels of Communication.

John Powell's 1975 book, *Why I am Afraid to Tell You Who I Am?*, describes five levels on which humans communicate. Understanding each level is essential for leaders.

Level 5: <u>**Small Talk**</u>. Shallow conversation, such as "How are you?" or "What are you doing?" Such conversation borders on the meaningless, but it may be better than awkward silence. A common, often reflex answer is "Fine." Communication remaining on this level is boring and little information is shared. In marriage, shallow conversation can lead to frustration and resentment.

Level 4: <u>**Factual Conversation**</u>. Information is shared, but without personal comments. You tell what has happened, but do not reveal how you feel about it. A wife may observe her partner leaving the house after dinner and ask, "Where are you going?" and he can give a factual answer, "Out." Friends who have not seen each other for a long-time may connect on this level, as they exchange information on people they know in common. However, the information shared tends to be about others only. Gossip (quasi-facts) may be found at this level.

Level 3: <u>**Ideas & Opinions**</u>. Real intimacy begins here. On this level, you risk exposing your own thoughts, feelings, and opinions. Because you can express yourself and verbalize personal ideas, your partner has a better chance to know you intimately. Level 3 typically occurs only after the waters have been tested and determined to be "safe." A topic is raised, your partner's opinion on the topic is revealed, and you judge that it is okay for you to proceed and share more personal information.

Level 2: <u>**Feelings & Emotions**</u>. Such communication describes what is going on inside you—how you feel about a situation. You verbalize feelings of frustration, anger, resentment, or happiness. If you honestly share with your partner in a give-and-take manner, showing interest in the other's feelings as well as in expressing your own, this level will enrich and enlarge your relationship. But give-and-take and expressing your own feelings about a situation does not need to occur at this exact moment. Instead, listening well may be more appropriate.

Level 1: **Deep Insight**. Rare insightful moments will occur when you are perfectly in tune with another in understanding, depth, and emotional satisfaction. Usually a peak experience or something deeply personal is related. Communication about such experiences often makes a deep impression on both parties and enriches the relationships.

Quality of Communication Levels

Quality	Level 5	Level 4	Level 3	Level 2	Level 1
Degree of Loneliness	High	Moderate	Low	Low	Lowest
Amount of Commitment	Low	Low	Moderate	High	Highest
Quality of Communication	Poor	Poor	Moderate	High	Highest
How "Personal"	Little	Little	Reserved	More	A lot
Intention/Meaning	None	None	Moderate	High	Highest
Degree of Safety	Low	Low	Moderate	High	Highest

Adapted from: Powell J. *Why Am I Afraid to Tell You Who I Am? Insights into Personal Growth.* New York: Fontana Press, 1975.

27.2. Resources needed:

Annex 27-1. Role-Play Scripts

27.3. In-class activities:

"The single biggest problem in communication is the illusion that it has taken place." George Bernard Shaw

Step 1. Questions?
Step 2. Quote.
Step 3. Exercise.

FIVE LEVELS OF COMMUNICATION

a. Role-Play Scripts.

Read each script in Annex 27-1 conversationally and do not add or subtract or embellish. The scripts are written to illustrate the differences between the different levels of communication.

Scripts 1, 2 and 3 are offered twice. They are first offered in a bundle, read sequentially with only a slight pause between them. This allows participants to compare and contrast the levels (Level 5, 4 and 3).

Then Script 1 (Level 5) is repeated with additional lines. Read it, then discuss it.

Then repeat Script 2 (Level 4) and discuss it.

And so on, through Script 4 (Level 2).

27.4. Discussion questions:

Per facilitator …

Which level(s) of communication are most appropriate, most common in pharmacy practice?

Match the term with the correct definition:

1. Deep insight	—	a. Communication in which you risk exposing your own thoughts, feelings, and opinions.
2. Factual conversation	—	b. Communication that describes what is going on inside you—how you feel about a situation.
3. Feelings and emotions	__	c. Communication where both parties are in tune with each another in understanding, depth, and emotional satisfaction.
4. Ideas and opinions	__	d. Information is shared, but without personal comments.
5. Small talk.	__	e. Shallow conversation, such as "How are you?"

27.5. After-class assignments:

A. Practice the communication techniques you learned in this Module in your everyday life.
B. Fulfill the before-class activities for the next Module assigned by your facilitator.

27.6. Bibliography, references, & resources:

Flashcards via Quizlet, https://quizlet.com/class/3716098/, Communication Depth (Powell) » 5 terms
Powell J. *Why Am I Afraid to Tell You Who I Am? Insights into Personal Growth*. New York: Fontana Press, 1975.

Annex 27-1. Role-Play Scripts

Separate annex documents available to facilitators upon request (LeadGrowShape@plei.org).

Volunteers will read each script conversationally; do not add or subtract or embellish. The scripts are written to illustrate the differences between the different levels of communication.

All other participants should listen to the volunteers, rather than reading along.

Scripts 1, 2 and 3 are offered twice. They are first offered in a bundle, read sequentially with only a slight pause between them. This allows participants to compare and contrast the levels (Level 5, 4 and 3).

Then Script 1 (Level 5) is repeated with additional lines. Read it, then discuss it.

Then repeat Script 2 (Level 4) and discuss it.

And so on, through Script 4 (Level 2).

SCRIPTS 1, 2 & 3 – FIRST READING, THREE IN A ROW

Script 1 (Level-5 Communication) – 1st Reading

Person 1: "Hi, how are you?"

Person 2: "I'm fine, thanks. How are you?"

Person 1: "I'm okay. Is that a new haircut for you?"

Person 2: "Why, yes, it is. Thanks for noticing."

Person 1: "Sure, I thought you looked different."

Person 2: "It is not a different cut, only freshly done."

Person 1: "Oh, well, it is good to see you."

Person 2: "Thanks, you too."

–END–

Script 2 (Level-4 Communication) – 1st Reading

Person 1: "Did you hear about Jeff's promotion to district supervisor?"

Person 2: "No, I didn't know he was up for promotion."

Person 1: "Yep. He has only been with the company for 2 years."

Person 2: "I thought he was only going to stay as long as the sign-on bonus criteria dictated."

Person 1: "Me too! This is a complete surprise!"

Person 2: "He must have been offered a lot of money or he must be misbehaving somehow."

Person 1: "Come on. Do you really think so?"

Person 2: "Well, why not? His reputation in school was such that this would not be a stretch of the truth."

Person 1: "Well, okay. I guess you are right. Hmmm..."

–END–

Script 3 (Level-3 Communication) – 1st Reading

Person 1: "I went to the movies recently. I saw *Spiderman*."

Person 2: "I finally got around to seeing it, as well. It was really good!"

Person 1: "Yea, I liked the action mixed in with the emotion and seriousness."

Person 2: "Yea, me too! My head began to hurt trying to follow all of the movement from building to building."

Person 1: "I got choked up when Uncle Ben said, 'With great power comes great responsibility.'"

Person 2: "I did too, but I had no idea he would die."

Person 1: "Me either. I felt so sad for Spiderman."

Person 2: "I did too! I got choked up. Thank goodness for the action scene immediately following."

Person 1: "I wish today's leaders would embrace that same kind of motto."

Person 2: "I had not thought about it, but I agree with you wholeheartedly."

Person 1: "Speaking to that, that is some shocking news on TV this morning, was it not?"

Person 2: "What part?"

Person 1: "Well, you know. The child-abuse scandal downtown..."

Person 2: "Oh, that." [Brushed off topic with a shrug]

Person 1: "Well, I have a young child. I often wonder if I would be aware of any violations if he was involved."

Person 2: "Why worry about something that has not happened?"

Person 1: "Well, I am not worried. I wonder if I would be open enough to pick up on it, as it was happening."

Person 2: "You are a good parent and you would! What do you think we should get for lunch?"

Person 1: "Well, there is this new restaurant that opened up..."

–END–

Script 1 (Level-5 Communication) – 2nd Reading

Person 1: "Hi, how are you?"

Person 2: "I'm fine, thanks. How are you?"

Person 1: "I'm okay. Is that a new haircut for you?"

Person 2: "Why, yes, it is. Thanks for noticing."

Person 1: "Sure, I thought you looked different."

Person 2: "It is not a different cut, only freshly done."

Person 1: "Oh, well, it is good to see you."

Person 2: "Thanks, you too."

–END–

1. What do you think about this exchange?

2. What do you think about the quality of this exchange?

3. What percent of time do you spend engaging in this kind of exchange?

4. What if one of the questions was answered differently.

Script 1 (Level-5 Communication) – 2nd Reading, Repeat with Alternate Text

Person 1: "Hi, how are you?"

Person 2: "I am fine, thanks." "How are you?"

Person 1 [*in serious, troubled voice*]: "Well, I am feeling troubled over all things I read about in the news these days: refugees and poverty and climate change. I wonder whether it would be wise to bring children into this world. It is such a troubling time… I am generally an optimist, but I am also a realist and find that I have a responsibility to think this decision through carefully."

–END–

What was different? What did you see in Person #2? How should Person #2 respond?

✍ _____ ⌨

Script 2 (Level-4 Communication) – 2nd Reading

Person 1: "Did you hear about Jeff's promotion to district supervisor?"

Person 2: "No, I didn't know he was up for promotion."

Person 1: "Yep. He has only been with the company for 2 years."

Person 2: "I thought he was only going to stay as long as the sign-on bonus criteria dictated."

Person 1: "Me too! This is a complete surprise."

Person 2: "He must have been offered a lot of money or he must be misbehaving somehow."

Person 1: "Come on. Do you really think so?"

Person 2: "Well, why not? His reputation in school was such that this would not be a stretch of the truth."

Person 1: "Well, okay. I guess you are right. Hmmm…"

–END–

1. What do you think about this exchange?

2. What do you think about the <u>quality</u> of this exchange?

3. What percent of time do you spend engaging in this kind of exchange?

✍ _____ ⌨

Script 3 (Level-3 Communication) – 2nd Reading

Person 1: "I went to the movies recently. I saw *Spiderman*."

Person 2: "I finally got around to seeing it, as well. It was really good!"

Person 1: "Yea, I liked the action mixed in with the emotion and seriousness."

Person 2: "Yea, me too! My head began to hurt trying to follow all of the movement from building to building."

Person 1: "I got choked up when Uncle Ben said, 'With great power comes great responsibility.'"

Person 2: "I did too, but I had no idea he would die."

Person 1: "Me either. I felt so sad for Spiderman."

Person 2: "I did too! I got choked up. Thank goodness for the action scene immediately following."

Person 1: "I wish today's leaders would embrace that same kind of motto."

Person 2: "I had not thought about it, but I agree with you wholeheartedly."

Person 1: "Speaking to that, that is some shocking news on TV this morning, was it not?"

Person 2: "What part?"

Person 1: "Well, you know. The child-abuse scandal downtown…"

Person 2: "Oh, that." [Brushed off topic with a shrug]

Person 1: "Well, I have a young child. I often wonder if I would be aware of any violations if he was involved."

Person 2: "Why worry about something that has not happened?"

Person 1: "Well, I am not worried. I wonder if I would be open enough to pick up on it, as it was happening."

Person 2: "You are a good parent and you would! What do you think we should get for lunch?"

Person 1: "Well, there is this new restaurant that opened up..."

–END–

1. What do you think about this exchange?

2. What do you think about the quality of this exchange?

3. What percent of time do you spend engaging in this kind of exchanges?

Script 4 (Level-2 Communication) – 1st Reading

Person 1: "You know, I just finished teaching this geriatrics course and I was amazed and somewhat saddened that my students discussed death as the textbooks said they would. They discussed it with a level of un-comfortableness and an air of disregard. Many of them could not understand why we were discussing it and this exasperated me. Even the students whom I have grown to respect behaved in this way."

Person 2: "That must have been hard for you to experience, but I'll bet you have grown tremendously based on all of the research you had to do for the class. What are your views on death as they relate to your parents?"

Person 1: "Well, I can honestly say that I better appreciate their wishes. As a small child, I can remember being afraid that my parents would not be with me throughout my life. They were supposed to be there; it was their job. I can remember praying that they would not leave me. Now, and especially after teaching the course, I no longer feel anxiety or anger when they discuss their wishes in my presence."

Person 2: "What are their wishes?"

Person 1: "Well, they would like comfort care only. They do not want to be engaged in care that will cause them to suffer more than they already would at that point. I never believed I could support this wish because of my needs and my belief about "their job." But now, I think that I am strong enough to acknowledge and respect their wishes. I would be a fierce advocate for making sure they had comfort care. I imagine that the joy that I would feel honoring their wishes would provide me with a bit of solace while I worked through my dark and lonely moments of grief due to their death."

–END–

b. Observations/comments: _____

The next questions are asked to help you establish a baseline for comparison later. Answer these questions in detail, either now or when you have enough time to ponder carefully. If you have not considered these ideas before, take some time soon to think about this and determine your position.

c. How do you define communication?

✎ _____ ⌨

d. What makes communication effective (e.g., necessary ingredients)?

✎ _____ ⌨

e. With whom do you communicate? Is it an effective interaction? Name individuals or groups that fall in to this category?

✎ _____ ⌨

f. Why make the effort to communicate?

✎ _____ ⌨

g. What makes the communication meaningful?

✎ _____ ⌨

Leaders and accomplished followers [Module 24 discusses followership] are responsible to continually improve their communication skills. Attention to this area contributes to high functioning teams; the opposite can happen if communication is ignored.

Module « 28 »   FOSTERING AUTHENTIC COMMUNICATION

☞ Learning Objectives:

Objective 1. To learn the communication technique known as Diamonds & Stones (more useful when participants already know each other to some extent).
Objective 2. To learn how candid feedback helps leaders improve.
Objective 3. To help participants express personal opinions about controversial issues confidentially.

"What we've got here is failure to communicate." Famous quotation from *Cool Hand Luke* (Warner Bros., 1967), spoken in the movie first by Strother Martin (as The Captain, a prison warden) and later, slightly differently, by Paul Newman (as Luke, a stubborn prisoner).

A lack of communication threatens many groups. If people are too polite or nonconfrontational, the group can suffer. But how can one bring up sensitive subjects? How can you tell someone the truth, if that person could feel insulted or ridiculed? This exercise demonstrates a useful method to help people open up and talk, particularly about difficult subjects.

28.1. Readings or activities before class:

Read and be prepared to discuss the text for this Module.

28.2. Resources needed:

3- by 5-inch cards [in Canada, that would be 76 by 127 mm] or other sheets of paper

28.3. In-class activities:

"Everything becomes a little different as soon as it is spoken out loud." Hermann Hesse

Step 1. Questions?
Step 2. Quote.
Step 3. Exercise.

DIAMONDS & STONES

It is frequently difficult to get people to open up and tell you what they really think or feel. This is particularly true when the subject being discussed is strongly emotional or personal.

Many people are shy about speaking in group situations, or choose not to speak out when they think their opinion is unpopular. Introverts may need a bit more time to reply to questions than extroverts do.

Despite this, leaders know the value of letting everyone have a chance to voice their opinion, and to hear unpopular opinions. Leaders are also keenly aware of the value of getting a "report card" on their personal

210

performance. It can be difficult to get people to say exactly what they think about one another, about each other's performance, or good and bad characteristics.

First, describe the scenario. Will the exercise evaluate the performance of the leaders of one of the student groups or the class officers or some other group of leaders for whom feedback is desired?

a. The entire Diamonds & Stones process should be communicated to the group before starting. This will facilitate each member feeling secure in the confidentiality of his/her personal responses.

b. Each participant is given a 3"x5" card. On one side of the card, the participant writes at the top of the card "DIAMONDS" and on the reverse side writes at the top of the card "STONES." The facilitator then asks each participant to take 5 minutes to silently write down responses to the following tasks:

▷ On the diamonds side, write down the three best characteristics or talents of the last leader of a group [ideally, someone known to all in the room]. What did you most admire about this person?

▷ On the stones side, write down the opposite, three major limitations of that leader.

Alternately, this tool can be useful to open discussions on emotional or personal topics, such as:

▷ A debate on changing a major policy of the group.

▷ A decision to expel a member of the group.

▷ A discussion on how to handle a major complaint against the group.

c. The facilitator collects the cards, shuffles them, and redistributes them to the participants, such that no one receives his/her own card. If this happens by chance, that participant hands back the card and picks another card at random, then the deck is shuffled again. If desired, the group can be divided into smaller discussion groups of four to eight people each. In either the large group, or smaller groups, each participant reads aloud the diamonds and stones answers and explains to the group in his/her **own words** his/her understanding of the statements on the card. The original author of the card is not allowed to speak or correct the spoken interpretation. A recorder for the group may wish to record a list of all the answers given.

d. If smaller discussion groups were used, reassemble the larger group. Each recorder briefly presents the list of reasons to support or reject. A group discussion, vote, or evaluation of the leadership of the group can now occur with everyone feeling satisfied with his/her opportunity to have a voice in the process.

e. Write down three or more topics you believe would be useful in which to conduct a "Diamonds & Stones" session with your group. Share these with the group.

28.4. Discussion questions:

When should (and when shouldn't) a pharmacist make himself or herself own to criticism?

28.5. After-class assignments:

A. Use the Diamonds & Stones exercise with some group you are involved in.
B. Fulfill the before-class activities for the next Module assigned by your facilitator.

28.6. Bibliography, references, & resources:

See Module Z

Module « 29 »   GETTING ALIGNED ON GOALS

☞ Learning Objectives:

Objective 1. To describe an information-gathering technique called nominal group technique.
Objective 2. To describe the utility of listening to ideas nonjudgmentally before comparing options.
Objective 3. To understand the importance of goals to an organization.
Objective 4. To consider how to match organizational goals to personal needs and goals of members.

This Module explores goal-setting, exploring an approach called the nominal group technique (NGT).

Where do we go from here? The oft-paraphrased advice of the Cheshire cat from *Alice's Adventures in Wonderland* is appropriate: if you do not know where you are going, it does not matter which route you take.

What are your personal goals? Do you want to own your own pharmacy, be director of your department, be elected to city council, get another degree?

We should also consider that when individuals come together to form groups, the individuals may see the goals of the collective in different ways. We will review proven techniques for identifying your own goals, your family's collective goals, the goals of everyone in your social group or pharmacy.

This Module describes the importance of enumerating specific group goals, so that all members of the team can pull in the same direction. It trains leaders in how to obtain information about members' desires for the organization.

29.1. Readings or activities before class:

Read and be prepared to implement the steps described below to conduct the nominal group technique.

29.2. Resources needed:

None other than this Module

29.3. In-class activities:

"You've got a bunch of mountains.
When you climb one, then you've got another one to climb and another one.
When you get to the top of one mountain, interest declines.
There's more work to be done." Maurice R. Hilleman

Step 1. Questions?
Step 2. Quote.
Step 3. Exercise.

DECIDE & RANK GROUP GOALS

SITUATION: While our group was caught up in the excitement of learning of the new P1 members, we neglected to take time to decide what we wanted our involvement in our group to accomplish. Now is the best time to answer "Why am I really involved in _____?"

NOMINAL GROUP TECHNIQUE

Step 1. Understand the process of nominal group technique:

a. Nominal group technique (NGT) is a means of obtaining information from a small group of participants (usually no more than 10 to 12) about their ideas and priorities. It is a good tool to use at officers' retreats or by committees and task forces.

b. Each participant spends 5 minutes silently writing down single word or short-phrase answers to the question, **"What are the specific goals I want our group to achieve?"** *[as you will see, it is also possible to insert other questions that can have multiple answers]* No talking is allowed. All thoughts should be written down, no matter how off-the-wall or unconventional. Creativity is encouraged.

c. A recorder asks for one answer from each participant in sequence, and writes them on a flip paper or white board. **NO COMMENTS** are allowed from the other participants, NO CRITICISM, *NOR ANY COMPLIMENTS.* This format prevents dominant members from monopolizing discussion. *Even shy people have full opportunity to provide input.* The absence of criticism is one of the most important features of the nominal group technique.

d. Each person in turn contributes an idea, going repeatedly around the circle. The recorder contributes the first idea in each round and writes it down. Each item should be numbered sequentially. Duplicate answers should not be repeated, but new ideas generated by a previous comment are allowed. Members who have contributed all their ideas may say "Pass" and the recorder goes to the next person. If a person who has said "Pass" subsequently thinks of a new idea, he or she may contribute it at his or her next turn. This process continues until everyone around the circle says "Pass."

e. The recorder reads each idea in turn and anyone who is confused about the meaning of the item should ask for clarification, but arguments for or against an idea are not allowed. The rules-keeper should be alert here to deny attempts at argument or persuasion. Consolidate any duplicate or similar answers.

f. From the list, participants choose their favorite ideas. USE SECRET BALLOTS (this is extremely important to prevent dominance by vocal participants). Each participant can vote for 10% of the total number of contributions. For example, if 64 ideas were generated, each participant should cast seven ballots, assigning 7 points to his favorite idea, 6 points to the next favorite, then 5, and so on, until finally, 1 point for the least favorite idea. To assure counting accuracy, ask each participant to print on the ballot the point value (P=) and the idea number (I=) and at least one word of the idea. Repeat these instructions as often as necessary to assure people do not invert the numbers accidentally.

g. All the vote scores are added up and reported to the team members. Each team member should record the goals in his or her syllabus. The top vote getters should be considered as the top priorities for the group.

h. The advantage of NGT is that answers to the question asked are provided with the minimum amount of *argument* and *persuasion.* Answers should be considered on their own merits, not on how well they were presented. If vociferous participants object to the results of the vote, point out that these are nonetheless the considered opinion of the whole group.

Step 2. Form purposeful groups. Members of fraternity A, fraternity B, APhA-ASP, CASPI, or any other social group can get together (but not more than 10 to 12 people per cluster), so that their exercise work can have practical value to them. Unaffiliated participants can gather together and agree quickly to organize the question for some common purpose, such as improving conditions of some kind on campus. Or they could explore whether the need is strong enough to form some new group on campus, that would tackle

goals no other group has yet focused on.
"What are the specific goals I want our group to achieve?" Top 10 responses:

a. _____

b. _____

c. _____

d. _____

e. _____

f. _____

g. _____

h. _____

i. _____

j. _____

Step 3. Recopy the top 10 answers onto one sheet of poster paper.

a. Develop an action plan, identifying specific activities designed to accomplish the goals listed. Name the office of the person most likely to be responsible for each activity.

b. Remember to differentiate between:

- **Goal:** What you want to have happen. The ends toward which effort and action are directed or coordinated.
- **Strategy:** The broad approach you chose to help reach your goal.
- **Tactics:** Devices or actions taken to achieve a larger purpose. Narrow approaches to implement the strategy for reaching your goal.
- **Tasks:** Pieces of work to be done, to implement your tactics

To accomplish a goal of increased fund raising, you may adopt a strategy of involving more members, using the tactic of distributing raffle tickets to each of them. The tasks involved would be obtaining prizes, printing the tickets, depositing the proceeds, *et cetera*.

29.4. Discussion questions:

How often should a pharmacy team go about goal setting? Monthly? Annually? Under what circumstances?

Nominal Group Technique: Optional Quiz

1. The primary advantage of the nominal group technique (NGT) is:

    a. Even shy people have full opportunity for input.

    b. Balloting is done orally.

    c. Participants can argue over their priorities.

    d. Very little time is required.

2. Which of the following is NOT a characteristic of the nominal group technique (NGT)?

    a. The absence of criticism.

    b. Participants may say "Pass."

    c. Persuasion is appropriate.

    d. Clarification is permitted if absolutely needed.

3. The word indicating what you want to have happen is:

    a. goal

    b. strategy

    c. tactic

    d. task

4. The word indicating the broad approach you chose to help reach your goal is:

    a. goal

    b. strategy

    c. task

    d. standard

5. In the nominal group technique, one should always compliment responses with which you agree.

    a. True

    b. False

29.5. After-class assignments:

A. Use the nominal group technique for information gathering, goal setting, or prioritizing with a group you are involved with.

B. Fulfill the before-class activities for the next Module assigned by your facilitator.

29.6. Bibliography, references, & resources:

Delbecq AL, VandeVen AH. A group process model for problem identification and program planning. *J Applied Behav Sci*. 1971;7:466–91.

Delbecq AL, VandeVen AH, Gustafson DH. *Group Techniques for Program Planning: A Guide to Nominal Group and Delphi Processes*. Glenview, Illinois: Scott Foresman & Co., 1975.

Flashcards via Quizlet, https://quizlet.com/class/3716098/, Goal Alignment » 4 terms

Justice J, Jang R. Tapping employee insights with the nominal group technique. *Am Pharm*. 1990;30:603-5.

Module « 30 »   MEETING MANAGEMENT, GROUP FUNCTION

☞ Learning Objectives:

Objective 1. To describe best practices for maximizing the utility of the time when people gather in meetings.
Objective 2. To describe strategies for identifying important needs an organization can fulfill.
Objective 3. To describe the relationship between need fulfillment and member engagement.

This Module is all about meetings. While meetings are an effective communication tool when managed properly, they can easily be ineffective, wasteful of time (time = money), and frustrating to both chairs and members. Fear not, we will teach you best practices in meeting management.

Every year, organizations that were once great suddenly disappear. Why? For many, the simple answer is that they became irrelevant, losing touch with the needs of the individuals they were created to serve. This program will guide participants through an inquiry regarding the needs their organization meets (or does not meet) for them, their peers, and the community.

30.1. Readings or activities before class:

Read and be prepared to discuss the following text during class.
After reading, complete Annex 30-4: Parliamentary Procedure Crossword Puzzle (or follow facilitator instructions).

Have you found yourself sitting in meetings that did nothing but eat up the clock? Have you chaired meetings with the same problem? Meetings are great opportunities for problem-solving and team-building. We will describe the secrets to make meetings worth the time invested in them.

Leaders and managers are frequently called upon to chair meetings of peers, subordinates, or associates. In some cases, the leader chairs an assembly of the whole group, in some cases a committee. Committee membership generally defines an action-oriented team, whose work will benefit the larger organization. The business and policy decisions of meetings, and the information exchange that accompanies them, are often of high significance and consequence to the groups involved.

Yet it is not unusual to hear members, and even chairs (chairmen and chairwomen), complain that meetings occupy too much time, more time than they are worth. And decision making is shamefully rare in many assemblies. The costs associated with bringing people together for meetings are considerable: hundreds of dollars per hour for just the time costs of a dozen pharmacists gathering in the same room. In this Module, we will look at the meeting process and propose ways for you to improve your meetings.

ON GROUP FUNCTION & DYSFUNCTION

Bradford claims that every meeting involves three simultaneous operations:
- task activity (work on the stated agenda),
- maintenance (attending to the needs of the members), and
- team building (strengthening group capacity to face future issues).

216

"In an effective, fully functioning meeting, all three operations will receive some attention. If the group needs to attend to a member's personal feelings or problems, it does so, and then returns to the task. If an opportunity for developing problem-solving skills among members occurs, the group diverts from the task to do some team building."

Events during the meeting that detract from proper group function include:

- reaction to the agenda (e.g., frustration due to insufficient information, an absent party influencing the "real" decision),
- conflict within the group (e.g., blocking the majority, punishing the chair, competition for influence, pressures from other groups),
- lack of communication skills (e.g., poor oral communication skills, poor listening skills, lack of assertiveness or proper confrontation skills),
- apathy (e.g., unproductive experiences, sense of hopelessness, perceived lack of influence, leader dominance, lack of interest in purpose), and
- fear of decision making (e.g., fear of responsibility or risk, disruption of status quo, avoidance of work).

Indications that a group is not functioning correctly include avoidance of the task, impatience among members, attacks on ideas before they are fully expressed, inactive listening, disagreement and polarization, subtle interpersonal attacks, discouragement, hip-pocket agendas, rejection of new group members, discouragement at the loss of a group member, rise or fall of noise level or tempo in the group, a string of unquestioned decisions coupled with lack of implementation of those decisions, or inability to make decisions.

Conversely, the characteristics of a mature group are involvement (a sense of ownership), assumption of responsibility by members for their own behavior and for contributing to the group, trust and caring, acceptance of diverse resources, active listening, self-examination without defensiveness, experimentation, acceptance of subgroups, dealing with differences forthrightly, recognition of flight behavior, acceptance of new members, and acknowledgment of hidden agenda.

MEETING FUNCTIONS & ROLES

The sense of identity that membership conveys to members is paramount to group function. According to Jay, meetings have one major advantage compared to other communication devices: **meetings define the team**. Those present belong; those absent do not.

Meetings are the place where the group updates what it knows as a group. Meetings allow understanding of the collective goals of the group and how individuals contribute to group success. Meetings enable commitment to group decisions.

Kelly uses the metaphor of drama and the theater to describe meetings. He alludes to protagonists and antagonists, each seeking approval of their individual agenda. He also notes the conflict between traditional democratic values and task-oriented values. The first favors free expression of opinions and protection of minorities, while the latter recognizes the need to develop consensus and meet schedules.

But meetings do not exist solely for their social function. Committees exist for action and reports of committee action are intended to enable further action. Leaders should convene a meeting to solve a problem, not just to gather together.

The committee chair is responsible for planning an agenda, conducting the meeting, maintaining records, getting action, and evaluating results. The role of the meeting conductor is that of a leader. The chair stimulates group thinking, encourages and channels discussion, weighs the value of expressed ideas, summarizes constructive suggestions, and seeks decisions.

Many authors concur that meeting leaders should not overly emphasize parliamentary procedure, because too much rigidity or aloofness by the chair is an abdication of responsibility to guide the meeting. Carnes calls the chair the clarifier of debate. Even General Henry M. Robert (of *Robert's Rules of Order*) allowed for mature groups to expedite the flow of business, so long as the rights of members were preserved.

Group decision making can be easily inhibited by a chair who rewards or punishes members for voicing opinions. Consensus can fool members into believing that decision making is their primary task and that implementing the decision is someone else's job. Bradford warns that meeting leaders should not accept the traditional expectation that responsibility for success rests solely on the leaders' shoulders. The challenge is to develop the group's collective sense of responsibility for group success. Sharing leadership via committee takes time, trust, and openness.

Student group meetings may be one of the hardest of all assemblies to lead. Because each of the members and officers is each other's peer, motivating should be done based on personal motivators and gain for the organization as a whole.

Several types of meetings are common:

- instructional (one-way communication),
- informational (multi-direction communication, networking),
- problem-solving,
- decision-making, and
- combinations of these.

Group meetings are usually combination-type events. Which types are favored at your pharmacy? Do they differ depending on the type of organization you belong to?

Kelly argues a significant distinction between middle- and top-management meetings. Mid-level conferences, he says, are more likely to be searching for the optimal solution; their differences will be differences of technical opinion. Conversely, upper-level sessions are more likely to be adversarial proceedings, where groups of opposing viewpoint struggle for dominance.

COMMON MEETING TRAPS

Here are some traps that may ensnare committee leaders and members. Possible solutions are also described:

Planning & Preparation:

- Planning with no data about the participants. Ask questions: who is coming? Who is essential to achieve the business of the meeting?
- Lack of involvement in the planning by those who will participate. Ask for input; develop their ownership of the program. Ensure that pre-reading materials are provided before the meeting to avoid spending time on basics, and thus allow for deeper discussion while the group is assembled.
- Equipment that does not work. Check everything beforehand; have contingency plans. Or, beautiful, but illegible, visual aids. Check everything.
- Same meeting, same time, same place, same seat. Suggest a change to provide a fresh outlook; it may range from a different seat to a different city.
- Holding meetings with no real reason or agenda. Put meaning into the program or cancel the meeting.
- No agenda, or one that omits a review of the purposes of this meeting. Communicate the purpose of the meeting to the members.
- Too many items or activities planned for the time available. Prioritize or run simultaneous subgroups.

During the Meeting:

- No sharing of the agenda. Share the plan to increase participation.
- Formal, classroom-style seating, implying that all wisdom comes from the front of the room. Use circles or U-shapes to facilitate communication.
- Action delayed while waiting for late arrivers. Have a discussion question ready to productively use the time of those present.

- Long, drawn-out speakers or reports. Give speakers time limits, give them a 2-minute warning, and stick to it. Do not call upon a speaker for a second time before soliciting input from others that have not yet spoken.
- Reliance on one expert. Use more than one resource person, so that alternatives can be fully explored.
- Long coffee breaks. Have refreshments in the room and continue discussion.
- Failure to deal with feelings of participants. If hostility is present, deal with it before moving on.
- No record kept of what was done or said. At the end of each meeting, recap who is responsible for which actions before the next meeting. Keep minutes or a journal.
- Neglecting to carry the group into the future. Make decisions and affirm commitments to follow through on decisions.

Chairs should establish their leadership early by starting on time, sticking to the agenda, using communication skills to stay in control, reaching desired outcomes, and concluding on time. Obstacles that may lead a meeting off course include monopolies, interruptions, lack of participation, and side comments or conversations. If the chair does not assert leadership, some other member of the committee will likely arise as the *de facto* leader.

Faced with one of these obstacles, the leader can get back on track by addressing the person presenting the obstacle, using paraphrasing to acknowledge understanding (of each party, if more than one are involved, such as in arguments), using summary statements or questions to clarify remaining difficulties, or restating the agreed-upon agenda to move discussion toward the desired outcome.

In some meetings, a small cadre may dominate discussion. While the speakers may be articulate and the meeting may be effective, dominance is usually not in the best interests of the organizations. Quiet members should be drawn out by directing questions their way or asking for an update on their work. Ensure that you offer a chance to speak to a quiet person before another person gets a second turn. Asking questions gives each person an opening to join the discussion. Another option is to assign specific research or stimulus questions before the meeting.

Alternately, vociferous participants may be the problem. Such members not only dominate the conversation, they are disruptive to the business of the meeting. Their personal agenda and the polarization they induce slow or prevent the organization from reaching its goals. Consider thanking such an individual for his or her contribution and quickly asking another person his or her opinion. Or ask this member to summarize his or her points in one or two sentences, with the comment that other business must be tended to. When the conversation goes off track into other topics, suggest that the conversation occur after the meeting or as part of a subsequent meeting's agenda item.

In some pharmacy departments, the assistant director conducts the meeting. Then, whenever the director speaks, it will tend to add special emphasis or impart guidance on the provision of pharmacy services. In this setting, the director's comments are remarkable for their presence.

To close meetings, the chair should confirm that speakers' messages have been received the interpreted as intended, assure that he or she has all the information and advice needed, use summary statements to make sure all information is understood and agreed upon, make necessary contracts to implement agreements, specify a timetable for agreed actions, and get a verbal receipt from affected members for all agreements and contracts. Also, take time to celebrate the good work that has occurred by listing out what was accomplished. This allows the group to bask in its productivity and feel appreciated. No committee should adjourn without a specific action plan, even if the plan is to do nothing.

OTHER MEETING TIPS

Attendance: Problem-solving meetings should rarely exceed 10 people. Informational ones can easily be larger. Limit attendance to those who can make useful contributions.

Purpose: Have a definite purpose for meeting. Recurring meetings (such as weekly staff conferences) should have a recurring need to be held. Produce action. Discuss only relevant topics; do not belabor extraneous issues.

Planning: Brief members in advance on goals and what you hope they can contribute. Plan your meeting in detail (including a timed agenda) and set priorities. Assemble starting questions with which to start (or perhaps restart) discussion. Name one meeting participant as discussion summarizer. Hold meetings early in the week, allowing for action during the same week. Have references available at technical-review meetings (e.g., Pharmacy & Therapeutics Committees).

Leading: Prepare a brief opening statement (to reiterate purpose, create mood, and establish ground rules. Start on time and state the time you expect to finish. Rarely should meetings exceed 60 minutes. Steer the meeting subtly, specifying and clarifying priorities, defining problems. Maintain a productive atmosphere, encouraging contributions, preventing friction. The leader's job includes providing direction and guidance.

When to have a meeting: Have a meeting if you want information or advice from a group, if you want to involve the group in solving a problem or making a decision, if an issue needs to be clarified, if the group itself wants a meeting, if a problem involves people from different groups, or if there is a problem but it is not clear what it is or who is responsible for dealing with it.

When not to have a meeting: Do not have meetings for personnel issues (e.g., hiring, firing, salary negotiations), when there is inadequate data or poor preparation, if a better communication medium is available, for confidential subjects, or if there is too much anger or hostility in the group. People need time to calm down before they can work collaboratively.

EFFECTIVENESS CRITERIA FOR COMMITTEES

Effectiveness criteria by which to evaluate committees; reflecting the discussion of action-orientation and respect for people advocated by Bradford, Jay, Kelly, Schindler-Rainman *et al.*, and others. Use these criteria to evaluate committees you lead or attend:

TASK-ORIENTED CRITERIA

1. Purpose of meeting clear

2. Agenda available to members

3. Participation encouraged

4. New ideas well received

5. Action to implement decisions well defined

6. Implementation confirmed at subsequent meetings

7. Agenda addresses future as well as present needs

8. Valid decision-making process

HUMAN-RESOURCES CRITERIA

9. Members identify with group

10. Members perceive ability to influence the group

11. Members accept responsibility for decisions

12. Members help each other

13. Members actively listen

14. Members willing to self-examine previous decisions

15. Members willing to experiment

16. Members trust subgroups

17. Members deal with differences forthrightly

18. Members accept expert opinion

DISCUSSION

This Module has scratched the surface on meeting management and group dynamics. We mean for this to be a thought-provoking Module, not an all-inclusive one. If we have raised questions in your mind about how to lead meetings more effectively, we have succeeded.

Mastering meetings can lead to a more successful, more satisfying work environment.

Here is a rule of thumb for better meetings: practice and more practice. Meeting facilitation is part art and part skill – style and ability, that is. Repeated efforts, trial and error, and learning from "mistakes" help us all become ever better. After each meeting, critique it. Plan for making the next meeting more productive and more participative.

30.2. Resources needed:

Annex 30-1. Roles & Activities for Your Group
Annex 30-2. Role Play with Parliamentary Procedure
Annex 30-3. Summary of Parliamentary Procedure

30.3. In-class activities:

"Organizations that do not see the relevance in meeting a great need must not see a great need in being relevant." Michael J. Negrete

"But this is the way we've always done it." Anonymous (too numerous to count)

Step 1. Questions?
Step 2. Quotes.
Step 3. Exercise.

MEETINGS MEET NEEDS

a. The pre-class reading discussed the conduct of a meeting in considerable detail. But think about it. The only reason to meet is to meet one or more needs. The needs of the group. The needs of individual member(s). With that in mind, let's do a few exercises.

b. The Paradox of Needs: Discuss in pairs, or as a large group:

   i. What are the various types of human needs?

   ii. Are individuals generally open to discussing their needs?

   iii. What do people think of individuals who openly and frequently discuss their own needs?

   iv. What does our society think of people or organizations who do a great job at meeting the needs of others?

   v. What accounts for differing views re: individuals who express their own needs *versus* those who meet the needs of others? What are the implications of this dichotomy?

Step 4. How Well Does Your Group Meet Identified Needs?

a. Reflect on your participation in this organization. Specifically, what personal needs did you believe would be fulfilled by joining this group and engaging in its activities (member recruitment, attending meetings, participating in committees, or running for office)? List those needs in the space below and be brutally honest. Do not worry if what you believed some time ago seems a bit superficial now. After all, your efforts to meet those needs are what set you on the path that led you here today; and that is what is important!

✍ _____ ⌨

b. Share your personal needs for joining your group, and discuss the following:

221

i. Do you believe your needs are representative of others in your group? Why?

ii. How have your needs evolved from the time you first thought about joining the group to now? Have certain types of needs become more important to you over time? If the answer is yes, what has changed to affect the level of their importance?

iii. Consider individuals who joined the group and have since "disappeared." What might you infer about their needs, then and now? How could you verify that? Why might it be important to verify it (rather than simply infer)?

Notes: ✍ _____ ⌨

c. Two general schemas exist to explain why people choose to do things. One is an "identity schema" in which people do something simply because they believe it is what people who possess their identity should do (e.g., I see myself as a leader and people who are leaders should join that organization). The other is a "cost/benefit schema," in which people do something because the tangible benefit they receive outweighs the cost of time, effort or money they must invest to receive it.

▷ Discuss with your partner which schema you believe drives participation for much of your group's members?

▷ What are the pros and cons of each schema?

Notes: ✍ _____ ⌨

d. Use the table in Annex 30-1 to make three lists of roles (e.g., offices, committees) and activities (e.g., programs, events) for a group you belong to.

▷ In the left-hand column, list roles and activities that clearly meet an identified need for the group, the community, or the members (as individuals) who serve in that role or activity.

▷ In the middle column, list roles and activities that are clearly intended to meet one or more identified need(s) but are not effective at doing so, irrespective of the reason.

▷ Finally, in the right column, list roles and activities that in your estimation do not serve any apparent need.

e. Pair-share your lists (from Step 4) and discuss the following:

▷ Which list was easiest for you to create? Why?

▷ What are some reasons why an organization might have a lot of roles or activities in the middle column?

▷ What are some reasons why an organization would have activities in the right column? Why would they continue to invest time and resources into them?

▷ From your experience, how easy is it to get volunteers for roles or activities from the left column? How about the middle column? And the right column?

▷ What are the costs to the organization, its members and its community for having a significant proportion of its roles and activities in the middle and right columns?

▷ What is the likely future for organizations that have most of their activities falling in the middle and right columns? Why?

Notes: ✍ _____ ⌨

Step 5. Increasing Participation by Meeting Needs

a. How big is your group's bull's eye? Answer the following questions:

i. Approximately how many members are on the roster of your group?

ii. Approximately how many members do most of the work?

iii. Divide your answer for #2 by your answer for #1 and multiply by 100:

iv. Fill in the portion of the circle that corresponds to your answer:

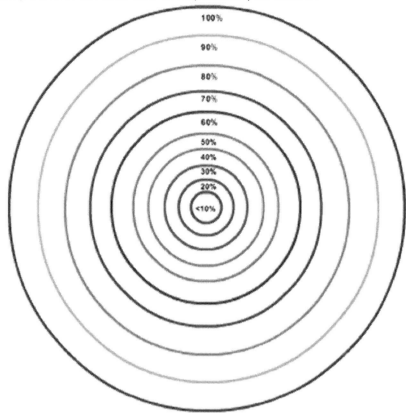

b. Share your results with a partner and pair-share on the following:

▷ Do you think the size of your bull's eye is typical of most volunteer organizations? Why?

▷ Why do you think most organizations do not have larger bull's eyes than they do?

▷ What might an organization do to expand their bull's eye?

Notes: ✎ _____ ⌨

g. List three commitments you will make to increase your group's ability to identify and meet needs of individual members.

By _____ (date) I commit to: ✎ _____ ⌨

By _____ (date) I commit to: ✎ _____ ⌨

By _____ (date) I commit to: ✎ _____ ⌨

Step 6. Role Play with Parliamentary Procedure. Use Annexes 30-2 and 30-3 to review rules of order for an assembly and conduct the role-playing exercise.

30.4. Discussion questions:

What kinds of meeting-management skills are needed by pharmacists who chair committees?
What kinds of meeting-management skills are needed by pharmacists who are committee members?

30.5. After-class assignments:

A. Work to expand the bull's eye of a group you belong to.
B. Fulfill the commitments you made to help your group identify and meet the needs of individual members.
C. Fulfill the before-class activities for the next Module assigned by your facilitator.

30.6. Bibliography, references, & resources:

Blake RR, Mouton JS. Overcoming group warfare. *Harvard Business Review* 1984;62:98-108.
Bradford LP. Some reasons for ineffective meetings. In: *Making Meetings Work: A Guide for Leaders & Group Members*. La Jolla, CA: University Associates. 1976.
Carnes WT. *Effective Meetings for Busy People: Let's Decide It and Go Home.* New York: McGraw-Hill, 1980.
Daily L. The formula for committee success. *Leadership 1987*. Washington, DC: Am Soc Assoc Exec, 1987.
DeMare G. *Communicating at the Top.* New York: John Wiley & Sons. 1979.
Flashcards via Quizlet, https://quizlet.com/class/3716098/, Group Dynamics » 8 terms; Parliamentary Procedure, Robert's Rules of Order » 17 terms
Jay A. How to run a meeting. *Harvard Business Review* 1976;54(Mar-Apr):43-57.
Kelly J. Surviving and thriving in top-management meetings. *Personnel* 1987;64(Jun):24-34.
Lee P. The P&T Committee secretary as facilitator. *Hosp Formulary* 1983;18:1039-1045.
Markowich MM. Using task forces to increase efficiency and reduce stress. *Personnel* 1987;64(Jun):34-37.
Robert HM III and others. *Robert's Rules of Order Newly Revised*, 11th ed. Boston: Da Capo Press, 2011. www.robertsrules.org.
Snook ID Jr, Zimmerman G. Management tools for modem day health administration. *Hosp Topics* 1983;61(1):1617.
Schindler-Rainman E, Lippitt R, Cole J. Some traps in planning and conducting meetings. In: *Making Meetings Work: A Guide for Leaders & Group Members*. La Jolla, CA: University Associates. 1976.
Trunzo TE. Group conflict—A challenge to participative management. *Hosp Topics* 1985;63(1):36-37.
Uris A. *The Executive Deskbook, 2nd ed.* New York: Van Nostrand-Reinhold Company, 1976.
US Junior Chamber [of Commerce, Jaycees]. Chairing Meetings, www.jci.cc/controlpanel/documents/USJC_LAG_Chairing_Meetings.pdf
US Junior Chamber [of Commerce, Jaycees]. Local Meetings, www.jci.cc/controlpanel/documents/USJC_LAG_Local_Meetings.pdf
US Junior Chamber [of Commerce, Jaycees]. Parliamentary Procedure, www.jci.cc/controlpanel/documents/USJC_LAG_Parliamentary_Procedures.pdf
US Junior Chamber [of Commerce, Jaycees]. Planning Meetings, www.jci.cc/controlpanel/documents/USJC_LAG_Planning_Meetings%20(1).pdf
Vancil RF, Green CH. How CEO's use top-management committees. *Harvard Business Review* 1984;62:65-73.

Annex 30-1. Roles & Activities for Your Group

Group: _____ ⌨

Separate annex documents available to facilitators upon request (LeadGrowShape@plei.org).

Make three lists of roles (e.g., offices, committees) and activities (e.g., programs, events) for a group you belong to.
  ▷ In the left-hand column, list roles and activities that clearly meet an identified need for the group, the community, or the members (as individuals) who serve in that role or activity.
  ▷ In the middle column, list roles and activities that are clearly intended to meet one or more identified need(s) but are not effective at doing so, irrespective of the reason.
Finally, in the right column, list roles and activities that in your estimation do not serve any apparent need.

Meets Identified Need(s)	Unable to Meet Identified Need(s)	Serves No Apparent Need
▸	▸	▸
▸	▸	▸
▸	▸	▸
▸	▸	▸
▸	▸	▸
▸	▸	▸

Annex 30-2. Role Play with Parliamentary Procedure

Separate annex documents available to facilitators upon request (LeadGrowShape@plei.org).

Target Audience: Novices and Intermediate Experience

Session Goal: To help participants practice how to participate in (and preside over) a business session using parliamentary procedure, according to the classic Robert's Rules of Order.

Situation: You are the delegate from your chapter to the 70th Grand Conclave of the Honorable Society of Left-Handed Pharmacists. You are attending a business session where several topics of discussion are being considered. The presiding officer is a renowned expert in parliamentary procedure and promises to teach by example how to make motions, make amendments, and generally move discussion along, both equitably and efficiently.

Purpose: Parliamentary law is used to conduct the business of an organization, balancing the rights of each member along with the rights of the assembly. Use these procedures to promote equality, and not as a weapon against those unfamiliar with them. A good officer presides over the group with impartiality. To be useful, each meeting needs an "agenda" or "order of business." To set policy and take actions, members introduce, discuss, adopt, or reject motions. A motion is an expression of what you want to accomplish. It is made simply by saying "I move..." after being recognized by the chair.

Background on parliamentary procedure:

a. Rules of Order provide common procedures for discussion (i.e., debate) and voting.

b. These rules put the whole assembly on an equal, well-understood footing. The various members speak in common terms.

c. Business is controlled by the will of the assembly, as reflected by voting.

d. This control is tempered by giving certain rights to individuals or to strong minority factions.

e. Undue strictness should not be allowed to intimidate members nor to limit full participation.

f. Deliberative assemblies want matters to be thoroughly discussed before acting.

g. If you don't understand, ask for information (Point of order!).

Committees and seconds ...

a. A "second" is concurrence by a second member of the assembly with the motion that someone else just made.

b. Procedurally, a committee report is the opinion of at least two people.

c. Because of this, no second is needed for a motion to accept a committee report. Two people already agree with it.

Before you speak...

1. Obtain the floor (the right to speak) by signaling the presiding officer (the "chair").

2. You must be recognized by the chair before you begin speaking.

3. No member can speak twice on the same subject until every else wishing to speak has spoken once. Ergo, choose your words carefully. Clear statements are more easily remembered by the assembly.

4. Direct your remarks to the chair. All remarks must be courteous. Avoid discussing personalities or motives.

▸

So, let's continue with a **practical exercise**. The agenda for the current session is open for new business.

Card 1. *[Say aloud:]* The official colors of this Honorable Society are "black and white." These honorable colors were adopted long ago and are so worthy of our respect. Yet, I must say it: these colors are outdated and should be brought into the digital age we live in now. I think the colors should be changed to "red-green-blue."

Presiding Officer responds: You are welcome to any opinion you would like. Do you have any business to propose to the Grand Council assembled? [Stating an opinion is all well and good, but it doesn't result in any organizational movement.]

Card 2. Presiding Officer, I move that this Honorable Society's colors be changed from "black and white" to "red-green-blue." ["I move..." is the key to action.]

Presiding Officer responds: It has been moved to change this Honorable Society's colors to "red-green-blue." Is there a second? [Repetition of the motion recognizes the importance of what just happens, and helps the group focus on a decision they will eventually need to make. Pause, then acknowledge the person seconding the motion.] ... Mr./Ms. Smith seconds the motion. Now, is there any discussion?

Card 2. Presiding Officer. *[pause to be recognized]* These changes do not go far enough. I would like to amend the motion by adding an additional change: I move to amend the main motion by substituting that the new colors be "cyan-magenta-yellow-black," rather than red-green-blue.

Presiding Officer responds: The motion to amend is in order. Is there a second to the amendment? [pause, then acknowledge the person seconding the amendment.] Mr./Ms. Jones seconds the motion. Is there any discussion on the amendment?

Card 3. Presiding Officer. *[pause to be recognized]* This is terrible. We can't make momentous decisions like this on a whim. What is the definition of "cyan"? What would it look like? Where does it appear on the PowerPoint color chart? And magenta? Do you mean purplish-red, reddish-purple, or mauvish–crimson? I move that this question be referred to the next round of Regional Conferences for consideration and debate. Only then should it be considered by the next Grand Conclave.

Presiding Officer responds: It has been moved to refer this motion and its proposed amendment to the next round of Regional Conferences. Is there a second? [pause, then acknowledge the seconder.] Mr./Ms. Brown seconds the motion. Is there any discussion on referring the question to the Regional Conferences?

Presiding Officer: Okay, we've thoroughly considered the various viewpoints. Unless there are further new perspectives, let us proceed to vote on the amendment....

Card 4 (part 1). Wait, a point of order! I rise to a point of order!

Presiding Officer: Yes, Left-Handed Pharmacist?

Card 4 (part 2). What is needed to pass the amendment? A majority or two-thirds?

Presiding Officer: ... Alright, that is settled. Let us proceed to vote on the amendment. All those in favor of the amendment....

Card 5 (part 1). Wait, a point of order!

Presiding Officer: Yes, Left-Handed Pharmacist?

Card 5 (part 2): Please restate the amendment to be voted on...

Presiding Officer: Good point – a good chair always makes clear what any given vote is about and which way to vote for various options. In this case, a yes vote would change "red-green-blue" to "cyan-magenta-yellow-black" in the proposed amendment. A no vote would reject that proposed amendment.

Now then. All those in favor of the amendment to substitute CMYK instead of RGB, please raise your hand. Thank you, you may lower your hands.

Now, all those opposed to the amendment, please raise your hands. Thank you.

The amendment _____ [*passes or fails*]

Presiding Officer: So, the amendment has been defeated. This means we return to the main motion before the assembly. Recall that the main motion, the original motion, is: that the Society's colors be changed from "black and white" to "red-green-blue." Is there any other discussion on the main motion?

Card 6. Wait, I call the question!

Presiding Officer: Really, why? Do you understand the meaning of that phrase or does it just sound cool? What does it mean to "call the question"? Let's talk about it …

Options: (a) It might be that the person "calling the question" wants to hold a vote on cutting off debate. That is the proper meaning of the phrase. Not many people realize this.

(b) More often, people mean it as: I really want to get on with the vote. Charitably, this could be assumed to mean: Do we have unanimous consent to proceed directly to the vote on the motion?

A benevolent presiding officer will realize that the well-meaning member might not really understand the meaning, and so could go with option b and test it by asking the group: Are we ready to vote? If there is objection by even a single person, then either a vote should be held on whether to cut off debate, or further discussion should be accepted.

Presiding Officer: Alright, are we ready to vote on the main motion: that the Society's colors be changed from "black and white" to "red-green-blue"? Hearing no desire for further discussion…

A yes vote would adopt the change in colors from B&W to RGB.

A no vote would reject the change in colors and the traditional black-and-white colors would remain in effect.

All those in favor of the motion raise your hand. [*count hands*]

All those opposed to the motion raise your hand. [*count hands*]

The motion fails. The colors remain the same – our time-honored colors of "black and white." Huzzah!

Presiding Officer: Now, let's rerun the example, without the explanatory parts, so you can see how smoothly and quickly the whole matter can be handled. [Do so.]

Presiding Officer: Next, let's have a general discussion of whatever topics you would like. Here are some possibilities.

- ‣ Nominations and elections
- ‣ Unfinished Business *versus* New Business
- ‣ What to do with "wise guys" who want to be smartest person in the room?
- ‣ Why would you want to table a motion?
- ‣ Caucus *versus* recess *versus* adjourn
- ‣ Discussion of sticky wickets you have been in previously.
- ‣ Define: Quorum. Majority vote (how to calculate).

Annex 30-3. Summary of Parliamentary Procedure

Separate annex documents available to facilitators upon request (LeadGrowShape@plei.org).

This is a reference document.

WHAT DO YOU WANT TO DO?

A. INTRODUCE BUSINESS: "I move to «adopt or some other verb» ..." or "I move that ..."

B. BRING TO A VOTE: "I call the question to a vote." or "I call the previous question."

C. AMEND: "I move to amend the motion by «describe what would change»..." If "friendly amendments" cannot be quickly agreed to, handle them in the classic fashion.

D. WITHDRAW A MOTION: "I withdraw my motion." Prevents the matter from coming to a vote. Needs NO second, is not debatable, not amendable, and requires a majority vote. However, before the chair states a motion, it may be withdrawn or modified by the maker without the consent of the group.

E. DISPENSE WITH A MOTION: Several ways to kill a motion (stop action):
   ▷ Table.
   ▷ Postpone either to a specific time or indefinitely.
   ▷ Object to consideration.
   ▷ Commit or refer to committee.

F. SUSPEND THE RULES: "I move to suspend the rules to allow ..."

G. NOMINATING AND VOTING

   1. Nominations do NOT require a second. Accept all nominations. Do not vote to close nominations. ["Seeing no further nominations, we proceed to the next order of business (perhaps voting) ..."]

   2. Voting: Votes may be changed until results are announced. If a vote results in a tie, the motion fails. Chair may cast a vote to break a tie. The chair always votes when voting by ballot.
      ▷ Voice vote: Yeas and nays. This is the usual method of voting, unless a motion is passed to use an alternate method.
      ▷ Request for roll call: Requires a second, is not debatable, requires a majority vote. "I move to conduct the vote by roll call."
      ▷ Ballot (secret vote): Requires a second, is not debatable, requires a majority vote. "I move to vote by secret ballot."
      ▷ General or unanimous consent: Used only when approval of the action is a matter of mere formality).

   Member: "I ask general consent to a vote of thanks to Pharmacist Jones for her outstanding work on the blood drive."

   Chair: "General consent is asked for a vote of thanks to Pharmacist Jones. Is there any objection? Hearing none {if none is made}, it is so ordered." If an objection is made, then there must be a second, debate, and vote on the vote to offer thanks.

H. REVERSE A PRIOR ACTION (assumes the action resulting from the prior motion can be reversed or has not yet been taken):
   ▷ Reconsider: Requires a second, is debatable, not amendable, requires a majority vote. May be made only by a member voting on the prevailing side. Must be made on the same day or on the next calendar day.

▷ Rescind: Requires a second, is debatable, amendable. If previous notice given, majority vote required. If not, needs 2/3 majority

I. APPEAL. Object to decision made by chair and ask assembly to overturn the chair's decision. Second required, debatable, amendable, majority vote.

J. QUESTIONS OF PRIVILEGE: These questions address matters that cannot wait. No second, not debatable, not amendable, majority vote.

K. WHEN IS TWO-THIRDS VOTE REQUIRED: Object to consideration / Suspend rules / Take up agenda item out of order / Bring previous question to vote / Close nominations.

L. FOR FURTHER INFORMATION: Less common motions are addressed in the text of Robert's Rules of Order, such as "objecting to consideration," reconsideration, orders of the day, limit or extend debate, rescind, fix time of next meeting, and others. See current edition of *Robert's Rules of Order Newly Revised,* www.robertsrules.org.

Summary Table of Motions:

You want to:	You say:	May you interrupt others?	Needs second?	Debat-able?	Amend-able?	Vote needed	
Adjourn a meeting	I move that we adjourn.	No	Yes	No	No	Majority	
Take a break	I move to recess for __ minutes.	No	Yes	No	Yes	Majority	
Complain about heat, *et cetera*	I rise to a question of privilege. ... Specifically, ...	Yes	No	No	No	No vote	↑ Order of precedence ↑
Delay	I move to lay the motion on the table.	No	Yes	No	No	Majority	
End debate and amendments	I call the (previous) question. – or – I move to close debate.	No	Yes	No	No	Two-thirds	
Postpone	I move to postpone discussion until ___.	No	Yes	Yes	Yes	Majority	
Arrange more detailed study	I move to refer the matter to the __ committee.	No	Yes	Yes	Yes	Majority	
Modify wording	I move to amend the motion by [changing / substituting / inserting] ...	No	Yes	Yes	Yes	Majority	
Introduce business	**I move that ...**	**No**	**Yes**	**Yes**	**Yes**	Majority	
Protest breach of rules or conduct	Point of order! – or – I rise to a point of order! [Then explain yourself...]	Yes	No	No	No	No vote	
Vote on a ruling from the chair	I appeal from the chair's decision.	Yes	Yes	Yes	No	Majority	
Suspend rules temporarily	I move to suspend the rules, so that ...	No	Yes	No	No	Two-thirds	
Verify voice vote by rising (standing)	I call for a division.	Yes	No	No	No	No vote	
Request information	Point of information!	Yes	No	No	No	No vote	
Take up a matter previously tabled	I move to take from the table ...	No	Yes	No	No	Majority	

Annex 30-4. Parliamentary Procedure Crossword Puzzle

Separate annex documents available to facilitators upon request (LeadGrowShape@plei.org).

Across

5. Introduce business
6. General consent
7. Delay a motion
9. Agree to a motion
11. Break

Down

1. Modify the motion
2. Protest breach of rules
3. Complaint about something
4. Supermajority
8. Secret vote
10. For more detailed study

Module « **31** »   PROBLEM-SOLVING

☞ Learning Objectives:

Objective 1. To describe the importance of identifying a clear problem statement.
Objective 2. To describe a systematic, step-wise process for problem-solving.
Objective 3. To discuss the importance of a continuous-improvement approach.

What's the problem here? Those four words form a crucial part of leadership, as one must name a problem before one can try to solve it.

This Module explores problem-solving and offers a step-wise approach that can be applied in many situations. You may have heard of the PDCA cycle, which stands for Plan-Do-Check-Act. We will use a similar, but slightly different approach based on eight questions.

31.1. Readings or activities <u>before class:</u>

Read and be prepared to discuss the text for this Module, including Annex 31-1.

31.2. Resources needed:

Annex 31-1. Problem-Solving Process (and Solution)

31.3. In-class activities:

"Too many problem-solving sessions become battlegrounds where decisions are made based on power rather than intelligence." Margaret J. Wheatley

Step 1. Questions?
Step 2. Quote.
Step 3. Exercise.

PROBLEM-SOLVING PROCESS: WHAT'S THE PROBLEM?

a. Divide into teams of four to eight people.

b. Find a solution to a problem using the Problem-Solving Process in Annex 31-1. [Several problem options are offered for you to choose from, but a real-life problem confronted by your group might be the best option.] Address each of the eight questions individually, methodically, in sequence. Do not jump to the next step prematurely. If you see more than one problem here, deal with each individually.

c. The emphasis in this exercise is on the <u>process</u> of problem solving, rather than the superficial issue of the apparent problem. The hardest or most divisive step is usually getting everyone to agree on the definition of what the problem is.

d. Be alert to differentiate causes, symptoms, and problems.

e. If you ever realize that you misstated the problem, go back to Step 1 and restate the problem.

f. After 20 minutes, return your attention to the whole group. Go through each question of the problem-solving process, one-by-one. See if the other teams agree with your assessment of the problem. How did assumptions made by the various teams affect the approaches used to resolve the problem?

g. What generic lessons did you learn about the process of solving problems?

h. Disciplined problem-solving is a useful technique to address any problem.

Scenario #1: Something confronting the group or the class. Or a situation provided by the facilitator…

Scenario #2: "Our group has been informed by the national headquarters that a $1,000 debt remains from the deadbeat members who allowed the group to go inactive three years ago. They are willing to help us eliminate our financial problem through our planning of a payment schedule. We must develop and follow a group budget for the next year. The national office needs a list of fund-raisers we plan to conduct, how we will implement them, and a report on what our expected profit will be. Their records show that we have also not completed payment of our own Initiation Fees ($1,000 remains unpaid). The national office wonders if the problem originated in our procedure of collecting dues from new members. If our records show differently, we must state our case in a formal letter which must be in the mail tomorrow morning (i.e., handed to the facilitator not later than his or her deadline)."

Scenario #3: One of your coworkers is habitually late and shirks duties consistently. A third coworker wants to tell the supervisor every time there is a gap in performance. Another coworker notes the "shirking coworker" has extenuating family circumstances. What should we do?

Scenario #4. Attendance at group meetings is declining. Commuters complain if meetings are held in the evenings; P3s complain if they are held on weekends; others complain about other times. You are on the group's executive committee. What is the problem? What do you recommend be done?

Scenario #5. The controlled substances inventory has been off by a disturbing amount each of the last three counts. You know you should try to determine the root cause of the discrepancy. This problem has not happened to you before and you are not sure what to do. If you seek advice from a peer, it might lead to a formal report, even though you have no idea why the count is off. If you seek help from your supervisor, you might be blamed for not supervising things well enough. What would be a reasonable approach to this sensitive situation?

Step 4. Proceed in a disciplined manner through the questions below. Be careful not to go too quickly through the first few questions, or you are likely to find yourself confused and bogged down in later questions. When in doubt, ask yourself: "What is the problem here?"

a. What's Going On? Define the problem(s) in this scenario. [What is the problem here? If more than one problem exists, tackle each one individually.]

✎ _____ ▦

b. What Do We Know? Gather facts, data, impressions, observations.

✎ _____ ▦

c. What Are the Root Causes? Which events led to which other events? Follow the dominoes backwards.

✎ _____ ▦

d. What Could We Do? What are your options? Generate several possible solutions.

✍ _____ ⌨

e. What's the Best Thing to Do? Evaluate your options using decision criteria [also explored in Module 32]. In other words, what factors should you consider in contrasting the alternate solutions? Compare the advantages and disadvantages of each option.

✍ _____ ⌨

f. How Do We Go About It? Plan the implementation of the solution you selected. Who will do what?

✍ _____ ⌨

g. Have We Solved the Problem? Implement the solution, then evaluate whether your solution actually solved the problem. Did it work? Does the problem persist?

✍ _____ ⌨

h. Can We Improve on What We Have Done? Adopt a continuous-improvement approach. If problem persists, redefine the problem and begin the cycle again.

✍ _____ ⌨

31.4. Discussion questions:

Per facilitator

31.5. After-class assignments:

A. Practice these disciplined problem-identification and problem-solving steps in your daily activities.
B. Fulfill the before-class activities for the next Module assigned by your facilitator.

31.6. Bibliography, references, & resources:

Flashcards via Quizlet, https://quizlet.com/class/3716098/, Problem-Solving Process » 8 terms
See also Module Z

Annex 31-1. Problem-Solving Process (and Solution)

Separate annex documents available to facilitators upon request (LeadGrowShape@plei.org).

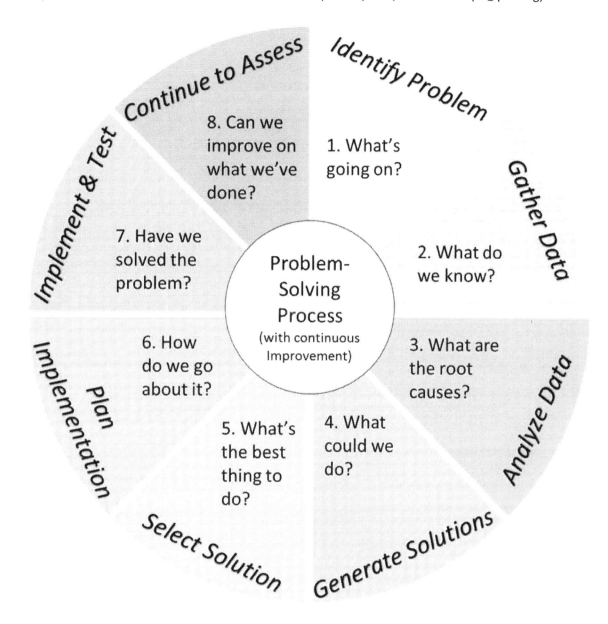

You may have your own responses.

Appropriate Questions	Example Answers
What's Going On? What is the problem? If more than 1 problem exists, tackle each one individually.	- No commitment to paying the debts of others. Others… - - -
What Do We Know?	…
What Are the Root Causes?	…
What Could We Do? What are our options?	- Pay all at once Others… - - -
What's the Best Thing to Do?	1. Select your decision criteria, such as impact on current members, national office's patience, competing resource needs, equity, *et cetera*. 2. Evaluate the options above using these criteria 3. Select best option. If the choice suggested by your decision criteria does not seem quite right, maybe your problem is misstated or your criteria are inappropriate.
How Do We Go About It?	Plan your implementation. Be specific. Be realistic. - Pay initiation fees first, then pay $250 per semester on old debt until resolved. Others… -
Have We Solved the Problem?	Implement the solution. Evaluate whether solution actually solved problem. - -
Can We Improve on What We Have Done?	▸

Module « **32** »   DISCIPLINED DECISION-MAKING

☞ Learning Objectives:

Objective 1. To describe a systematic, step-wise process for objectively making decisions.
Objective 2. To differentiate between Limits and Desirables when establishing decision criteria.
Objective 3. To understand the importance of weighting among decision criteria.

Do you consider yourself indecisive, decisive, impulsive, or _____? If you're deciding which movie to see, you don't need to do too much planning. If you're impulsive when buying a candy bar, we won't complain – as long as you eat your fruits and vegetables too.

But if you are about to pay a lot of money for something, or if you are about to dedicate a lot of time based on a decision, you'd be well advised to take your time and think things through.

This Module addresses disciplined decision-making. More specifically, it explains decision matrices and how they can be used to organize your decision-making. The key teaching point is to think carefully about your «decision criteria» – the concepts that allow you to compare and contrast your options. Our scenario will involve which new car to purchase, but you'll find ways to apply this step-wise method in lots of other ways too.

32.1. Readings or activities <u>before class</u>:

Study the text of the in-class exercise and be prepared for the decision-matrix exercise in class.
Perform the recalculation exercise described in Annex 32-1.

32.2. Resources needed:

Annex 32-1. Decision Matrix: Car Choice

32.3. In-class activities:

"Information is a source of learning. But unless it is organized, processed, and available to the right people in a format for decision making, it is a burden, not a benefit." William Pollard

Step 1. Questions?
Step 2. Quote.
Step 3. Exercise.

DECIDING HOW TO DECIDE

a. When confronted with a major decision, how do you go about the process of deciding? Do you consult experts, use a bit of the seat-of-the-pants approach, or just flip a coin? Each of these can be appropriate. Find out the right situations to apply each.

As a teaching scenario, we will use a new car purchase to illustrate how decision matrices can help organize your thinking and enable a disciplined decision-making process. This kind of approach is suitable for many big decisions, such as deciding between job offers, whether to rent an apartment or buy a house, or many other multi-factor decisions where slowing down and considering each of the factors individually would be advisable.

Scenario: A wealthy aunt recently died and left you $90,000 in her will. Aunt Begonia was known to be a little eccentric and it carried through in her will: She always thought you studied too hard, so she stipulated that the money had to be spent on a new car, although if there was any money left over, you could keep or spend that money as you wish.

Now, your parents are the executors of the will. Before they will disburse the money to you, they want to use the situation to teach you to sharpen your decision-making skills. They want to see a detailed description of the criteria by which you will choose which new car you will buy.

From all the preceding Modules in this course, you have become increasingly self-aware and so you jot down some subjective and objective factors that you want to balance in deciding which new car to select:

- Roominess: You have lots of friends, so you want a car that seats at least four people.
- Mileage: You are a frugal person, so you would prefer a car that gets good gas mileage.
- Reliability & Value: Your parents taught you to spend your money wisely, so you want a car with a good Kelly Blue Book® (KBB) customer-satisfaction rating.
- Fuel Range: Your home town is a long way from campus, so you want a vehicle that can get you home on one tank of gas.
- Performance: You may be frugal, but you have always been envious of mega-horsepower cars. What if…?

Instead of studying for midterm exams, you find visions of automobiles dance in your head: A bright red Ferrari 458 Italia, a dependable Ford Fiesta hatchback, the venerable BMW 7 series, a Tesla Model S (hey, Aunt Begonia was an environmentalist…). Vrrooom goes the Ferrari! No, be practical with the Fiesta. But that BMW is so seductive. No gas needed with the Tesla…

"Stop!" your parents shout. Organize your thoughts. Gather the relevant facts. Settle on some decision criteria. Write it down!

So, you gather these facts into Table 32-1.

Options Criteria	Ferrari 458	Ford Fiesta	BMW 7 series	Tesla Model S
Seats	2	5	5	7
Miles/gallon	14	29	23	89e
KBB (out of 10)	9.4	7.0	8.2	9.6
Fuel range (mi)	318	384	474	260
Horsepower	570	197	320	362
Price	$245K	$23K	$77K	$81K
Cash left over	Debt	$67K	$13K	$ 9K

But that doesn't help. Tesla's mileage! BMW's range! Fiesta's value! Ferrari's horsepower!

"Stop!" your parents shout. How can you better organize your thoughts? Well, I could see how many first-place ranks each option gets: I could rank order the cars for each of the criteria… Okay, let's try that. Let's give the most points to the car with the most favorable result for each of the criteria. That would look like Table 32-2.

Options / Criteria	Ferrari 458	Ford Fiesta	BMW 7 series	Tesla Model S
Seats	1	2	2	3
Miles/gallon	1	3	2	4
KBB (out of 10)	3	1	2	4
Fuel range (mi)	2	3	4	1
Horsepower	4	1	2	3
Price	1	4	3	2
Cash left over	1	4	3	2

Now it is a tie: both the Tesla and the Fiesta have two 4's (best within the row) and two 3's, as well. But I really like the lines of that BMW! Oh, what should I do?

"Stop!" your parents shout. Are all these criteria equally important? No, you admit sheepishly.

Step 4. So, let's take it one step at a time:

a. First, which of these criteria are absolutely essential? These are dichotomous criteria (also known as go/no go criteria or limit criteria) where a "no" answer or a "no go" situation means that the choice is either acceptable or not. There is no middle ground. In this case, only one criterion is an absolute one, a limit, insofar as the car must seat at least 4 people.

b. Okay, which of the other criteria are more important than the others? We will put a weighting factor on the important criteria. Well, mileage and range sorta go together, but mileage is really important to me. And some cash left over would help a lot on my budget. Horsepower can wait until I get a real job. I have not had time to look up what that KBB Customer Rating really means – is it reliability as in few trips to the mechanic, or is it more like happiness with the new car smell? That one is a little important, but not too much.

c. Okay, now we are ready to proceed to Annex 32-1 and populate the fields in the decision matrix.

32.4. Discussion questions:

Per facilitator ...
What kinds of projects warrant the disciplined decision-making process described here? In a personal life? In a professional life?

Match the term with the correct definition:

1. Alternatives	__	a. A choice made after thinking about it
2. Criterion	__	b. Absolute criteria – must be fulfilled
3. Decision	__	c. Choices, alternatives
4. Decision matrix	—	d. List of values in rows and columns that enable one to systematically identify, analyze, and rate relationships
5. Desirables	__	e. Options, choices
6. Facts	__	f. Other criteria, not absolute requirements
7. Limits	__	g. Position within a hierarchy
8. Options	—	h. Something that is used as a reason for making a judgment or decision

9. Rank	__	i. Something that truly exists or happens
10. Weighting	__	j. The relative importance accorded to something

32.5. After-class assignments:

A. Apply the decision-matrix approach to your next big purchase or job choice.
B. Fulfill the before-class activities for the next Module assigned by your facilitator.

32.6. Bibliography, references, & resources:

Flashcards via Quizlet, https://quizlet.com/class/3716098/, Disciplined Decision-Making » 10 terms
See also Module Z

Annex 32-1. Decision Matrix: Car Choice

Separate annex documents available to facilitators upon request (LeadGrowShape@plei.org).

Step 1. State the purpose for making a decision.

Step 2. Establish decision criteria (e.g., cost, quality, performance, capabilities)

Step 3. Separate criteria into

a. *"LIMITS"* These are absolute criteria that can veto an alternative, making them go/no go criteria. For example: "seating for at least 4 passengers"). And

b. *"DESIRABLES"* These are relative criteria, such as miles per gallon or cash left over. To each "desirable" criterion, attach a weight. For example: mpg is more important than range, horsepower and KBB rating are hardly important at all. If so, then weight mileage and cash left over with a factor of 5, give range a factor of 2, and give horsepower and KBB factors of 1 each. As we get into further steps, we will multiply the weighting factor for each desirable criterion by the rank orders determined in Table 32-2.

So, is any car ruled out because of limits? Yes, the Ferrari 458 Italia. Sigh, it's a 2-seater. That's it, consider it no further in this analysis. [If you suddenly decide passenger capacity isn't very important, then you are letting emotions overrule objective decision-making. Maybe someday…

Steps 4 and 5. Generate and Compare Alternatives. This table shows the general scheme. Below it appears another table that has been partially filled in.

Alternative A		Alternative B		Alternative C	
Limits	Go ?	Limits	Go ?	Limits	Go ?
a. b. c.	Go/No go Go/No go Go/No go	a. b. c.	Go/No go Go/No go Go/No go	a. b. c.	Go/No go Go/No go Go/No go
Desirables	Rank * Wgt = Product	Desirables	Rank * Wgt = Product	Desirables	Rank * Wgt = Product
a. b. c. d.	a. b. c. d.	a. b. c. d.	a. b. c. d.	a. b. c. d.	a. b. c. d.
Total:		Total:		Total:	

Step 6. Identify favored alternative based on results of steps 4 & 5.

Let's fill in the matrix for our scenario:

Alternative A Ford Fiesta Hatchback ST			Alternative B BMW 7 series			Alternative C Tesla Model S		
Limits	Go/no go?		Limits	Go/no go?		Limits	Go/no go?	
a. Seats ≥ 4 b. c.	Go		a. Seats ≥ 4 b. c.	Go		a. Seats ≥ 4 b. c.	Go	
Desirables	Rank * Wgt = Product		Desirables	Rank * Wgt = Product		Desirables	Rank * Wgt = Product	
a. MPG	3 * 5	15	a. MPG	2 * 5	10	a. MPG	4 * 5	20
b. Kelly Blue Bk	1 * 1	1	b. Kelly Blue Bk	2 * 1	2	b. Kelly Blue Bk	4 * 1	4
c. Fuel range	3 * 2	6	c. Fuel range	4 * 2	8	c. Fuel range	1 * 2	2
d. Horsepower	1 * 1	1	d. Horsepower	2 * 1	2	d. Horsepower	3 * 1	3
e. Cash left over	4 * 5	20	e. Cash left over	3 * 5	15	e. Cash left over	2 * 5	10
Total:	43		Total:	37		Total:	39	

So, the Fiesta is preferred based on your stated criteria and weighted preferences. The Tesla came in second and the BMW third. You can set up your computer with a background image of the Ferrari 458 Italia for free.

But what if you had selected different criteria as being most important? Let's say you assigned KBB customer rating a weight of 4, upgraded fuel range to a weight of 4 and downgraded MPG to a weight of 2, leaving the other weights the same. Which car would be preferred under those conditions?

The lesson in this recalculation exercise is that the weights are pivotally important to the process. As you will see, changing those numbers can completely reverse the results.

It took a lot of work to get this far. You wouldn't go to this much effort to choose among candy bar choices. Under what conditions might you go to this effort?

Module « **33** »   CONFLICT MANAGEMENT

☞ Learning Objectives:

Objective 1. To identify symptoms and causes of conflict.
Objective 2. To explore means of resolving conflict.
Objective 3. To understand how growth and improvement can come from conflict.

This Module explores conflict: how to recognize and categorize conflict, and how to use various interpersonal skills to help resolve it. This exploration takes us into four types of conflict, five actions, and five conflict-resolution methods.

We tackle a scenario to illustrate what to do. As usual, the face-to-face discussion puts the human face on what to do.

33.1. Readings or activities <u>before class</u>:

A. Reread Annex 16-1 on the four conversation types, especially performance (PC) and closure (CC).
B. Read and be prepared to discuss Annex 33-1, which summarizes five basic methods for resolving conflict, their effect, when to use them and when not to use them.
C. After reading, complete Annex 33-2: Conflict-Assessment Crossword Puzzle (or follow facilitator instructions).
D. Read and be prepared to discuss the following text.

TYPES OF CONFLICT: Know what kind of conflict you are in:

<u>Factual level</u>: Are my facts different from your facts? Are my facts really facts or merely assumptions? (e.g., do you think we have a surplus of $500 in the budget when I know we have a $250 shortfall?)

<u>Process level</u>: Does the conflict center on your way of doing things *versus* my way of doing things? (e.g., do I worry about getting every comma in place while you are just concerned with getting "close enough"?)

<u>Purpose level</u>: Do you have different goals? Is one trying to maximize professional services while the other is trying to maximize profits?

<u>Values level</u>: Core human values can give rise to deep-rooted conflicts: abortion *versus* adoption, euthanasia, *et cetera*.

ACTION STEPS:

<u>Identify</u>: Face the fact that you are in a conflict. Identify the type of conflict you are in.

<u>Listen</u>: Let the other person know you are interested in how he or she looks at the problem. This is the hardest part.

<u>Speak</u>: Just as you listened to your partner in this conflict, now it is your turn to explain your perspective. Use "I" statements to indicate you recognize your views as your own and not infallible truths.

<u>Seek</u>: (a resolution together): What are your areas of agreement? Try to collaborate to reach your common goals.

<u>Follow-through:</u> Implement the plan the two of you have assembled.

33.2. Resources needed:

Annex 33-1. Five Basic Methods for Resolving Conflict
Annex 33-2: Conflict-Assessment Crossword Puzzle

33.3. In-class activities:

"For good ideas and true innovation, you need human interaction, conflict, argument, debate." Margaret Heffernan

Step 1. Questions?
Step 2. Quote.
Step 3. Exercise.

CONFLICT ASSESSMENT & INTERVENTION PLANNING

a. SITUATION: Evidence of a serious split in the group along class lines is being noticed. The P2 members do not seem to associate much with the older and younger members. They do not spend much time together during group activities and only two of them attended the last three group meetings. Is the problem serious? What do we do about it?

When one P2 was asked to comment on the problem, he said, "It's not my fault that we all have labs together and want to study together. That's one of the biggest reasons I joined, so I could have close friends to study with. Get off my back! You P3s and P4s pal around together too! Nobody says much about it, though, because there are fewer of you around than there are P2s."

Even this week, the P2s have been clinging together. They have been insisting on deciding issues their way. A crisis may be near since the P2s are objecting to a plan to "require" a certain amount of community service from each member each month (actually, it was a <u>goal</u> of five hours per person). "Forget it, you know P3 year is the toughest," one of them said, "I'll just go inactive if you try to push that kind of policy through." Many grumbles of agreement were audible from the P3 section.

b. What do you do to defuse this situation? How do you prevent splits from occurring? This can seem like a tall order. So, break it into steps, to make it more manageable.

c. First seek to understand. As an individual, consider each of the following questions and jot down answers to each:

What can you do to accomplish defuse the situation?

What is the benefit of asking other P2s individually?

When might it be a good idea to address the P2s as a group?

d. Is this really a problem? Is it serious or is it only your perception that it is a pressing problem? How might you broaden your thinking about the situation?

✎ _____ ⌨

e. Expand the help circle. What is the role of an advisor or faculty member in this situation? How might this individual offer support? How can you present an objective summary of the situation? Why would it be important to offer an objective view of the situation?

✎ _____ ⌨

f. Taking action. After you appreciate the situation, what might you do to address the situation? For example, how can you share what you have learned in a way to express care and concern for the P2s, acknowledge how they feel, and advocate for their retention in the group? How might you engage them to determine what will work for them and what will work for the overall group? What tools might you use to start a successful conversation with the group [Module 28 explains the Diamond & Stones exercise].

g. Write out some statements you might use to help understand the situation. What specifically would you say? How will you convey that you acknowledge their concerns and the importance they offer the group as vibrant contributors? How can you facilitate feedback from them to improve your ability to create an environment where they would want to participate fully? Circulate the statements among two or three people. As they listen to your statements, they should consider how they might receive them (if they were a P2 hearing them) and offer feedback/edit statements directly to you. Continue to circulate until your statements have received feedback.

✎ _____ ⌨

EFFECT OF ASSUMPTIONS & GOSSIP

Step 4.

a. When is the last time you made an assumption?

b. When is the last time you took something personally?

✎ _____ ⌨

c. Making assumptions and "taking things personally" (which most people do) can serve to ravage resources quickly. These create problems in relationships and insert drama where it would be non-existent otherwise. Feelings can be hurt; expectations may be missed because of the belief that the other person "should have known." A big assumption we suffer from: we will be rejected by others, so we are not free to express ourselves individually and thus we don't.

d. How many times do we WONDER why a greater number of people do not participate in group activities? How easy has it been to label a subgroup of people as apathetic or dead weight pulling down the group? How many times do we take a pulse after recruitment activities to find out why someone made an alternate choice so that the group can learn from it?

e. You do not have to make assumptions when you know the truth (in other words, be sure you really understand the situation). Asking questions when misunderstandings or ignorance arises circumvents the power of assumptions.

✎ _____ ⌨

f. What does it mean to gossip?

Briefly describe a situation in which you engaged in a form of gossip.

247

✎ _____ ⌨

g. Gossip (considered from the individual's perspective). Can be any idea shared with another that influences perception. Examples include:

▷Movie reviews.

▷Listening to classmates ahead in the program concerning classes, professors and preceptors.

▷The "hermit neighbor" feared by all small children.

Gossip can shape perceptions before the individual is exposed to the person or situation and formulate an opinion for himself or herself.

How many people attended an event because of what someone SPECIFICALLY said?

How many people had a preconceived idea about the experience based on what someone SPECIFICALLY said?

How often do our leaders guide us and stop there to ALLOW us to have our OWN EXPERIENCES and SHAPE our OWN PERCEPTIONS?

✎ _____ ⌨

h. Gossip is a broad term and relevant to many every day experiences. Gossip in this sense does not necessarily indicate "he said, he did" type of events. Again, it can be any idea shared with another that shapes the receiver's interpretation.

✎ _____ ⌨

Step 5.

Scenario #1: You are working in your pharmacy. An unknown person walks up to you and pleasantly says "Hello" and tells you they do not have insurance and they want to know the price of their prescription. You quickly inform her that the order would cost around $40 and you offer to fill it. The person kindly thanks you for the information, declines to have the prescription filled, and walks out.

a. What can you say with certainty about the unknown person?

✎ _____ ⌨

b. Can you assume that they left happy and are okay?

✎ _____ ⌨

Scenario #2: You are working in your pharmacy. An unknown person walks up to you and pleasantly says "Hello" and tells you they do not have insurance and they want to know the price of their prescription. You quickly inform her that the order would cost around $40 and you offer to fill it. She yells: "This is highway robbery!" and "You health-care workers are all alike – vultures preying on the sick and dying!"

c. What about now? What can you say for certain is happening with this person?

✎ _____ ⌨

d. Anything we say is speculation, really. It is made up/our story. We do not know the root upon which

248

this is based – in either case (Scenario #1 or 2).

 e. If there is a complex correlation between behavior and motivation, how can we be relatively sure we understand where someone stands when we interact with them?

 ✎ _____ ⌨

 f. What do you think about the threat of making assumptions in either case?

 ✎ _____ ⌨

 g. It is important to acknowledge that each person is motivated by different reasons at different times to different degrees and his or her action(s) in response to a situation may affect our motivation. For example, in Scenario #1, you might be motivated to do nothing more because you perceive no follow up is required (person seems fine). In Scenario #2, you might be motivated to get the person physically out of the pharmacy quickly so that others do not overhear the ruckus. You might also be motivated to do nothing, because the person is yelling at you and you don't set prices but merely "work here."

 ✎ _____ ⌨

Consider the impact to relationships when assumptions are made. What is gained? What is risked?

 ✎ _____ ⌨

33.4. Discussion questions:

Per facilitator …
How might a pharmacist use conflict-management techniques within a pharmacy team?
How might a pharmacist use conflict-management techniques with one or more patients?
Facilitator discretion: Use of Annex 33-2. Conflict-Assessment Crossword Puzzle

 Conflict Management: Optional Quiz
1. Which is NOT a method of resolving conflict?
 a. Denial
 b. Dominance
 c. Negotiation
 d. Delegation
 e. Collaboration
2. Compromise is appropriate when:
 a. Both parties have enough leeway to give.
 b. Time is available to complete the process.
 c. The issue is relatively unimportant.
 d. Power comes with the position of authority.
3. Collaboration is NOT appropriate when:
 a. The original inflated position is unrealistic.
 b. Abilities and commitment are not present.

249

c. Losers have no way of expressing need.

d. The issue is important.

4. Which is NOT a type of conflict?

a. Values level

b. Purpose level

c. Factual level

d. Individual level

5. Which is NOT a step in the resolution process?

a. Identify

b. Negotiate

c. Listen

d. Follow-through

33.5. After-class assignments:

A. Observe behavior of people around you in terms of conflict. Apply the conflict-management techniques described here.

B. Fulfill the before-class activities for the next Module assigned by your facilitator.

33.6. Bibliography, references, & resources:

Flashcards via Quizlet, https://quizlet.com/class/3716098/, Conflict Types & Action Steps » 8 terms; Conflict Resolution » 5 terms

Ford J, Ford L. *The Four Conversations: Daily Communication That Gets Results*. Oakland, CA: Berrett-Koehler Publishers, 2009. www.bkconnection.com

Hart LB. *Learning from Conflict.* Addison-Wesley Publishing Co., 1981.

See also Module Z.

Annex 33-1. Five Basic Methods for Resolving Conflict: A Summary

Separate annex documents available to facilitators upon request (LeadGrowShape@plei.org).

Method	What Happens When Used:	Appropriate to Use When:	Inappropriate to Use When:
Denial or Withdrawal	Person tries to solve problem by denying existence. Results in win/lose situation.	Issue is relatively unimportant; timing is wrong; cooling-off period is needed; short term use only.	Issue is important; when issue will not disappear, but build.
Suppression or Smoothing	Differences are played down; surface harmony exists. Results in win/lose in forms of resentment, defensiveness, and possible sabotage if issue remains suppressed.	Same as above, also when preservation of relationship is more important at the moment.	Reluctance to deal with conflict leads to evasion of an important issue; when others are ready and willing to deal with issue.
Power or Dominance	One's authority, position, majority rule, or a persuasive minority settles the conflict. Results in win/lose if the dominated party sees no hope for itself.	When power comes with position of authority; when this method has been agreed upon.	Losers have no way to express need, could result in future disruptions.
Compromise or Negotiation	Each party gives up something to meet midway. Results in win/lose if "middle of the road" position ignores the real diversity of the issue.	Both parties have enough leeway to give; resources are limited; when win/lose stance is undesirable.	Original inflated position is unrealistic; solution is watered down to be effective; commitment is doubted by parties involved.
Collaboration	Abilities, values & expertise of all are recognized; each person's position is clear, but emphasis is on a group solution. Results in win/win for all.	Time is available to complete the process; parties are committed and trained in use of the process.	The conditions of time, abilities, and commitment are not present.

Adapted from: Hart LB. *Learning from Conflict.* Addison-Wesley Publishing Co., 1981.

Annex 33-2. Conflict-Assessment Crossword Puzzle

Separate annex documents available to facilitators upon request (LeadGrowShape@plei.org).

Across

4. Resolution step where you show how much your interest in understanding the other side
5. Resolution step searching for areas of agreement and common goals
7. Conflict type centered on verifiable statements *versus* assumptions
8. Resolution step where you Implement your joint plan

Down

1. Conflict type centered on your way *versus* my way of doing things
2. Resolution step featuring acknowledgement of the type of conflict you are in
3. Conflict type centered on your way *versus* my core values
5. Resolution step where you explain your perspective
6. Conflict type centered on your way *versus* my goals

Module « **34** »   SHAPING YOUR ENVIRONMENT

☞ Learning Objectives:

Objective 1. To explore organizational and personal behavior under stressful circumstances.
Objective 2. To test problem-assessment and decision-making skills in a series of realistic practice scenarios.
Objective 3. To shift conversions to the point where you are asking the questions, as a means of regaining control in stressful circumstance.

The stress and pressure in our day-to-days lives can be daunting. It's easy to feel that "they" have control and we are merely pawns. But that is not your only choice. Indeed, if you seek help from others, if you are the one who is asking the questions, you will exert your autonomy and regain a degree of control that will lift your mood, brighten your day, and help restore your spirit.

This Module is designed to help you realize how much control you have in shaping your environment, even when it seems like others are in control.

34.1. Readings or activities <u>before class</u>:

Re-read Annex 16-1, Performance Conversations & Closure Conversations. Be prepared to discuss.
Read and be prepared to discuss this passage about the Pegasus Grille. Then reflect on how can you make your practice setting a "Pegasus Grille."

A Culinary Oasis: It's No Mirage. How one man's enterprise makes the chow line a dining experience.
Julian E. Barnes, *U.S. News & World Report*, December 6, 2004.

CAMP LIBERTY, IRAQ—At most of the dining facilities at this sprawling American military base next to the Baghdad airport, the grapes look awful, the steak is all gristle, and the desserts, well, never mind.

But at the Pegasus chow hall here, such culinary misdemeanors simply aren't tolerated. Every afternoon, Joe Pradarits culls the bad fruit from the good to create a gorgeous platter of watermelon, pineapple, kiwi, and, yes, purely perfect grapes. Then there's the Sunday prime rib. Ed Sholes III marinates that baby for two full days, then cooks it up medium rare and slices it as thick as each soldier wants. At night, there are banana splits, smoothies, five different pies, and three different kinds of cake ....

Fine dining, of course, is as much about the ambience as the food. At Pegasus, the institutional white walls are festooned with sports banners. The plastic tables are draped with green tasseled tablecloths that complement the handsome gold window treatments. The servers all wear toques blanches—tall, white chef's hats. And then there are the lights: The harsh fluorescent bulbs have been removed, replaced by ceiling fans with warm tungsten bulbs.

The man behind this unique culinary oasis is a retired Army cook with a missionary's zeal and a talent for infecting others with his creative drive. Retired from a 25-year career as a Marine Corps and Army cook, Floyd Lee has come to Iraq to create the perfect soldier's dining experience. ...

Every day, the 1st Cavalry soldiers who dine at Pegasus find Lee making his rounds, checking that everything is just right. "I work the front of the house," he says. "You have to know the diner." ...

253

"He's like a 200,000-watt light bulb with ideas going off in his head all the time," says Sholes, a New Orleans resident who oversees the Pegasus kitchen. ...

Lee's feat is all the more remarkable because he gets his food from the same source as the other dining halls. The basic fare is the standard 21-day Army menu. But the staff at Pegasus is always looking for ways to spice up a recipe or add a little extra zip. ... Every day, Lee puts out two containers, one labeled Texas Sweet Tea and one labeled Carolina Sweet Tea. It is the same stuff, but the arguments about which is better go on for days.

... Iraq can grind down even the most gung-ho soldier. The tours last mostly for a full year, the workweek is seven days long, and workdays can stretch to 18 hours or more. ... So sometimes all they have to look forward to is a meal. "They are in danger over here," says Lee. "... As I see it, I am not just in charge of food service; I am in charge of *morale*."

What are five ways you can make your workplace or college setting like the Pegasus Grille?

1. ✎ _____ ⌨

2. ✎ _____ ⌨

3. ✎ _____ ⌨

4. ✎ _____ ⌨

5. ✎ _____ ⌨

34.2. Resources needed:

Annex 34-1. Selected Ways to Improve Your Pharmacy Work Life

34.3. In-class activities:

"Life is an escalator. Ask the people ahead of you for advice from where they stand, from what they can see." John D. Grabenstein

Step 1. Questions?
Step 2. Quote.
Step 3. Exercise.

SCENARIOS: SHAPING YOUR ENVIRONMENT

a. Align into subgroups of two to three people each, so you can share possible solutions at appropriate points.

b. Think about the two following scenarios:

▶

Scenario #1. "You are at the mall."

a. The clerk scans one of your purchases twice – you notice. What do you do?

b. At lunch, you bite into your "hot" food and find it cold. What do you do?

c. Your companion wants to visit a different store than you do. What do you do?

Ask the participants how they dealt with the scenarios at the mall. Would they suffer in silence? Or would they shape their environment to their own liking?

Scenario #2. "You are at work."

a. The prescription order in front of you seems improper for this patient. What do you do?

b. The pharmacy technician supporting you keeps slipping away for unexplained absences during the shift. What do you do?

c. The pharmacist on an earlier shift left multiple problems or questions unresolved (what really irks you is that this keeps happening repeatedly) – you respond by …

Regarding the scenarios at work: Assume that you are new in the job and are not sure what one should do… what one is allowed to do by the company. Who would you turn to for coaching?

▸

Step 4. Now proceed with several of the following scenarios.

a. For each scenario, independently identify a possible solution. Take 2 minutes to annotate Workbook.

b. Then huddle and have each participant share a solution with the small group. Record ideas in Workbook. Take 2 minutes to do so. The group picks one of the solutions to share with the whole assembly.

c. Consider another scenario and repeat steps above.

Scenario #3: "Absences." The pharmacy technician supporting you keeps slipping away for unexplained absences during the shift. How should you respond?

✎ _____ ▦

Scenario #4: "Left-Overs." The pharmacist on an earlier shift left multiple problems or questions unresolved. You are on duty now and need to deal with the mess. What really irks you is that this keeps happening repeatedly. How should you respond?

✎ _____ ▦

Scenario #5: "Choices." An angry patient is criticizing you in a loud voice, while several other customers are watching (and listening). Your partner, standing beside you, is pointing to the telephone, whispering that Dr. Smith insists on speaking to you immediately. What should you do?

✎ _____ ▦

✎ _____ ▦

Scenario #6: "Priorities." Assume you have a 6-year-old daughter. Her school play is Wednesday afternoon. Fortunately, you are off on Wednesday afternoon. But late on Tuesday, your boss asks whether you can work Wednesday (including afternoon hours) to cover for a sick coworker. What should you do?

Points to consider:

▸ Answer to the acute situation

▸ Answer suitable for the long term

▸ Any differences by setting: community, inpatient, nursing home, office?

- When, how to engage managers in this situation?
- Look for patterns.
- If you cannot change physical environment? (change your response)

Step 5. Consider Annex 34-1 with Jacobs' "Ways to Improve Your Pharmacy Worklife." We are all in this together. If you could sum up all the experiences of people in the room, it would span centuries. If we work together and share our accumulated knowledge, experience, and wisdom, we can accomplish a lot.

Am I in this alone? No way! Ask for help – with confidence and without shame. You cannot be expected to know everything, even if you are a health-care professional who should know – even if we are reluctant to admit we need help.

Who would you ask for help? Ask your buddies, your coworkers, your partners for their opinions. Ask if they have been faced with similar dilemmas; learn how they approached the situation. Recognize that not all suggestions will be applicable or will be the optimal way to address the situation. These are not easy topics and there is rarely "one right answer," since there may be other varied factors that may influence the situation. Listening to others may be enough to help you determine what makes sense for the situation you have at hand. Share your ideas, your findings.

Step 6. Applying These Lessons to Help Others.

a. To overcome aimless juggling of tasks and the underlying reason (fear of failure) for not examining what it is that we keep in midair, we can learn to recognize behaviors associated with failure that might undermine or prevent assessment of what is being juggled by people around us.

b. So, close your eyes and picture yourself in your workplace or a college setting. What comes to mind in terms of the behaviors of colleagues in terms of failure?

c. Aimless juggling of "priorities" (and less important tasks) challenges our ability to establish balance in our lives. This includes the time dedicated to our work, as well. It is not enough to identify our priorities (what we juggle and why) or to acknowledge why we cannot let go of something for fear we might let others down. We may not come right out and say that we are afraid of feeling like we are failing or perceived by others as having failed. But failure may manifest through in behavior. If we can learn to recognize how people behave in response to failure, we can see it – either in ourselves (primary) or in others (secondary) and do something to help. In *Failing Forward*, John C. Maxwell describes behaviors that are often related to failure, such as:

Paralysis	Purposelessness	Blame
Procrastination	Self-pity	Hopelessness
Excuses	Wasted energy	Despair
Fear	Suffering	

d. Now that you are thinking about it, to what degree do these exist in your work environment or college setting? What happens in the pharmacy when one or more of these behaviors is demonstrated by one person? Does it matter whether they are a clerk or a certified technician or a pharmacist?

e. Let's explore some of the things that can be done each day, so we can put ourselves in a better position to help others identify their priorities and align with what will make them (and us collectively) happy, fulfilled, or satisfied.

34.4. Discussion questions:

Per facilitator

34.5. After-class assignments:

A. The next time you are in a stressful situation, try to pull back and think of the ways you could take control (asking questions, reframing the situation, reminding the other party of other facts). Even if you can't do this in the heat of the moment, reflect on what you might do next time in a similar situation.
B. Fulfill the before-class activities for the next Module assigned by your facilitator.

34.6. Bibliography, references, & resources:

Ford J, Ford L. *The Four Conversations: Daily Communication That Gets Results*. Oakland, CA: Berrett-Koehler Publishers, 2009. www.bkconnection.com

Gladwell M. *The Tipping Point: How Little Things Can Make a Big Difference.* NYC: Little, Brown & Co., 2000.

Jacobs MR. *101 Ways to Improve Your Pharmacy Worklife*. Washington, DC: American Pharmacists Association, 2001.

Annex 34-1. Selected Ways to Improve Your Pharmacy Worklife (Jacobs)

Separate annex documents available to facilitators upon request (LeadGrowShape@plei.org).

Idea #	Ways to Improve Your Pharmacy Worklife
3	Set a standard pickup time for special orders.
7, 40	Train patients to call 24 hours in advance for refills. Require 24 hours' notice for compounded prescriptions.
13	Change from "customer" to "patient."
14	Display your credentials.
20	Post "canned responses" by each of the phones.
25	Don't duplicate effort – type information directly into the computer.
33	Have a weekly "meeting on paper."
36	Redirect long-winded patients.
37	Use an OTC consultation form.
38, 49	Put drugs away using basket organizers. Prioritize prescriptions using colored baskets.
41	Condition patients to call their doctors for refills.
42	Hand the patient the telephone right in the pharmacy.
47	Use technicians' help with prescription transfers.
51	Have technicians fill all prescriptions.
53	Use appointments for extended counseling sessions.
80	Stop apologizing to doctors and nurses.
92	Create a business card or redesign the one you have.
97	Teach inhaler technique at the consultation window.
99	Fax "SOAP notes" to medical records.

Adapted from: Jacobs MR. *101 Ways to Improve Your Pharmacy Worklife.* Washington, DC: American Pharmacists Association, 2001.

See book for all 101 ways, plus detailed discussion.

Module « 35 »   STAYING BALANCED

☞ Learning Objectives:

Objective 1. To help participants find balance in personal and professional lives and live a more fulfilling life.

Objective 2. To help participants take ownership of workplace morale.

Objective 3. To model the LIMS technique of questions and empathy to prevent crisis and diffuse difficult situations. Listen – Isolate – Mirror – Solve.

We intend to enlighten participants on how knowing and understanding one's self can help individuals do more for themselves and others.

Stress management, avoiding burnout. Would rat race or treadmill be a good word to describe your pharmacy practice or life? Do you find yourself getting exasperated and impatient with greater frequency? We will show you ways to manage stress and turn it to your advantage.

Turn the tables and get to the point where you are asking the questions.

Oh, at the very end of this Module, we talk about money.

35.1. Readings or activities before class:

Read and be prepared to discuss the text for this Module.

35.2. Resources needed:

Annex 35-1. Money & Self-Awareness

35.3. In-class activities:

"Life is like riding a bicycle.
To keep your balance, you must keep moving." Albert Einstein

Step 1. Questions?
Step 2. Quote.
Step 3. Exercise.

PRESSURE-PROOF PROFESSIONALS

a. Read Rudyard Kipling's passage from "If…" and comment on it as a warm up for the session.

If…

If you can keep your head when all about you
Are losing theirs and blaming it on you,

If you can trust yourself when all men doubt you,
But make allowance for their doubting too;

...
If you can fill the unforgiving minute
With sixty seconds' worth of distance run –
Yours is the Earth and everything that's in it,
And – which is more – you'll be a *professional my friend*!

- (Joseph) Rudyard Kipling, circa 1895

'man my son' in the original

b. There is great joy in a job well done and at the highest level. Duress can dismantle your well-meaning and empathetic self and ability to focus. You, as the professional, can come to work armored with an:

i. attitude of gratitude,

ii. ownership of your problems, and

iii. courage to model your pressure-proof professionalism to others.

An attitude of gratitude will keep you smiling!

So many employees look at their employer and their clients as the enemy, when it is the employees who apply for and accept the jobs; these individuals are responsible for choosing the profession, too. An attitude of gratitude is taking time to establish or re-establish those aspects of the job that bring you joy.

Step 4. What are five things you really love about your (current or recent) job? List them in your Workbook.

a. _____

b. _____

c. _____

d. _____

e. _____

Step 5. Arriving at workplace #1. Follow facilitator instructions.

Step 6. Now, the opposing question: "What are five things you really dislike about your (current or recent) job? List them in your Workbook.

a. _____

b. _____

c. ✍ _____ ⌨

d. ✍ _____ ⌨

e. ✍ _____ ⌨

Step 7. Arriving at workplace #2. Follow facilitator instructions.

Step 8. What is the worst job you can think of? Name five things that make it a "horrible" job.

a. ✍ _____ ⌨

b. ✍ _____ ⌨

c. ✍ _____ ⌨

d. ✍ _____ ⌨

e. ✍ _____ ⌨

Step 9. Discuss the answers. How does your job look now?

Step 10. Model the Pressure-Proof Professional. The LIMS technique described below is a tool that can help you deal with difficult patient situations. Listen – Isolate – Mirror – Solve.

Listen – Do not interrupt until they are finished, so you gain all available information. Ask clarifying questions. Use "I understand …" (if you do understand). Or say "I heard you say that …"

Isolate – What is their real concern? Example: Are they angry the physician wrote for a prescription they cannot afford? Are they taking it out on you? Or are they scared that they have just been diagnosed with something they fear and their anger at the prescription price is only a secondary problem? If applicable, isolate that they want a less-expensive medicine and you will be happy to be part of the solution by …

Mirror – their expressed needs. Try stating it in a sentence, like "I understand that…" Or "I heard you say that…" For example, "I understand the doctor wrote for an expensive medicine and that you would prefer something less expensive. Is that correct?" Let them agree or disagree. Or they may engage with you as being on their side now. "Yes, that's what I want…" or "No, what I really meant was…" Refrain from saying "I understand," because you may be told you have not had the same experience.

Solve – "Well, let me call the doctor and try to get you something less expensive. Just have a seat and we'll get right on this for you…"

Pearl: The person in control is the person asking the questions.

a. People do not always want answers to their problems or in response to their 'rant'; often, they just want to know someone cares. Patients coming into your pharmacy are no different. The pharmacy is usually the last stop before they get home and the pharmacist (or pharmacy technician) is the last person with whom they interact (and sometime unload upon). Let the patient know you are their advocate, particularly if the patient is upset. Let them know you value their time and money – let them know you value them.

b. Practical Exercise.

TIME VALVE

<u>How long</u>? {often said in a huff, as in "How long is this going to take?"}

(Possible answers: I understand you are in a hurry…when did you want to pick it up? That would be about 15 minutes. Would you like to have a seat or come back in a little bit?)

<u>How much</u>? {often said in a huff, as in "How much is this going to cost?"}

I was shorted three pills. Why do you always short me pills?

All you have to do is put a sticker on it, why does it take so long?

Why can't you fill my Vicodin® again? I told you I lost the bottle yesterday.

Why do you always charge me so much?

Can you ring all of this up?

The goal is to get back in charge and manage your situation on your own terms. One way to do that is to get back to the point where you are asking questions.

You can be a pressure-proof professional and cultivate a pressure-proof practice by

▸ maintaining an attitude of gratitude and the smile that goes with it,

▸ being intentional about morale and keeping people upbeat, and

▸ by using questions to keep in control.

Spirit of Aloha

"It's being true to yourself first, and then you can be true to everybody else with genuine aloha. It's the love that you would share with a child, that you love, your child! It's the same love you would share with a complete stranger. That's Aloha." – Titus Kinimaka, highperformancesurf.com

35.4. Discussion questions:

Per facilitator

35.5. After-class assignments:

A. Review and consider the comments about Money & Self-Awareness in Annex 35-1.
B. Fulfill the before-class activities for the next Module assigned by your facilitator.

35.6. Bibliography, references, & resources:

Canfield J. *The Success Principles: How to Get from Where You Are to Where You Want to Be.* New York: Harper Collins, 2005.
Flashcards via Quizlet, https://quizlet.com/class/3716098/, L-I-M-S » 4 terms

Annex 35-1. Money & Self-Awareness

Separate annex documents available to facilitators upon request (LeadGrowShape@plei.org).

For you to ponder as you make your way in the world...

This Workbook spends a lot of time helping you become more self-aware, typically using workplace and team examples. We would be remiss if we did not spend just a little time and space to address what happens when self-awareness intersects with money and financial affairs. We make no effort here to teach you the basics of money management, cash flow, investment, researching credit card deals, or retirement plans. Our role is to help you understand yourself better.

It is indisputable that who you are and what motivates you will translate into how quickly money accumulates or slips through your fingers. All the earlier lessons about understanding your core values and priorities apply here.

- As you make a big purchase, are you excited or nervous or both?
- The last time you made a financial mistake, were you chagrined or ashamed or _____?
- Are you open to acknowledging that you have made or might make financial mistakes?

Few people have a completely rational relationship with money. For most, money is encumbered with more or less emotional and psychological baggage. This emotional overlay affects how prudently or imprudently we make financial decisions.

Many of our money emotions come from the way our parents handled money and discussed their finances. That could be good or bad. You might have seen free-spenders or you might have seen methodical savers.

Regardless, it is important for you to find a good balance between spending and saving. Debt is justifiable if it helps you purchase a long-term asset (like a college degree or a house). But do not finance a vacation at credit-card interest rates. Avoid paying fees whenever possible.

Some general principles:

▷ Spend less than you earn
▷ Invest early and frequently
▷ Pay off debt, use credit sparingly
▷ Build assets and create passive income

If you don't understand the push-and-pull (lift and drag) of any of those principles, learn more.

With the stock market and some other investments, risk and reward travel together. Diversify. Start your retirement savings early and take full advantage of the magic of compound interest. Expect the stock market to have up and down cycles. Beware of overconfidence when markets rally. Trust your long-range plan when markets decline. Certainly by the time you have children (maybe before), write a will and take out life insurance. With insurance, be able to compare and contrast term *versus* whole insurance.

At the end of the day, budgets reflect your values. What you spend money on (things you can touch, experiences, donations) say a lot about what you stand for and who you are. Look at your budget every month. If you don't like what you see, change it.

Explore your own financial values, financial priorities, and financial balance with these questions:

- How do you feel about earning money?
- What does money mean to you?
- How does buying something make you feel?

- How does saving for the future make you feel?
- How do budgeting and tracking expenses make you feel?
- How do you feel when financial markets are up?
- How do you feel when financial markets are down or volatile?
- How do you feel about your financial future?

Notes: ✍ _____ ⌨

Financial professionals can be excellent sources of information and advice, but be sure to understand their compensation systems. To be blunt, find out if they are paid by commissions earned on payments you make to them, which could encourage overuse of the products they sell. Just ask. And be sure it's an answer you understand, not jargon.

Here are a few approaches to moving forward:
- If your employer offers to match investment funds you set aside, be sure to maximize the match. Consider it free money.
- Automate your saving and investing with routine deductions from your paycheck or automatic bank transfers each payday or each month. Pay yourself first.
- Adopt a financial strategy that helps neutralize your emotions during stressful periods.
- Take small steps toward better financial behaviors like bi-weekly family budget meetings.
- Forgive yourself for mistakes and get back on track as quickly as possible.

[*Optional*] Look at the "mental models" written by Joshua Kennon, beginnersinvest.about.com/ Consider starting with "Investing Basics."

Or see www.joshuakennon.com/about-dot-com-investing-for-beginners-directory/. Consider starting with "The Basics."

See also investor.gov and consumerfinance.gov.

Notes: ✍ _____ ⌨

Module « **X** »   THE BIG GAME OF LIFE

☞ Learning Objectives:

Objective 1. To be happy.
Objective 2. To be fulfilled.
Objective 3. To help other people.

X.1. Readings or activities <u>before class:</u>

Read for enjoyment, advancement, and fulfillment, even when there is no class assignment.
A few ideas appear in Module Z.

X.2. Resources needed:

Support from others.
The ability to be self-critical.
A vision of a better tomorrow.

X.3. In-class activities:

"A mind that is stretched by a new experience can never go back to its old dimensions."
Oliver Wendell Holmes, Jr.

Step 1. Questions?
Step 2. Quote.

X.5. After-class assignments:

Learning never ends.
The crowning glory of life is to serve.
Take another look at the Values-Interests-Strengths-Needs (VISN) Chart in Annex 3-2. Adjust any entries that
    need to be updated.

Module « Y » EVALUATION

☞ Learning Objectives:

Objective 1. To evaluate this Workbook and the course curriculum, to itemize improvements that could improve the next edition of the Workbook and the next iteration of the class.
Objective 2. To distribute resources for further leadership development.
Objective 3. To reach closure after all the interpersonal sharing.

Y.1. Readings or activities <u>before class:</u>

Ponder how you will fill out Annex Y-1, Annex Y-2, and Annex Y-3.

Y.2. Resources needed:

Print out Annex Y-3 before class, so that you can turn it in to your facilitator after you complete it, to help improve the next iteration of this Workbook.
Annex Y-1. Self-Assessment vis-à-vis CAPE Competencies for Student Leaders
Annex Y-2. Personal Leadership Assessment (second iteration)
Annex Y-3. Critique of Workbook

Y.3. In-class activities:

"And any skill can be developed, strengthened and enhanced given the motivation and desire along with practice and feedback, role models, and coaching.." Posner BZ. J Lead Educ. 2009;8(1):1-10.

Step 1. Questions?
Step 2. Quote.
Step 3. Self-Evaluation. Let's think back to the opening session of the class. You might want to a look at the text in Module 1 to refresh your memory.
   Refresh your memory of the definitions of the four key elements addressed by this Workbook:
   Self-awareness – Examine and reflect on personal knowledge, skills, abilities, beliefs, biases, motivation, and emotions that could enhance or limit personal and professional growth.
   Leadership – Demonstrate responsibility for creating and achieving shared goals, regardless of position.
   Innovation & entrepreneurship – Engage in innovative activities by using creative thinking to envision better ways of accomplishing professional goals.
   Professionalism – Exhibit behaviors and values that are consistent with the trust given to the profession by patients, other healthcare providers, and society.
   a. How would you explain to someone who knows you well which of your attitudes and behaviors have changed since the beginning of the course, with respect to these four elements?

Self-awareness – ✍ _____ ⌨

Leadership – ✍ _____ ⌨

Innovation & entrepreneurship – ✍ _____ ⌨

Professionalism – ✍ _____ ⌨

b. Next, jot down some notes about yourself, regarding the competencies for pharmacy student leader development, listed in Table 1-A:

✍ _____ ⌨

c. Complete Annex Y-1, to help you assess where you stand in leader development vis-à-vis becoming a pharmacist.

d. Complete Annex Y-2, to help describe your perception of your leadership qualities and skills.

Step 4. To critique the Workbook, use Annex Y-3. Hand in the completed Annex to your facilitator, to help improve the next iteration of this Workbook. You can also use Appendix 8 to send us feedback.

Step 5. To critique the course, use the form or process provided by your facilitator.

Step 6. See the resources for further self-development in Module Z.

Y.5. After-class assignments:

Take another look at the Values-Interests-Strengths-Needs (VISN) Chart in Annex 3-2. Adjust any entries that need to be updated.

Annex Y-1. Self-Assessment vis-à-vis CAPE Competencies for Student Leadership Development

Separate annex documents available to facilitators upon request (LeadGrowShape@plei.org).

Leadership Knowledge	Self-Assessment (I can…, I will…, I need to…)
Competency 1: Explain the importance of leadership in pharmacy.	▸
Competency 2: Recognize that leadership comes from those with and without titles.	▸
Competency 3: Distinguish between leadership and management.	▸
Competency 4: Describe the characteristics, behaviors and practices of effective leaders.	▸
Personal Leadership Commitment	
Competency 5: Demonstrate self-awareness in leadership.	▸
Competency 6: Engage in personal leadership development.	▸
Leadership Skill Development	
Competency 7: Develop a shared vision for an initiative or project.	▸
Competency 8: Collaborate with others.	▸
Competency 9: Lead members of a team.	▸
Competency 10: Develop knowledge of organizational culture.	▸
Competency 11: Outline change processes.	▸

Source: AACP CAPE Janke KK, Traynor AP, Boyle CJ. Competencies for student leadership development in doctor of pharmacy curricula to assist curriculum committees and leadership instructors. *Am J Pharm Educ*. 2013 Dec 16;77(10):222. www.ncbi.nlm.nih.gov/pmc/articles/PMC3872941/pdf/ajpe7710222.pdf

Annex Y-2. Personal Leadership Assessment (second iteration)

Separate annex documents available to facilitators upon request (LeadGrowShape@plei.org).

A. Rank yourself on how well you exhibit these leadership *qualities:*

Quality:	Low			High	
1. Self-confidence	1	2	3	4	5
2. Respect for and confidence in others	1	2	3	4	5
3. Ability to empower or challenge others	1	2	3	4	5
4. Fairness, being equitable	1	2	3	4	5
5. Ability to work with people at any level	1	2	3	4	5
6. Ability to communicate with others	1	2	3	4	5
7. Expertise, knowledge within a subject	1	2	3	4	5
8. Ethical behavior	1	2	3	4	5
9. Creativity	1	2	3	4	5
10. Willingness to take a calculated risk	1	2	3	4	5
Sum of scores:	▶				
Mean score (sum ÷ 10):	▶				

B. How well do you translate your leadership talents into action? Rank yourself on how well you use these leadership *skills*:

Skill:	Low			High	
1. Delegate	1	2	3	4	5
2. Motivate, inspire	1	2	3	4	5
3. Coach, counsel, develop	1	2	3	4	5
4. Encourage teamwork	1	2	3	4	5
5. Serve as a model	1	2	3	4	5
6. Discover/create new opportunities/goals	1	2	3	4	5
Sum of scores:	▶				
Mean score (sum ÷ 6):	▶				

Note: This instrument has not been psychometrically validated. The scores are suitable for introspection only.

C. From the items in the boxes above, list three aspects of your leadership *capacity (qualities)* you would like to continue to improve. Then list three aspects of your leadership *skills (behavior)* you would like to continue to improve:

Capacity/Qualities:

a. _____ b. _____ c. _____

Skills/Behavior:

a. _____ b. _____ c. _____

      Why are these items important to you? For what future purpose will they serve to address what you wrote above?

      ✍ _____ ⌨

      How will you go about improving in each area? What specific steps might you take or to whom might you ask for help? What could you do in the next weeks to get started?

      ✍ _____ ⌨

D. For which of these aspects of leadership has this Workbook been the most effective in helping you?

      ✍ _____ ⌨

E. How have you most changed since the opening day of this course?

      ✍ _____ ⌨

Annex Y-3. Critique of Workbook

Separate annex documents available to facilitators upon request (LeadGrowShape@plei.org).

Please answer the following questions by circling the appropriate rating:

Rate the content of the Workbook [*Lead←Grow→Shape*].
   a. Outstanding   b. Good   c. Satisfactory   d. Fair   e. Poor

Rate the usefulness of the Workbook [*Lead←Grow→Shape*].
   a. Outstanding   b. Good   c. Satisfactory   d. Fair   e. Poor

This Workbook [*Lead←Grow→Shape*] helped the course meet its objectives.
   a. Strongly Agree   b. Agree   c. Disagree   d. Strongly Disagree

The Workbook [*Lead←Grow→Shape*] helped develop one or more of my leadership traits or skills.
   a. Strongly Agree   b. Agree   c. Disagree   d. Strongly Disagree

Please indicate anything you particularly liked about the content or format of this Workbook:

   ►

_____

   ►

_____

Please indicate anything you particularly disliked about the content or format of this Workbook:

   ►

_____

_____

If you had viewing difficulties on Kindle®, tell us as much as you know:

Hardware type: _____

Software (app) type: _____

Software (app) version: _____

Describe problem: _____

PROGRAM CRITIQUE

1. This program has been valuable to my work and studies.
   a. Strongly Agree   b. Agree   c. Disagree   d. Strongly Disagree

2. This program has been valuable to me personally.
   a. Strongly Agree   b. Agree   c. Disagree   d. Strongly Disagree

3. My facilitator(s) had the tools needed to do the job.
   a. Strongly Agree   b. Agree   c. Disagree   d. Strongly Disagree

   What was lacking? _____

4. What have you learned about leadership?

   _____

5. What have you learned about yourself?

   _____

6. What part of the Workbook did you consider most valuable? Why?

   _____

7. What part of the Workbook did you consider most confusing or least valuable? Why?

   _____

8. What topic would you have liked to spend more time on?

   _____

9. How should we improve this Workbook the next time we revise it?

   _____

Module « Z »   WHERE TO GO FOR MORE

This class (and this Workbook) have barely scratched the surface in the arena of personal development and leadership. Exercise your curiosity and keep learning. Just like Carnegie Hall, the best way to get to leadership is to practice, practice, practice.

The AACP Argus Commission of 2008-09 recognized that different student pharmacists will want differing levels of leadership-development content. Their prediction of how this could sort out appears in Table Z-1.

If you are one of the ones who wants more, keep reading…

Student Groups, Community Groups, Pharmacy-Practice Associations: These are the natural laboratories where student pharmacists can learn many skills, including interpersonal and leadership skills. Serve on a committee, chair a committee, run for office, lead when you have positional authority, lead when you have no position to brag about. This course helped prepare you. Now go practice and shape the future. APhA, ASHP, CPhA, and many other national practice-based associations offer training programs in leadership, management, and other skills. Check them out.

Independent Study: Colleges often offer opportunities for independent study to foster the skills, attitudes, and values needed for self-directed lifelong learning. Formal and informal learning activities will help you develop new competencies, enhance your professional practice, and achieve your career goals. For example, see: Boyd B, Williams J. Developing life-long learners through personal-growth projects. *J Lead Educ.* 2010;9(2):144-50. www.journalofleadershiped.org/attachments/article/148/Boyd_and_Williams.pdf

Co-curricular Activities: Get involved with planning and conducting any of these: Assemblies, grand rounds, advocacy programs, legislative-process discussions, health fairs, clinical-skills competitions, networking within multi-campus organizations, business-plan competitions, interprofessional seminars, post-graduate roundtables, formulary-review competitions, community outreach, or wherever your imagination takes you. Adapted from: Ross LA, *et al. Am J Pharm Educ.* 2013 Dec 16;77(10):220.

Think Outside Pharmacy – Web-Based Courses: A wide variety of personal-development courses are available on the Internet. One example is the Institute for Healthcare Improvement (IHI) Open School (www.ihi.org/education/ihiopenschool/Pages/default.aspx). This and similar programs can help you advance professionalism and interprofessional understanding and collaboration.

Residencies: Blend leadership and other self-development topics into a pharmacy residency. For examples, see one of the following articles.

Bartelme KM, Bzowyckyj A, Frueh J, Speedie M, Jacobson G, Sorensen TD. Experience and outcomes of a pharmaceutical care leadership residency program. *Innov Pharm.* 2014;5(3):168.

Fuller PD. Program for developing leadership in pharmacy residents. *Am J Health-Syst Pharm.* 2012;69(Jul 15):1231-3.

Gallina JN, Jeffrey LP, Temkin LA, Cardi V. Management seminar miniseries for training pharmacy residents. *Am J Hosp Pharm.* 1985;42:320-2.

Knoer SJ, Rough S, Gouveia WA. Student rotations in health-system pharmacy management and leadership. *Am J Health-Syst Pharm.* 2005;62(Dec 1):2539-41.

Sorensen TD, Biebighauser SM. Pharmaceutical care leadership: An innovative pharmacy practice residency model. *JAPhA.* 2003;43(Jul-Aug):527-32.

Noteworthy Leadership Development Practices in Schools of Pharmacy:

Creation of a culture of expectation for involvement as leaders.

Establishment of opportunities for leadership in student organizations.

Provision of role models and mentors for leadership.

Establishment of ways for valuing and recognizing efforts.

Promotion of leadership development programs for students and faculty members.

Integration of leadership building skills throughout the curriculum.

Source: Ross LA, Janke KK, Boyle CJ, Gianutsos G, Lindsey CC, Moczygemba LR, Whalen K. Preparation of faculty members and students to be citizen leaders and pharmacy advocates. *Am J Pharm Educ*. 2013 Dec 16;77(10):220. www.ncbi.nlm.nih.gov/pmc/articles/PMC3872939/pdf/ajpe7710220.pdf

FEED YOUR BRAIN; ENHANCE YOUR SELF-AWARE SELF:

Start a habit of walking into any bookstore and checking out the shelves full of books on leadership and improving yourself in various ways. Even the books that seem to be business-focused usually explore human-relationship principles that easily can be transferred from the business world to the pharmacy world.

If the content of one of these books looks interesting, read it and see how it can advance you on your journey in leading.

Book Synopsis 1 – How to Get Your Point Across in 30 Seconds

Frank MO. *How to Get Your Point Across in 30 Seconds—Or Less.* New York: Simon & Schuster, 1986.

The title says it all.

- Your objective
- Who's listening?
- The right approach
- The hook
- Your subject
- Ask for it
- Paint a picture

Book Synopsis 2 – 7 Habits of Highly Effective People

Covey SR. *The 7 Habits of Highly Effective People*. New York: Simon Schuster, 1989. Covey advocates attaining goals by aligning oneself to what he calls "true north" principles.

- Be proactive.
- Begin with the end in mind.
- Put first things first.
- Think win-win.
- Seek first to understand, then to be understood.
- Synergize.
- Sharpen the saw.

Book Synopsis 3 – The Speed of Trust

Covey SMR, Merrill RR. *The Speed of Trust: The One Thing That Changes Everything*. New York: Free Press, 2006. https://www.cu.edu/sites/default/files/ExecSummaries-The_Speed_of_Trust.pdf
The Four Cores of Credibility™

1. Integrity, 2. Intent, 3. Capabilities, 4. Results.

Integrity and Intent are character cores. Capabilities and Results are competency cores.

The 13 Behaviors of High Trust™

1. Talk Straight
2. Demonstrate Respect
3. Create Transparency
4. Right Wrongs
5. Show Loyalty
6. Deliver Results
7. Get Better
8. Confront Reality
9. Clarify Expectations
10. Practice Accountability
11. Listen First
12. Keep Commitments
13. Extend Trust

The 7 Low-Trust Organizational Taxes™

Redundancy

Bureaucracy

Politics

Disengagement

Turnover

Churn

Fraud

Book Synopsis 4 – 21 Indispensable Qualities of a Leader

Maxwell JC. *21 Indispensable Qualities of a Leader: Becoming the Person Others Will Want to Follow*. Thomas Nelson, 1999.
1. CHARACTER: Be a Piece of the Rock
2. CHARISMA: The First Impression Can Seal the Deal
3. COMMITMENT: It Separates Doers from Dreamers
4. COMMUNICATION: Without It You Travel Alone
5. COMPETENCE: If You Build It, They Will Come
6. COURAGE: One Person with Courage Is a Majority
7. DISCERNMENT: Put an End to Unsolved Mysteries
8. FOCUS: The Sharper It Is, the Sharper You Are
9. GENEROSITY: Your Candle Loses Nothing When It Lights Another

10. INITIATIVE: You Won't Leave Home Without It

11. LISTENING: To Connect with Their Hearts, Use Your Ears

12. PASSION: Take This Life and Love It

13. POSITIVE ATTITUDE: If You Believe You Can, You Can

14. PROBLEM SOLVING: You Cannot Let Your Problems Be a Problem

15. RELATIONSHIPS: If You Get Along, They'll Go Along

16. RESPONSIBILITY: If You Won't Carry the Ball, You Cannot Lead the Team

17. SECURITY: Competence Never Compensates for Insecurity

18. SELF-DISCIPLINE: The First Person You Lead Is You

19. SERVANTHOOD: To Get Ahead, Put Others First

20. TEACHABILITY: To Keep Leading, Keep Learning

21. VISION: You Can Seize Only What You Can See

https://vialogue.wordpress.com/2010/08/29/21-indispensable-qualities-of-a-leader-notes-review/

Book Synopsis 5 – The Four Conversations

Ford J, Ford L. *The Four Conversations: Daily Communication That Gets Results*. Oakland, CA: Berrett-Koehler Publishers, 2009. www.bkconnection.com

- ▸ Initiative Conversation
- ▸ Understanding Conversation
- ▸ Performance Conversation
- ▸ Closure Conversation

Book Synopsis 6 – The Four Agreements

Ruíz DM. *The Four Agreements: A Practical Guide to Personal Freedom*. New York: Amber-Allen, 1997.

1. Be impeccable with your word.

2. Don't take anything personally.

3. Don't make assumptions.

4. Always do your best.

Book Synopsis 7 –Five Voices

Kubicek J, Cockram S. *5 Voices: How to Communicate Effectively with Everyone You Lead*. New York: Wiley, March 2016; 5voices.com

- ▸ Nurturer: Champion of People. Concerned about relational health and harmony of the group.
- ▸ Connector: Champion of Relationships and Strategic Partnerships. Rallies people to causes and things they believe in.
- ▸ Pioneer: Champion of Results and Progress. Approaches life with an "Anything is possible!" attitude.
- ▸ Creative: Champion of Innovation. Outside the box thinker.
- ▸ Guardian: Champion of Responsibility and Stewardship. Respects and values logic, order, procedure, and process.

TABLE Z-1. THREE TIERS OF LEADERSHIP DEVELOPMENT ACTIVITIES (AACP ARGUS REPORT, 2008-09)

Activities for ALL students	Activities for the MAJORITY of students	Activities for a FEW students (~10-20%)
Didactic exposure to basic leadership theory and practice	Additional elective didactic or experiential coursework for leadership insights and skill development	Campus or business leadership programs, tracks or electives; dual degree programs in business or health administration
Observation exposure to identified leaders	Experiential exposure to identified leaders	"Make something work" – hands on experience in leading or changing program, process, new practice activity, *et cetera*.
Exposure to mentor(s) and mentoring concepts	Alumni-student, faculty-student and student-student collaboration	Service as officers of local student professional organizations or in campus organizations
Committee membership and team learning activities and experiences	Honors Program, leadership retreats	Regional or national involvement and recognition (national practice associations, fraternities, Phi Lambda Sigma, other groups)
Community volunteer activities and exposure to issues	Mentoring of students for specific leadership roles (committee chairs, project leadership)	Completion of requirements for a leadership designation upon graduation or a dual degree (e.g., MBA)
Participation in professional association meetings or activities	Service on committees of student organizations, both within school and larger academic and social communities; committee chairs	Leadership rotations as part of the advanced pharmacy practice experience
Service learning activities	Formal assessment of leadership traits and potential	

Source: Kerr RA, Beck DE, Doss J, Draugalis JR, Huang E, Irwin A, Patel A, Raehl CL, Reed B, Speedie MK, Maine LL, Athay J. Building a sustainable system of leadership development for pharmacy: Report of the 2008-09 Argus Commission. *Am J Pharm Educ*. 2009;73(Suppl):S5.

Appendix 1. Selected Accreditation Standards for Schools of Pharmacy

1. Accreditation Council for Pharmacy Education (ACPE), Standard 4 – 2016
2. Canadian Council for Accreditation of Pharmacy Programs (CCAPP) [Conseil Canadien d'Agrément des Programmes de Pharmacie], Standards 19, 21, and 33 – revised 2014

1. ACPE Standard 4: Personal & Professional Development – 2016

The program imparts to the graduate the knowledge, skills, abilities, behaviors, and attitudes necessary to demonstrate self-awareness, leadership, innovation and entrepreneurship, and professionalism.

Key Elements	Addressing this Topic	
	Module #s	Other Material
4.1. Self-awareness – The graduate is able to examine and reflect on personal knowledge, skills, abilities, beliefs, biases, motivation, and emotions that could enhance or limit personal and professional growth.	3, 6, 8, 9, 11, 12, 24, 35	▸
4.2. Leadership – The graduate is able to demonstrate responsibility for creating and achieving shared goals, regardless of position.	1, 2, 4, 5, 7, 8, 10, 13-15, 18, 19, 21-23, 25-34	▸
4.3. Innovation and entrepreneurship – The graduate is able to engage in innovative activities by using creative thinking to envision better ways of accomplishing professional goals.	16, 17, 20	▸
4.4. Professionalism – The graduate is able to exhibit behaviors and values that are consistent with the trust given to the profession by patients, other healthcare providers, and society.	12	▸

Source: ACPE, https://www.acpe-accredit.org/pdf/Standards2016FINAL.pdf

2. CCAPP Accreditation Standards 19, 21, and 33, for First Professional Degree in Pharmacy Programs – revised 2014

Standard 19: The Faculty must have suitable mechanisms to develop student leadership and professionalism, forums for student dialogue, and must ensure adequate communication of student opinions and perspectives.

Standard 21: The Faculty must provide an environment and culture that promotes professional behaviour and harmonious relationships among students, faculty, administrators, preceptors and staff.

Criterion 21.3: The Faculty must implement strategies and activities to strengthen the professional culture of the student experience. Examples of Evidence:

▷ Participation in professional curricular and extracurricular activities

▷ Service learning, volunteer experiences, community-engaged scholarship, social accountability or similar initiatives

▷ Participation in student inspired interprofessional activities

▷ Other professional activities, such as white coat ceremonies and student-developed codes of conduct, honour codes, and policies to guide student body relationships with the pharmaceutical industry with respect to the receipt of gifts or other benefits.

Standard 33: The Faculty must use and integrate a variety of teaching and learning methodologies that have been shown through evaluation of the academic program to produce graduates who have met the required educational outcomes.

Criterion 33.2: Teaching strategies and technologies must support the needs and learning styles of diverse learners, while appropriately developing the knowledge, skills, attitudes and judgment required of the pharmacy graduate. Examples of Evidence:

▷ ...Development of critical thinking, problem-solving, and oral and written communication skills supported through the application of information and other instructional technologies, laboratory experiences, practice- and decision-support tools, case studies, guided group discussions, problem-based learning cases, and simulations and other practice based exercises (where appropriate, these techniques should involve actual or standardized patients, pharmacists, and other health care professionals)

▷ Promotion of the development of life-long learning habits through an emphasis on active, self-directed learning and the fostering of ethical responsibility for maintaining and enhancing professional competence

▷ Procedures for student to assume responsibility for their own learning (including assessment of their learning needs)

▷ Development of personal learning plans, and self-assessment of their acquisition of knowledge, skills, attitudes, and values and their achievement of desired competencies and outcomes

▷ Teamwork and collaboration examples

Source: CCAPP, http://ccapp-accredit.ca/wp-content/uploads/2016/01/CCAPP_accred_standards_degree_2014.pdf

Appendix 2. Educational Outcomes & Associated Leadership Competencies

1. AACP's Center for the Advancement of Pharmacy Education (CAPE), Educational Outcomes & Associated Leadership Competencies – 2013
2. Association of Faculties of Pharmacy of Canada (AFPC) [Association des Facultés de Pharmacie du Canada] Educational Outcomes for First Professional Degree Programs in Pharmacy, Vancouver, June 3, 2010

1. CAPE Domain 4 – Personal & Professional Development

4.1. Self-awareness (Self-aware) – Examine and reflect on personal knowledge, skills, abilities, beliefs, biases, motivation, and emotions that could enhance or limit personal and professional growth.

Examples of Learning Objectives*

4.1.1. Use ***metacognition*** to regulate one's own thinking and learning.

4.1.2. Maintain motivation, attention, and interest (e.g., ***habits of mind***) during learning and work-related activities.

4.1.3. Identify, create, implement, evaluate and modify plans for personal and professional development for the purpose of individual growth.

4.1.4. Approach tasks with a desire to learn.

4.1.5. Demonstrate persistence and flexibility in all situations; engaging in ***help seeking*** behavior when appropriate.

4.1.6. Strive for accuracy and precision by displaying a willingness to recognize, correct, and learn from errors.

4.1.7. Use constructive coping strategies to manage stress.

4.1.8. Seek personal, professional, or academic support to address personal limitations.

4.1.9. Display positive self-esteem and confidence when working with others.

4.2. Leadership (Leader) – Demonstrate responsibility for creating and achieving shared goals, regardless of position.

Examples of Learning Objectives*

4.2.1. Identify characteristics that reflect ***leadership*** versus ***management.***

4.2.2. Identify the history (e.g., successes and challenges) of a team before implementing changes.

4.2.3. Develop relationships, value diverse opinions, and understand individual strengths and weaknesses to promote teamwork.

4.2.4. Persuasively communicate goals to the team to help build consensus.

4.2.5. Empower team members by actively listening, gathering input or feedback, and fostering collaboration.

4.3. Innovation and Entrepreneurship (Innovator) – Engage in innovative activities by using creative thinking to envision better ways of accomplishing professional goals.

Examples of Learning Objectives*

4.3.1. Demonstrate initiative when confronted with challenges.

4.3.2. Develop new ideas and approaches to improve quality or overcome barriers to advance the profession.

4.3.3. Demonstrate creative decision making when confronted with novel problems or challenges.

4.3.4. Assess personal strengths and weaknesses in *entrepreneurial skills*

4.3.5. Apply *entrepreneurial skills* within a simulated entrepreneurial activity.

4.3.6. Conduct a risk-benefit analysis for implementation of an innovative idea or simulated entrepreneurial activity.

4.4. Professionalism (Professional) – Exhibit behaviors and values that are consistent with the trust given to the profession by patients, other healthcare providers, and society.

Examples of Learning Objectives*

4.4.1. Demonstrate altruism, integrity, trustworthiness, flexibility, and respect in all interactions.

4.4.2. Display preparation, initiative, and accountability consistent with a commitment to excellence.

4.4.3. Deliver *patient-centered care* in a manner that is legal, ethical, and compassionate.

4.4.4. Recognize that one's professionalism is constantly evaluated by others.

4.4.5. Engage in the profession of pharmacy by demonstrating a commitment to its continual improvement.

* Colleges or schools are encouraged to expand or edit these example learning objectives to meet local needs, as these are not designed to be prescriptive.

Source: AACP, www.aacp.org/resources/education/cape/Pages/default.aspx;
www.aacp.org/resources/education/cape/Open%20Access%20Documents/CAPEoutcomes2013.pdf

2. Association of Faculties of Pharmacy of Canada (AFPC) [Association des Facultés de Pharmacie du Canada] Educational Outcomes for First Professional Degree Programs in Pharmacy, Vancouver, June 3, 2010

Educational Outcomes

Care Provider: Pharmacy graduates use their knowledge, skills and professional judgement to provide pharmaceutical care and to facilitate management of patient's medication and overall health needs.

Communicator: Pharmacy graduates communicate with diverse audiences, using a variety of strategies that take into account the situation, intended outcomes of the communication and the target audience.

Collaborator: Pharmacy graduates work collaboratively with teams to provide effective, quality health care and to fulfill their professional obligations to the community and society at large.

Manager: Pharmacy graduates use management skills in their daily practice to optimize the care of patients, to ensure the safe and effective distribution of medications, and to make efficient use of health resources.

Advocate: Pharmacy graduates use their expertise and influence to advance the health and well-being of individual patients, communities, and populations, and to support pharmacist's professional roles.

Scholar: Pharmacy graduates have and can apply the core knowledge and skills required to be a medication therapy expert, and are able to master, generate, interpret and disseminate pharmaceutical and pharmacy practice knowledge.

Professional: Pharmacy graduates honour their roles as self-regulated professionals through both individual patient care and fulfillment of their professional obligations to the profession, the community and society at large.

Source: www.afpc.info/sites/default/files/AFPC%20Educational%20Outcomes.pdf

Appendix 3. Oath of a Pharmacist, Commentary, & Pledge of Professionalism

1. USA: Oath of a Pharmacist, Commentary, Pledge of Professionalism
2. International: Oath/Promise of a Pharmacist, FIP

1. USA: Oath of a Pharmacist, Commentary, Pledge of Professionalism

OATH OF A PHARMACIST

The revised Oath was adopted by the AACP House of Delegates in July 2007 and has been approved by the American Pharmacists Association.

"I promise to devote myself to a lifetime of service to others through the profession of pharmacy. In fulfilling this vow:

▸ I will consider the welfare of humanity and relief of suffering my primary concerns.

▸ I will apply my knowledge, experience, and skills to the best of my ability to assure optimal outcomes for my patients.

▸ I will respect and protect all personal and health information entrusted to me.

▸ I will accept the lifelong obligation to improve my professional knowledge and competence.

▸ I will hold myself and my colleagues to the highest principles of our profession's moral, ethical and legal conduct.

▸ I will embrace and advocate changes that improve patient care.

▸ I will utilize my knowledge, skills, experiences, and values to prepare the next generation of pharmacists.

I take these vows voluntarily with the full realization of the responsibility with which I am entrusted by the public."

Source: www.pharmacist.com/oath-pharmacist,
www.aacp.org/resources/studentaffairspersonnel/studentaffairspolicies/Documents/OATHOFAPHARMACIST2008-09.pdf

COMMENTARY ON OATH OF A PHARMACIST

The Oath of a Pharmacist is based on the "Oath and Prayer of Maimonides" with input from the American Pharmaceutical Association (APhA) and the American Association of Colleges of Pharmacy (AACP). The Board of Directors of AACP approved the Oath of a Pharmacist in 1983 and has made it available to every college and school of pharmacy.

The characteristics of a professional pharmacy practitioner are described in the Oath such that we obtain an understanding of the meaning of the word "professional." Professionals devote their lives to a significant social value. Pharmacy is a learned profession requiring individuals to dedicate themselves voluntarily to acquiring and maintaining exceptional knowledge and skills in order to provide pharmaceutical care in an ethical context.

The first two statements of the Oath describe a commitment to the service of humankind, the welfare of humanity, and the relief of human suffering as the pharmacist's primary concerns. Further, these statements emphasize that this commitment is lifelong in nature and should be practiced without discrimination. Specifically, the concept of pharmaceutical care embraces a covenantal relationship with the patient and other healthcare providers to ensure that optimal therapeutic outcomes are attained.

The next two statements accentuate the character of a pharmacist in exceeding the knowledge and skills of all others in providing pharmaceutical care and services to the public and other health professionals. A lifetime of learning in pharmacy is necessary to maintain one's professional stature and to provide services inherent with membership in the profession. The acquisition of knowledge and skills by pharmacists must serve to advance the profession. Professional competency involves participation in organizations that support and speak for the profession. Pharmacists promote unity within the profession and enthusiastically accept the responsibilities and accountability for membership in the profession.

The next two statements characterize the pharmacist's commitment to live a life characterized by faithfulness to high moral principles and ethical conduct. This is manifested not only in abiding by and enforcing the laws governing the practice of pharmacy but also in assuring that the laws support the primary mission of the profession, the delivery of pharmaceutical care. Pharmacists must exhibit moral and ethical conduct in their daily interactions with patients and other healthcare providers. Pharmacists dedicate themselves to excellence in their knowledge, skill, and caring because they adhere to high moral and ethical principles. This enables them to maintain a covenantal relationship with society.

The next statement describes pharmacy as a profession where change must be embraced rather than resisted. Pharmacists must actively participate as agents of change, focusing on improving healthcare. The last statement of the Oath describes the pharmacist as voluntarily making these vows with a full understanding of the responsibility they impose.

Professionalism requires constant attention. The seeds of professionalism are sown when students begin their preparation for pharmacy school, are cultivated and nurtured in pharmacy school, and are brought to fruition and maintained during their careers as pharmacists. Becoming a professional means more than learning the science of pharmacy. It means mastering the art of pharmaceutical care in service to one's fellow human beings. This service must be carried out with dignity, integrity, and honor as reflected in this Oath.
Developed by the American Pharmaceutical Association Academy of Students of Pharmacy and the American
Association of Colleges of Pharmacy Council of Deans Task Force on Professionalism, June 26, 1994.

PLEDGE OF PROFESSIONALISM

As a student of pharmacy, I believe there is a need to build and reinforce a professional identity founded on integrity, ethical behavior, and honor. This development, a vital process in my education, will help ensure that I am true to the professional relationship I establish between myself and society as I become a member of the pharmacy community. Integrity must be an essential part of my everyday life and I must practice pharmacy with honesty and commitment to service.

To accomplish this goal of professional development, I as a student of pharmacy should:

- ▸ DEVELOP a sense of loyalty and duty to the profession of pharmacy by being a builder of community, one able and willing to contribute to the well-being of others and one who enthusiastically accepts the responsibility and accountability for membership in the profession.
- ▸ FOSTER professional competency through life-long learning. I must strive for high ideals, teamwork and unity within the profession in order to provide optimal patient care.
- ▸ SUPPORT my colleagues by actively encouraging personal commitment to the Oath of Maimonides and a Code of Ethics as set forth by the profession
- ▸ INCORPORATE into my life and practice, dedication to excellence. This will require an ongoing reassessment of personal and professional values.
- ▸ MAINTAIN the highest ideals and professional attributes to ensure and facilitate the covenantal relationship required of the pharmaceutical care giver.

The profession of pharmacy is one that demands adherence to a set of rigid ethical standards. These high ideals are necessary to ensure the quality of care extended to the patients I serve. As a student of pharmacy, I believe this does not start with graduation; rather, it begins with my membership in this professional college community. Therefore, I must strive to uphold these standards as I advance toward full membership in the profession of pharmacy.

Source: APhA-ASP, AACP Council of Deans Task Force on Professionalism; June 26, 1994

2. International Pharmaceutical Federation (FIP, Fédération International Pharmaceutique): Oath/Promise of a Pharmacist

As a pharmacist, I vow to serve humanity and to support my profession's ideals and commitments.
- I shall be guided in all dimensions of my life by the highest standards of human conduct.
- I shall apply the full measure of my knowledge and abilities to supporting the health and well-being of all those I serve.
- I shall always place the needs of all those I serve above my personal interests and considerations.
- I shall treat all those I serve equally, fairly and with respect, regardless of gender, race, ethnicity, religion, culture or political beliefs.
- I shall protect the confidentiality of personal and health information entrusted to me.
- I shall maintain my professional knowledge and competence throughout my career.
- I shall support the advancement of knowledge and standards of practice in pharmacy.
- I shall nurture the preparation of future members of my profession.
- I shall use all opportunities to develop collaborative practice with all healthcare professionals in my environment.

In taking this solemn oath / making this promise, I honor those who have supported my development as a pharmacist and commit myself never to act in a manner that is contrary to these vows.

Source: Adopted by the FIP Council on 31 August 2014, in Bangkok, Thailand, www.fip.org/pharmacist-oath

Appendix 4. Code of Ethics for Pharmacists

PREAMBLE. Pharmacists are health professionals who assist individuals in making the best use of medications. This Code, prepared and supported by pharmacists, is intended to state publicly the principles that form the fundamental basis of the roles and responsibilities of pharmacists. These principles, based on moral obligations and virtues, are established to guide pharmacists in relationships with patients, health professionals, and society.

I. A pharmacist respects the covenantal relationship between the patient and pharmacist.

Considering the patient-pharmacist relationship as a covenant means that a pharmacist has moral obligations in response to the gift of trust received from society. In return for this gift, a pharmacist promises to help individuals achieve optimum benefit from their medications, to be committed to their welfare, and to maintain their trust.

II. A pharmacist promotes the good of every patient in a caring, compassionate, and confidential manner.

A pharmacist places concern for the well-being of the patient at the center of professional practice. In doing so, a pharmacist considers needs stated by the patient as well as those defined by health science. A pharmacist is dedicated to protecting the dignity of the patient. With a caring attitude and a compassionate spirit, a pharmacist focuses on serving the patient in a private and confidential manner.

III. A pharmacist respects the autonomy and dignity of each patient.

A pharmacist promotes the right of self-determination and recognizes individual self-worth by encouraging patients to participate in decisions about their health. A pharmacist communicates with patients in terms that are understandable. In all cases, a pharmacist respects personal and cultural differences among patients.

IV. A pharmacist acts with honesty and integrity in professional relationships.

A pharmacist has a duty to tell the truth and to act with conviction of conscience. A pharmacist avoids discriminatory practices, behavior or work conditions that impair professional judgment, and actions that compromise dedication to the best interests of patients.

V. A pharmacist maintains professional competence.

A pharmacist has a duty to maintain knowledge and abilities as new medications, devices, and technologies become available and as health information advances.

VI. A pharmacist respects the values and abilities of colleagues and other health professionals.

When appropriate, a pharmacist asks for the consultation of colleagues or other health professionals or refers the patient. A pharmacist acknowledges that colleagues and other health professionals may differ in the beliefs and values they apply to the care of the patient.

VII. A pharmacist serves individual, community, and societal needs.

The primary obligation of a pharmacist is to individual patients. However, the obligations of a pharmacist may at times extend beyond the individual to the community and society. In these situations, the pharmacist recognizes the responsibilities that accompany these obligations and acts accordingly.

VIII. A pharmacist seeks justice in the distribution of health resources.

When health resources are allocated, a pharmacist is fair and equitable, balancing the needs of patients and society.

Adopted by the American Pharmacists Association, October 27, 1994. www.pharmacist.com/code-ethics

🍁 In Canada, codes of ethics for pharmacists are promulgated by provincial colleges [boards] of pharmacy.

Appendix 5. The Albert B. Prescott Pharmacy Leadership Award

An award for leadership by a young pharmacist was established by Phi Delta Chi in 1987. The Albert B. Prescott Pharmacy Leadership Award is given annually to a pharmacist no more than 10 years into his or her career. The recipient delivers a scholarly lecture on issues such as pharmacy as a profession, leadership, or future trends in pharmacy practice or education.

Albert Prescott was dean of pharmacy at the University of Michigan from 1870 to 1905. A maverick, he was rebuffed by APhA for his heretical view that pharmacy should be an education-based profession – not an experienced-based trade. The credentials committee at the 1871 APhA convention rejected Prescott as unworthy of being seated as a voting delegate. But Prescott persevered. By the 1890s, Prescott's vision and convictions were proven correct. The rest of the country began to follow Prescott's lead. Ironically, he was eventually elected president of APhA in 1899, and became the first president of the organization we now know as the American Association of Colleges of Pharmacy (AACP), when it was founded in 1900.

Today, the Prescott Pharmacy Leadership Award is coordinated by the Pharmacy Leadership & Education Institute (PLEI), with major support from the Phi Lambda Sigma Pharmacy Leadership Society.

1987 Walter L. Fitzgerald, Jr. Impact of the winds of change on the leadership needs of the profession of pharmacy. *ΦΔX Communicator* 1987 Fall:2-4.

1988 Lucinda L. Maine: A universal goal for pharmacy. *ΦΔX Communicator* 1988 Sum:12-6.

1989 Heidi M. Anderson-Harper: Leadership: Back to the future. *ΦΔX Communicator* 1990 Fal:8-9.

1990 Janet P. Engle: Leadership & professionalism in pharmacy. *Am J Hosp Pharm.* 1991:1559-62.

1991 Kathleen D. Lake: Leadership. *ΦΔX Communicator* 1997 Spr:7-10.

1992 John M. Coster: Pharmacy, politics, & public policy. *Am J Hosp Pharm.* 1992:1759-62.

1993 Mary Eloise Stoikes: Through my pharmacy picture window. *ΦΔX Communicator* 1995 Fall:15-9.

1994 Mitchel C. Rothholz: Pharmacy organizations leading the way. *ΦΔX Communicator* 1996 Win:6-8.

1995 Kelly Hasty Kale: Politics & the profession. *ΦΔX Communicator* 1997 Sum:8-11.

1996 Timothy L. Tucker: Our future: Where does it begin? *ΦΔX Communicator* 1998 Sum:6-7.

1997 Nancy A. Alvarez: Searching for utopia. *ΦΔX Communicator* 1998 Sum:8-10.

1998 Christopher J. Decker: Primary lessons: A call for unity in American pharmacy. *JAPhA* 1998;38(Jul/Aug):431-5; *J Pharm Soc Wisc* 1998;May/Jun:9-13.

1999 Jeanne Ann Stasny: Patients' access to care—At the center of pharmacy's rebirth. *JAPhA* 1999;39(Jul/Aug):458-60.

2000 Tina Penick Brock: Will pharmacy survive or will it prevail? A complex systems approach. *JAPhA* 2000;40(5 Suppl 1):S25-9.

2001 Edwin H. Adams: Perspectives on pharmacoacademics. *JAPhA* 2001;41(Sep/Oct):S25-7.

2002 Christopher R. McCurdy: Pharmacy education: From Prescott to pharmacogenomics. *JAPhA* 2002;42(5):688-91.

2003 Jennifer Cerulli: Reaching beyond the pharmacy bench: Impressions of academic community pharmacy practice. *JAPhA* 2003;43(5 Suppl 1):S10-4.

2004 John D. Musil: What is leadership? [lecture not published]

2005 Bradley P. Tice: Advancing pharmacy through entrepreneurial leadership. *JAPhA* 2005;45(5):546-53.

2006 Michael J. Negrete: Lessons learned, lessons shared: What pharmacy needs to do to make the most of the profession. *JAPhA* 2006;46(5):556-9.

2007 David A. Medvedeff: Real leaders wear running shoes: Myriad variables need to be evaluated and strategies developed for lifelong career in pharmacy. *JAPhA* 2007;47(5):576-8.

2008 Macary Weck Marciniak: Just do it! Advancing the profession through innovation, advocacy, and mentorship [lecture not published]

2009 Scott Evans: Providing maximal patient care, improving patient safety: Being good isn't always good enough. *JAPhA* 2009;49:489-91.

2010 Jeffrey J. Neigh: Developing future pharmacy leaders. *JAPhA* 2010;50(4):468-70.

2011 (#25) Timothy W. Cutler: The pharmacy profession and health care reform: Opportunities and challenges during the next decade: If we only see the glass half full or half empty, we will never be able to fill it completely. *JAPhA* 2011;51:477-80.

2012 Conan MacDougall: The nonpharmacologic basis of therapeutics: To get to the next level in interprofessional patient care, pharmacists need to recognize the social and interpersonal aspects of medical decision making. *JAPhA* 2012;52:454-6.

2013 Robert Schoenhaus: Embracing our roles as medication navigators. *JAPhA* 2013;53(4):362-4.

2014 Sonak D. Pastakia: Designed to fail, reengineered to succeed. *JAPhA* 2014;54(4):350-4, 356.

2015 Alex J. Adams: Toward permissionless innovation in health care. *JAPhA* 2015;55(4):359-62.

2016 (#30) Joshua J. Neumiller: Diabetes education: Leadership through action. *JAPhA* 2016;56(6):611-14.

A reproduction of Robert A. Thom's "A Revolution in Pharmaceutical Education," featuring Dean Albert B. Prescott and his students at the University of Michigan, circa 1883, from the Parke-Davis & Co. series "Great Moments in Pharmacy," 1956. Reproduced with permission of the American Pharmacists Association, which owns the original collection. Phi Delta Chi has sponsored and holds a license for use of this image.

Appendix 6. Translations, for Leaders

A first step in cross-cultural understanding is translation. This list offers a few simple options for "leader" (via translate.google.com), to help get conversations started.

English	Leader
Afrikaans	Leier
Arabic	قادة
Bengali	নেতা
Chinese	領導
Czech	Vůdce
Danish	Leder
Dutch	Leider
Esperanto	Ĉefo
Filipino	Lider
French	Chef, dirigeant
German	Leiter
Greek	Ηγέτης
Gujarati	નેતા
Hawai'ian	Alaka'i
Hebrew	לעצב
Hindi	नेता
Hmong	Thawj coj
Hungarian	Vezető
Indonesian	Pemimpin
Italian	Capo
Japanese	リーダー
Korean	리더
Malay	Ketua
Pashto	مشر
Persian	رهبر
Portuguese	Líder
Punjabi	ਆਗੂ
Russian	Лидер
Spanish	Líder
Swahili	Kiongozi
Swedish	Ledare
Thai	ผู้นำ
Turkish	Lider
Urdu	لیڈر
Vietnamese	Lãnh đạo
Zulu	Leader

Appendix 7. Pithy Reflections on Leadership

Never tell people how to do things. Tell them what to do and they will surprise you with their ingenuity. – LtGen George S. Patton, Jr.

Do not begrudge the time you spend developing, coaching, and helping your people to grow so they can carry on when you are gone. It's one of the best signs of good leadership. – Bernard Baruch

Chief Lessons

Begin within.

Explore who you are, what makes you fulfilled.

Put smile back into your practice and your life.

What is important? Align your priorities with your values.

Take charge; mold your environment to your own liking.

If you cannot mold your environment, you can control how you react to it!

Enjoy the ride; your destination is a long way off.

Coach and let yourself be coached.

Is your Ferris wheel loaded, balanced, in motion?

a. Leaders challenge the process
b. Leaders share their vision with associates
c. Leaders enable others to act
d. Leaders model the way
e. Leaders motivate

Follow me

Lead by example (work hard yourself)

You catch more flies with honey than vinegar

Criticize in private, praise in public

Take care of people; they will take care of you

Do not fear delegation, it's how leaders succeed

People support what they help create

Tell people what to accomplish, not how

Leaders dare to be different

Be the advisor to your successor

Be accessible; really listen

Change for improvement, not just for the sake of change

Ask for criticism; use it

Face tough situations head on

Ask for facts and advice; know the difference

Be consistent

Accept mistakes gracefully, encourage success next time

Give credit where due; do not hog the spotlight

Set specific goals and high standards; respect excellence

Keep people informed

Use "we" and "our team," instead of "I" and "you"

Reinforce responsible behavior

Be first for disagreeable tasks (like paying dues)

Delegate! Resist temptation to micromanage

Elevate the values and aspirations of others, rather than *appealing* to the wants and needs of others

Inspire

Characteristics of leadership (U.S. Army): dependability, unselfishness, loyalty, justice, courage, bearing, sound judgment, integrity, knowledge, endurance, enthusiasm, initiative, tact, and decisiveness.

LDRSHIP: Loyalty Duty Respect Service Honor Integrity Courage (U.S. Army Core Values)

On Learning More Leadership

a. See learning as a continual process of growth and development

b. Test yourself, challenge yourself

c. Use mistakes to grow

d. Use frustrating experiences as an opportunity to stretch yourself

e. Talk with peers about what is happening

g. Be both a teacher and a learner

h. Use your current strengths to build new strengths

i. Ask for feedback on your behavior and progress

LEADERSHIP PEARLS

1 – One of the requirements for being a successful leader is making time to sit and read and just learn more about the task.

2 – Leadership is not a scientific subject; a great deal depends on components that are not entirely clear.

3 – They never really put themselves into the job until they understand what their personal roles are in making the project happen.

4 – The leader has no more important concern than helping all the people involved reach the conclusion that they are important to the undertaking and that it is important to their world.

5 – People work for fulfillment, appreciation, and companionship.

6 – Volunteer organizations have the advantage that very few people initially join without being interested in the work.

7 – Most leadership is negative in that it is dedicated at not failing. Not failing is not the same as succeeding.

8 – Few things are more important for the leader than making certain that people who deserve appreciation receive it.

9 – The leader must be a walking, talking, visible example of what the ethics of the business are to be. Example is all.

10 – Becoming locked into a plan is lazy management.

11 – Running a business is like managing a flowing river.

12 – Nothing will happen unless individuals have something they want to accomplish and go for it.

13 – People who are going to run something need a much broader understanding of the world than they can

get from specialized magazines.

14 – Every organization needs a planned method of recognizing the people who make contributions to the success of that organization.

15 – A specific team for a specific task should also have a specific time limit on its life.

16 – Families are much harder to run than big companies.

Adapted from: Crosby PB. *Running Things: The Art of Making Things Happen.* New York: McGraw Hill, 1986.

DEFINING LEADERSHIP

Leadership is many things. It is patient, usually boring coalition building.... It is altering agendas so that new priorities get enough attention. It is being visible when things are going awry, and invisible when they are working well. It is building a loyal team at the top that speaks more or less with one voice. It is listening carefully much of the time, frequently speaking with encouragement, and reinforcing words with believable action. It is being tough when necessary, and it is the occasional naked use of power—or the "subtle accumulation of nuances, a hundred things done a little better," as Henry Kissinger once put it. Most of these actions are what the political scientist James MacGregor Burns in his book *Leadership* calls "transactional leadership." They are the necessary activities of the leader that take up most of his or her day. – Peters TJ, Waterman RH Jr. *In Search of Excellence.* New York: Warner, 1984.

A DEFINITION OF LEADERSHIP

"The process of persuasion and example by which an individual (or leadership team) induces a group to take action that is in accord with the leader's purposes or the shared purposes of all." – John W. Gardner

BETTER TEAM BUILDING

   – start with premeeting networking

   – map out a team mission

   – define roles

   – create a group identity

   – draw a game plan

   – use liberal doses of "we" and "our"

   – do not be a "fact hog"

   – encourage networking

   – encourage play time

   – reinforce the team concept

   – use humor

   – develop an open atmosphere

Adapted from Belzer EJ. Twelve ways to better team building. *Working Woman* 1989;14:12-4.

ON LEADERSHIP

"...the concept of leadership is crucial to the revolution now under way—so crucial that we believe the words "managing" and "management" should be discarded. "Management," with its attendant images—cop, referee, devil's advocate, dispassionate analyst, naysayer, pronouncer—connotes controlling and arranging and demeaning and reducing. "Leadership" connotes unleashing energy, building, freeing, and growing. As Warren Bennis, a major figure in the current rethinking process, says, "American organizations have been overmanaged and underled...." – Peters TJ, Austin N. *A Passion for Excellence: The Leadership Difference.* New York: Random House, 1985.

- Understand what underlies our capabilities and desire to perform
- Analyze each individual's support needs
- Use delegation to develop people's capabilities to perform
- Use motivation to develop people's desires to perform
- Coach individuals effectively to develop new capabilities, maintain good levels of performance, and engage proactively
- Provide meaningful feedback and performance evaluation for continuous improvement.

Appendix 8. Feedback: Suggestions to Improve the Next Edition

Separate documents available to facilitators upon request (LeadGrowShape@plei.org).

To suggest improvements for the next edition, send feedback to LeadGrowShape@plei.org.

In Module _____, the following section is troublesome (describe problem) ...

✎ _____ ⌨

In Module _____, the following section should be changed ...

✎ _____ ⌨

In the next edition, please include a module on _____.

What else should we know, so we can improve?

✎ _____ ⌨

If you are having viewing difficulties, tell us as much as you know:

Hardware type: _____ ⌨

Software (app) type: _____ ⌨

Software (app) version: _____ ⌨

Describe problem: ✎ _____ ⌨

Thank you for helping us grow better!   *Nancy, Gary, Michael, & John*

About the Editorial Board

Nancy A. Alvarez, PharmD: Assistant Dean for Experiential Education & Continuing Professional Development at Chapman University, Irvine, CA; 1997 recipient of the Prescott Pharmacy Leadership Award, 2000 president of Phi Lambda Sigma Pharmacy Leadership Society, 2017 president of the American Pharmacists Association. According to StrengthsFinder®, she provides Input, Arranger, Responsibility, Learner, Intellection.

Gary J. Keil, II, PhD: Co-founder and director of Growth Leaders Network, motivational speaker and positive psychology coach, and holistic wellness advocate; previously, global pharmaceutical strategic planning and competitive intelligence executive and long-standing chronic pain researcher for AstraZeneca. According to StrengthsFinder®, he contributes Ideation, Positivity, WOO, Input, Strategic.

Michael J. Negrete, PharmD: Assistant Academic Vice President, Samuel Merritt University, Oakland, CA; 2006 recipient of Prescott Pharmacy Leadership Award; previously, vice president for clinical & educational affairs for California Pharmacists Association (2012-2013) and chief executive officer for Pharmacy Foundation of California (2006-2011). According to StrengthsFinder®, he leverages Maximizer, Connectedness, Ideation, Strategic, Activator.

Colonel (Retired) John D. Grabenstein, PhD, served 27 years as a pharmacist in the Medical Service Corps of the U.S. Army. He directed the Military Vaccine Agency, where he organized "Immunization University" to train clinicians from many health disciplines. In 1989, he led the team that developed the first Leader-Development Seminar for Phi Delta Chi. In 1996, he led the team that wrote the first curriculum for APhA's Pharmacy-Based Immunization Delivery Program. In 2006, he joined Merck Vaccines, where he serves as global director for medical affairs. Via StrengthsFinder®, he supplies Analytical-Achiever-Learner-Connectedness-Relator.

SUGGESTED CITATION

Alvarez NA, Keil GJ II, Negrete MJ, Grabenstein JD. *Lead←Grow→Shape: A Prescription for Life-Long Leader Development, Workbook 2017*. East Hanover, NJ: Pharmacy Leadership & Education Institute, January 2017.

Pharmacy Leadership & Education Institute

Acknowledgements

This work has its origins with the first Leader-Development Seminar (LDS) conducted by Phi Delta Chi for its collegiate members in August 1989 in Monterey, California. After the 16th LDS in 2016 and the umpteenth separate leader-training program conducted by the Pharmacy Leadership & Education Institute (PLEI), this book was a natural next step.

The Editorial Board expresses its gratitude to the PLEI Board of Directors and to Phi Delta Chi's Executive Council for their support and encouragement over the decades. Each of us acknowledges the dozens of mentors, family members, and leader-exemplars from whom we have learned throughout the course of our lives – we are enriched and enabled to undertake this work. And we aren't afraid to say in public that we love them!

For Module 15, we are grateful for the video creativity and contributions of Richard A. Marasco, PharmD, in 1992. Tony A. Guerra, PharmD, contributed to the Finding Balance elements (now Modules 34 and 35) in 2008. Likewise, we are grateful to so many, throughout pharmacy, who have participated in our various leader-development laboratories since 1989. Our current thinking has been shaped by their engagement and feedback.

Thanks also to the facilitators (and their students) who critiqued early editions, to help us give you a better experience:

- Michael Manolakis (LDS #1, 1989), PharmD, PhD, and Wingate University, 2016
- Cynthia A. Naughton, PharmD, and North Dakota State University, 2016
- Jennifer A. Tilleman, PharmD, and Creighton University, 2016
- I. Shane Trent, PharmD, MBA, and South College, 2016
- Cathy L. Worrall, PharmD, and South Carolina College of Pharmacy (MUSC Campus), 2016
  ... and many others.

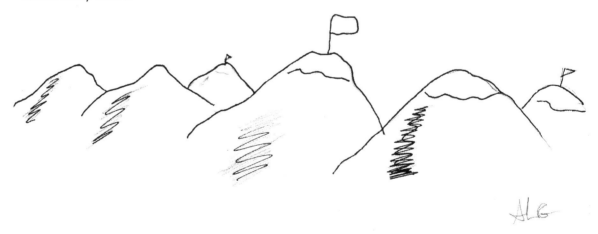

"You've got a bunch of mountains.
When you climb one, then you've got another one to climb and another one.
When you get to the top of one mountain, interest declines.
There's more work to be done." Maurice R. Hilleman

Index

Pharmacy Leadership & Education Institute

Made in the USA
Middletown, DE
05 May 2017